Charles Edward Whitehead

Wild Sports in the South

The Camp-Fires of the Everglades

Charles Edward Whitehead

Wild Sports in the South

The Camp-Fires of the Everglades

ISBN/EAN: 9783337254018

Printed in Europe, USA, Canada, Australia, Japan

Cover: Foto ©Andreas Hilbeck / pixelio.de

More available books at **www.hansebooks.com**

Phew! what a tussel! "Go it, pups!" sez Marthy, holdin' up her light. "Go it, yaller backs!" That old woman "as clear g'it—well, she was.—PAGE 389

WILD SPORTS IN THE SOUTH;

OR, THE

CAMP-FIRES OF THE EVERGLADES.

BY

CHARLES E. WHITEHEAD,

TRANSLATOR OF "GERARD THE LION KILLER."

> "Yet let us sing,
> Honor to the old bow-string;
> Honor to the bugle horn;
> Honor to the woods unshorn."

WITH ILLUSTRATIONS BY EHNINGER, TAIT AND OTHERS.

NEW YORK:
DERBY & JACKSON, 119 NASSAU STREET.
1860.

Entered according to Act of Congress, in the year 1860, by
DERBY & JACKSON,
In the Clerk's Office of the District Court of the United States for the Southern District of New York.

W. H. Tinson, Stereotyper.   Geo. Russell & Co., Printers.

THIS VOLUME

IS DEDICATED,

WITH FEELINGS OF THE PROFOUNDEST RESPECT AND VENERATION,

TO THE

BIG BEAR OF THE WAKASSARE RIVER,

AND THE

FRIENDS WHO WERE IN AT HIS DEATH.

PREFACE.

The larger portion of the Sketches contained in this volume were contributions made by the Author to "The Spirit of the Times," a few years ago, under the title of "Camp-Fire Stories," and as some of them have been floating about in other papers, this statement seems necessary, lest the reader may regard these "twice-told tales" as lacking in originality.

Nothing more is claimed for this volume than that it contains pleasant reminiscences of hunting life and adventure in the peninsula of Florida, and counterparts of tales, some of them remembered, some of them fancied, that frontier hunters tell when assembled at night around their camp-fires.

The Author does not ask that each story shall be regarded as having occurred literally as written; but he believes the spirit of the tales, the description of natural scenery, and the fragments of Indian history to be correct, and he has carefully striven not to offend the keen observation and long experience of his hunting comrades at the South whose eyes will scrutinize these pages, by any allusion to natural history which is not exactly true. If the book will recall the Author pleasantly to their minds, or awaken the remembrance of grand old sports and merry camp-fires in the States of the South, its object is attained.

CONTENTS.

	PAGE
INTRODUCTORY,	9
THE CAMP FIRE,	20
A BEAR IN THE CAMP,	40
THE DANGERS OF FIRE-HUNTING,	51
THE PLANTATION HOUSE OF "FAR AWAY,"	61
THE PANTHER'S CUB,	75
THE DEER HUNT,	86
THE FIRESIDE AT FAR AWAY,	106
THE STILL HUNT,	119
THE FLORIDA POCAHONTAS,	143
THE FLORIDA POCAHONTAS, CONTINUED,	159
THE BATTLE ON BONDA KEY,	175
THE HISTORY OF AN OLD FRIEND,	195
THE DROWNED LANDS,	208

CONTENTS.

	PAGE
The Skin of the Tiger-Cat,	239
Supper,	245
Home Again,	265
The Burial,	285
Indian History,	295
A Bear in Difficulty,	303
How we conquered Halleck Tustenuggee,	311
The "Painter" in the Pig Pen,	327
Poke receives a Cur'osity and tells a Yarn,	341
Woodland Choruses,	354
Life in the Light-house,	366
Tracking the Enemy,	372
Smoking out the Enemy,	382
Besieging the Light-house,	393
Mike and Tiger Tail play Chess,	404
The Surrender at Discretion,	416

WILD SPORTS IN THE SOUTH.

CHAPTER I.

INTRODUCTORY.

"O flourish, hidden deep in fern,
   Old oak I love thee well,
A thousand thanks for what I learn,
   And what remains to tell."

TENNYSON.

A GOODLY creation is a tree! Its mast-like trunk, supporting a thousand branches that weave and interweave, fretting the blue air with their tracery; lithe to the wind, stubborn to the storm, the pillars bend but do not break, in the long-drawn leafy aisles of God's cathedral. Its roots, far-reaching, with tiny fibres probe the earth for moisture, and send the life-blood through the arteries to the fragrant blossoms and the topmost leaves that "clap their little hands in glee with one continuous sound." To its shadow not only the beasts of the field come for shelter, but millions of insects seek a home under the rough folds of its bark, or weave their cradles in its rocking boughs. On its branches the birds build their nests, and in its hollows the squirrel and the hooting owl conceal their young, and the wild bee stores its sweets, while both day and night the buds breathe their perfume, and the wind, the rustling leaves, and its feathered guests, chant an anthem of praise.

If it be a pleasant thing to see one plant thus munificently endowed, how does it delight the heart to look down the forest, where trees of every hue and form stand in countless numbers, and their shade, with its perpetual twilight, makes a new climate, where new flora gem the sheltered earth, where parasite plants and vines festoon the trees with corridors, gay with flowers, or purple with clustered fruit, where the moss takes the place of grass, and the last year's leaves fill the hollows—where the wild bird and timid game make their home, and gambol in the unrestrained indulgence of natural instincts! To this scene add the brook cluttered with stones and filled with leaves, the open river tenanted with aquatic birds, and making vistas in the woods, and, lastly, the deep blue of the sea, fringed with the white of the breakers, and complaining of its limits, and you will have the view that is to be met in nearly every sea-coast forest in the land. But in the woods of the far southern States, and more particularly in the Florida peninsula, Nature develops new beauties, and excites further thoughts of praise to its Creator.

> There simmer first unfauld her robes,
> And there they langest tarry,

bringing in her train the fragrance of the earth, with the colors of the sky, decking her tallest trees with flowers proportioned to their grandeur. There the lakes and rivers are broad and deep, and teem with curious animal life. There the birds of the air are painted with crimson, and sing in dialects consonant with the voluptuous clime. There the great queen lily rides the lagoon, where drooping moss from the live oaks so curtain its retreat that no eye ever sees it but the wild bird's, and there the earth is so prolific of her fruits that there is abundance for all the crowded forest. No single life is forgotten, and the minute insect that feeds on the pollen of the tiger lily, lives as abundantly as the alligator that takes his toll from the whole animal creation.

Thus from year to year have the seasons come and gone; animal and vegetable life has reached its limit of years, has fallen and decayed, and wealth that would have enriched a nation has only formed the subsoil for another age, nor eye of man has seen, nor pen of man has told, the wonders of that inner forest that was barred by nature and the Seminole from the civilized world.

Under such a wood, near where the Stinhatchee River empties its dark waters into the Gulf of Mexico, at Deadman's Bay, the grey light came to my eyes as I lay wrapped in my blanket, by the smoldering camp-fire, a few years ago. Hunters and negroes were all still buried in dreams, and the weary hounds lay stretched around indiscriminately among the sleepers. No tent was raised, for the elements required none, though a screen of boughs had been built as a break-wind, and to keep the reflected heat near the fire. Here and there were scattered accoutrements, or the relics of the last night's meal, feathers of birds, skins of beasts, antlers of deer. The serried leaf of the palmetto fringed us around like a hedge, and above us the tassels of the pine trees just began to be discernible against the morning sky. Once in a while a bird twittered in the trees, now and then a sound like dropping rain was heard, where some animal shook the dew-laden branches. All else was still, save the quiet murmur of the sea on the beach, some little distance off. Its low roar lulled me; I shut my eyes to the coming dawn, and turned over in my blanket. How pleasant is that second sleep at the grey twilight!

I know not how long I slept; but when I awoke the negroes had rekindled the fire, and a pleasant fragrance of cooking meats mingled with the pine scent of the forest. I started to my feet, and taking my gun, sauntered down the bank of the river, partly for a walk, and partly to search for game. The air was clear and cool, and all nature seemed to be coming forth to salute the day. The quail whistled in the distance, the grey and fox squirrels leaped from bough to bough, or half descending the great trunks of the oak trees, challenged with pert gestures the passers-by. Long trains of cormorants sailed overhead to their feeding grounds, and with measured beat the ibis and heron were slowly passing seaward. I saw the ducks feeding on the margins of the river, and the various tribes of woodpeckers, jays, and hawks, flitting among the trees; but none of these excited my attention: they were rather the constant sights that one sees without regarding. At length the gobble of a turkey came faintly on the air. I have heard that sound often before, and trust to hear it many times hereafter, but I can never listen to its first clear note without a flutter of delight, that I verily believe is greater far than that of its sweetheart, as she listens from the jungle to this the loud love-call of her mate. It apparently does not strike the ear, but the heart, and then tingles outward through every nerve. There may be something in this of early association, but it is one of the pleasantest that a man has in this world, and which so often makes him rich when he has never a son. I stopped short and listened for a repetition of the sound, to tell from what direction it came, and also for any answer that might come back, as by directing my course toward the latter I could intercept the cock when he should take his course. The hundred little beings that talked around me in their various tongues were all speaking. The forest that I thought so still, was now, when attentively listening, full of life. How distinctly now came the booming of the sea, and the distant tap of the ivory-billed woodpecker! Yet I could hear no cluck of hen, or responsive gobble of the younger cocks of the brood. Again the call was repeated. First a low chuckle, and then the rich guttural vowels poured out in a hurried volume. It domineers over every other sound by reason of its peculiarity. There is no manner of representing it in language, though the negroes have a song that ends in a turkey chorus, which might be written thus: Chug-u-logga, chug-u-logga, chug-u-logga-chug. In the liquid negro *patois* it is not dissimilar. Having taken the bearings of the turkey by his sound, and mentally estimated his distance, I ran on ahead, during a time equal to the interval between his calls, and then stopped and listened. In a moment the call resounded through the woods near me. I walked carefully forward, sheltering myself behind clumps of alders and trunks of trees, and having gone what I thought was a sufficient distance, waited and watched attentively. Again the note sounded, but it seemed in the air. I cast my eye upward, and there, perched on the dead and topmost boughs of a tall sycamore, from whence he could overlook the surrounding forest, stood my friend. His erect and slender form was drawn up to its full height, his little head turned quickly to the right and the left as he surveyed the forest below him, lit up by the same early sun that was burnishing his own glossy breast. I could imagine the view he was eying, and it must have been the conscious pride of a chieftain viewing his native heaths and hills that drew his form to such stately proportions. From where he sat he overlooked river and lake, broad lagoon and open ocean, and hundreds of low lying islands; he saw savannahs covered with reeds and osiers, and shady with tapering canes, where bred the crab, and trailed the snail and centiped; he heard the pattering rain of pecan and of beech-nuts on the upland,

and saw the pawpaw bear its luscious fruit; shady glens and pools of water invited to repose, and in fancy's eye his lazy harem lay beneath those trees, shuffling with their wings the clear white sand of the hummocks that bounded the sea. All this he saw, and then swelling his throat, he sent forth his clear alarm, herald of the morn, and gathering cry of his clan.

I understood his feeling, and yet raising my rifle I took aim at him (strange contrariety of man) and fired. A half-uttered gobble was suppressed, and spreading his wings he sailed away in a slanting direction. "Missed," I ejaculated, as I saw him skating along **like a** hawk. Just then, without an indication, he rolled over in the air and came crashing through the boughs of the pine **trees to the earth.**

I ran to my prize. His heavy beard and long spurs showed him to be an old gobbler, probably one of those lonely birds that, expatriating themselves from their flocks, wander about in self-doomed celibacy. Throwing **my** game over my shoulders, I returned to camp and to breakfast, well contented with my success.

If the reader is **desirous** of knowing what is a wild turkey, by turning to Audubon's, Wilson's, or Bona- **parte's** Ornithology, he will discover it to be of the gallinaceous order, with conical papilla on the forehead, neck corrugated, beset with cavernous caruncles, frontal caruncle blue and red, and with scutellate toes, scabrous above and papillæ beneath, etc. After pondering on this description he may suspect that his ideas on the subject may be rather confused, he may doubt if he would be able to sketch the bird from the description given, and may desire to hear it described in simpler language.

If so, let him imagine a full-grown black turkey cock of the domestic species made shy and cautious in its movements, restless with its head and neck, high stepping over obstacles with its bare, sinewy legs, and erect, slender and game-like in its bearing. The wild turkey is to its barnyard kinsman what the racehorse is to the carthorse. See him in the early morn as he stands on some elevation, and welcomes the dawn, and announces to his family his movements for the day. His scarlet wattles lie pendent on a neck that one moment curves like a swan's and in another is erect like a crane's; his comb is a soldier's plume, his eye is full and hazel black, gleaming with something of a human look from his shapely head, covered by the wrinkles of skin and a few scattered hairs, and tinged with blue and red. His neck swells very gradually to his body, and is burnished with a gloss of brown and gold that varies with every light. There is no pomposity or clumsiness about his air; on the contrary, his whole manners are those of an accomplished gallant and a warrior.

You see him among the hens. Their gentle looks are on him, and they follow his unspoken directions with perfect readiness. They ramble hither and thither as fancy leads them beneath the wild plum-trees, picking the stray fruit that has ripened before its season and fallen to the ground, then a russet persimmon or a choice pecan-nut shaken down by last night's wind. Their leader casts his eye from side to side, scanning everything that moves. Now a caressing love-note is uttered to his favorite hen; then, drawing himself to his full height, he gives a glance of scrutiny into the woods ahead of him, where the little pine trees open an extended vision. Passing a rotten stump, with a stroke of his stalwart leg and claws he tears down the rotten bark. A half inclination of the head, more graceful than that of any gentleman, defers to the nearest hen a curd-white grub that has rolled out from the wood, and with a low cluck of acknowledgment she picks it up. Now with one foot half raised, he searches for the cause of a sudden noise. Ah! it was only that opossum, and the turkeys care little for him when they are in a flock together, and now in passing he leaps up and catches a beetle that was crawling in a bush above him, now a may-apple, then a spider or plethoric tadpole stranded in the hollow of the receding waters, are all espied by these wandering gipsies, and immediately appropriated. At length they reach the banks of a river; there is a little hurry among the young hens. They don't like large streams: there are alligators and garfish in the water, and wild-cats and eagles prowling around the banks, yet the river is to be crossed, and they are not half so good at flying as they are at running. Indeed they would walk round the head of it, had they not learned that all Florida rivers connect, in some way, one with another. As it is, they walk up and down a little while on the high bank, clucking and purring, with an occasional pick at some misplaced feather, just as an old lady smooths down her apron before expressing any decided opinion. The cock may occasionally spread his fan if the sun shines brightly where he stands, and utter his loud thrumming sounds like the roll of a drum. He has eyed for some minutes a low-limbed juniper tree, standing near, and presently, after much examination, flits into it. Up go the hens in succession, and from the juniper they all fly to the upper limbs of a dead cotton-wood standing hard by. There is a continuation of the cluckings and notes of preparation, and then with the gobbler in the van, they launch themselves out in the air, and with broad extended pinions float in a slanting direction across the river, landing on the opposite side, at the edge of the underbrush, and are immediately lost to view.

I remember a pretty incident in connection with a turkey hen falling under my own eye, demonstrating a knowledge of character on her part.

I had taken my stand on the end of St. Rosas Island, off Pensacola, to watch for deer that the hounds were driving. After my arrival I noticed a turkey hen come skimming to the ground, and presently walk toward a knoll of grass a few yards from my place of concealment. Her anxious look and her feigned attitude of indifference immediately showed me that she was near her nest, and taking a little pocket spy-glass I carried with me to watch the water channels, I presently saw her settle herself down among some low willows, until I could discern nothing but her head.

Shortly afterward a fox came by, and coming across the trail of the turkey he turned short about, and throwing up his sharp nose, scented the different spears of grass the bird had touched, and then taking up her trail, commenced following it slowly and cautiously toward where she was sitting. With noiseless foot and undulating body he wound along in the trail, when suddenly, to my surprise, I saw the turkey hen leave her willow clump, and returning on her own trail, walk directly toward the fox. She picked hither and thither, in a nonchalant manner, and when within some ten or fifteen yards of her enemy, who had crouched in the sparse grass when he first saw her coming, she diverged slowly to the right, and the fox, as she turned aside, recommenced his crawlings, keeping his eye on the bird and leaving the trail he had been previously following. In this way they progressed some hundred yards in a direction contrary to her nest, when coming near a low tree, with a soft chuckle, which seemed to say, as plain as accent could make it, "what a fool you are," she flitted up in the tree.

The fox being then on open ground, at once knew himself discovered, and raising from his crouching position, after one or two longing looks, and a whimper of disappointment, trotted over the sandhills, and was lost to sight.

CHAPTER II.

THE CAMP FIRE.

" Under the shore his boat was tied,
 And all her listless crew
Watched the grey alligator slide
Into the still bayou."

LONGFELLOW.

"Turkey buzzard?" sarcastically cried my friend and hunting comrade, Poke, as, returning to camp, I laid my game down, and seated myself by the blanket that was serving for a table, and around which Poke, the hunter Mike, and the two negro boys were busy at their breakfast.

"Spring turkey?" inquired Mike, in delicate allusion to the age of my turkey.

It was generally the habit of the party to quiz each other at every success, and even mishaps were treated as sources of amusement.

"Da is har nuff to pizen all Floridy," said Scipio Africanus, raising the long tassel of beard hanging at the turkey's breast.

"Pooh!" said Poke, "I don't believe in that nonsense; it wouldn't kill a cat."

"Jis you try him, da's all; ya cut em up fine, and put

um in de grog or de bread, and don't he work um? Din't ole Ma'm Lize, on de Robinson plantation, take off Maussa Robinson? She be real nigger witch! Ole man, he took sick, and all ee doctors in Swanna couldn't cure him all winter, an' in de spring he die ob turkey beard. Dat's Gospel!"

"You nigga, mussen come cooking 'fore our fire, or we be habin' turkey beard too," retorts Cæsar, as with his black muscular arms, bare to the shoulder, he elbowed his darky brother aside to put a dish of meat before the party.

The sight of the smoking food brought every man's thoughts and fingers to the subject before him. The huge roll of cookery smelled good, but was by no means comely to look at. As layer after layer of green leaves were pulled off, there presently rolled out what might have been a pig in civilized life, but which we immediately recognized as an oppossum. His skin and hair adhered to the wrappings that had been bound around him, and which kept him from the ashes and the burning coals, and nothing now remained but the steamy fat little carcass that would have made a vegetarian forego his creed. Added to this there was a venison steak and some corn-bread, and Poke had a canteen of whisky hid away (the sensual dog!) and we feasted like kings, or rather as kings are supposed to feast, with great good humor and monstrous appetites, but which I verily suspect kings rarely have. Each one pulled at the 'possum, or cut strips from the venison, as he liked, and as fast as one cake was eaten, another would be ready on the stone in front of the fire. Beyond the circle sat the hounds, awaiting, with expressive attitude, the stray bits that were handed them from time to time; and joke, and tales, and future plans, were one by one rehearsed with laugh and hopeful wishes.

Poke was a jolly fellow. A critical judge of character might have said he was a little lazy, but none of us were critical, and who could blame a man who never lost his temper in all his life? His face was like an orange, so full and gentle, and the soft flaxen curls that clustered tight around his head were like a child's. A shrewd observer, he never saw a leaf changing color but he inquired the reason, and with his gentle air read human character with great facility. He seemed to know everything, medicine, and the arts, and the commonest little handicraft, and the greatest human theories, and he would discourse up to his waist in a miry slough upon the beauties of some aquatic plant as gracefully as in a parlor on the color of a painting. His true name was Earnest Pollock. His acquaintances called him Doctor, for he had studied medicine at Paris; the newspapers call him the Honorable Mr. Pollock, for he had once been appointed bearer of dispatches to Russia: I called him Poke, for I loved him. Poke was short in stature, and ready to talk. In this respect he was the counterpart of Mike, or Michael Hone, or Mike the Spook, as he was termed by different classes of people. Mike was gaunt, though not over tall, slow in his motions, and very quiet in whatever he did. There was no pretension or ostentation about him, and so far did he carry this negative virtue, that he never mentioned himself if he could avoid it, and no one could tell his intentions or anticipate his motives until the act was done. A leather dress, and a **leather cap,** the same colored shoes and belt, with a blue flannel shirt, buttoned in front **by** two polished alligator's teeth, was the invariable costume of the hunter. **Once he had a** cabin at Tampa, where he would come **and** go with such uncertainty that he obtained the name of Mike the Spook. Thence, at evening, when the set**tlers with** anxious eye regarded the forest that environed them, dreading the whoop of the Seminole on every wind, Mike would flit into the shadow, and begone a **month or** more, appearing again on the limits of the peninsula at Fort Dallas. The great interior wilderness was his home, and in its solitudes he had acquired his taciturnity. His voice was low and singularly musical. He might not speak for hours, the indication of his finger and the expression of his countenance being sufficient for all ordinary language, yet when he did, his tone was as effective as a command. The villagers at Micanopy called him Injun Mike, and said they never saw him **come or go** but in a storm, and they, hunters as they were, seemed afraid of his reckless will and strong arm.

Mike acted as guide in our wildwood roamings. He had undertaken it partly from a liking for me, and partly, as I suspected, from mere curiosity to see the Doctor and myself in the woods, for he would sometimes sit by the hour in his silent way, watching our motions and conversation. He never added a word, but if his opinion was asked, and the subject one that had been in the range of his observation, he answered the querist in the simplest manner. There he sat by the fire that morning; I remember him as if painted before me. His mahogany face wrinkled in kindly lines, and his chin covered by a long, thin beard. He was smoking in the Spanish fashion, rolling cigarettes from dried leaves across his knees, and his quizzical eye wandered over us with a considering look, as though we were children. A big, black and dun hound, with a melancholy face, stood beside him; it was said either of them could track a bear by the scent. He had acquired the Indian habit of inhaling smoke for some minutes, and then driving it out of his mouth and nostrils in dense volumes, as a whale fills his lungs with water, and then spouts it into the air.

The negro boys, Scipio and Cæsar, regarded him with feelings of respectful veneration. He excelled them in all their own handicraft. He knew every tree in the woods, and its uses; the habits of wild game, vegetable poisons, and the best manner of cooking; he could swim, ride, hunt, and shoot better than they. He had a close acquaintance with the Indians, and, the boys said, with the devil, and therefore there was a superstitious awe in regard to him, that was exhibited to no one else.

Besides the human members of our party, there were a dozen dogs of high and low degree. Mike had two;

they were long-eared, sad-looking hounds, with fierce **eyes.** I had a couple; one was a hound, and one a terrier. The negroes had four or five; you could not tell pre**cisely how many,** for they would appear and disappear like sprites, and sometimes one would be gone for a week or more, and then come to light at the **most** unexpected **moment.** The Doctor had one, and **his** name was Wag. Now there were two ways of seeing this dog, and therefore two ways of describing it. If he should be regarded through the Doctor's eyes, he was a Gelert in courage, of the sagacity of a fox, and so graceful and beautiful, and of such winning ways, that all the world loved him. But **any** one else in speaking of him would have called him a rusty, ragged, ill-tempered mongrel, with an elfish disposition for mischief. He stole our food, he frightened our game, he howled away our sleep, and whenever he saw vengeance coming he slunk away to his master's protection. He knew he did evil, and, with one eye on his pursuer, and his tail wagging, he would stand until standing was no longer safe, and then run for his life. Why the Doctor loved that dog I never could divine. He said he found him when a pup, and rescued him from some boys who had a rope around his neck preparatory to giving him a swing; if so, his humanity brought sad discredit on the canine race.

It is beyond the scope of my story to describe the toils and successes of each day in the campaign which had commenced that morning. Scenes of hourly interest to the actor, and adventures which to the hunter and naturalist would be beyond expression exciting, would be dull to the reader. Therefore, in a long winter's trip, that extended from the Suwanee River almost to Okechobee Lake, I can only recall those scenes that remained most strongly on my mind after the lapse of months, and which sometimes, when my brain is most active, will come up to me in my dreams, when in sleep I hear the wash of waves and the ringing music of hounds and guns, and the frantic rush of the chase in the deep everglades of the Seminoles. Yet there are many little minutiæ of an extended hunt to explain, as they form the regular duties of camp life.

After the breakfast has been dispatched, the one saucepan, one coffee-pot, and two tin coffee cups, are neatly cleaned, the two little vagabond horses which are possessed by the party are caught and led up with leading ropes around their necks. They are vicious, ragged-looking little beasts, but invaluable as pack-horses. On their backs we strap a couple of blankets folded in half; over that a little open frame-work, in which and to which we may fasten anything that is to be carried. This novel pack-saddle resembles a kitchen chair turned upside down. In it is put the little box containing our salt, pepper, vinegar, cloves, lard, etc., little matters, but of great use—we familiarly called the box "the kitchen;" also a small keg of powder, a bag of shot, another of bullets, caps, needles, thread, scissors, etc., then a joint of venison, or a turkey, or any article of food, the Doctor's trophies, skins of birds, skulls of animals, or strange flowers or sketches. Then the coffee-pot, frying-pan, etc., are hung on the perpendicular legs of the saddle, two axes are strapped to the sides, and the ponies move off after making two or three malicious kicks at the dogs and bystanders. Mike leads the van with a cat-like motion, his long rifle lying on his arm, and followed by his dogs. I generally came next in line, then the negroes and the ponies, and then the Doctor. We passed for the most of our time through an open pine country with a sandy soil. Here and there a grove of closer vegetation could be seen, and now and then a pool of water, surrounded by oaks and cypress, but generally the long vistas of slender trees would only be interrupted by some climbing plant, or the high knolls that traversed the country, following the general course of the drainage of the water. We only made one march a day of about eight hours, and then selecting some spot for the beauty of its location, or the abundance of its game, we pitched our camp, built our fire, turned out our horses, that is to say our ponies, and made ourselves as much at home as though we never expected to change. There were many days that we never broke up our camp, for the great abundance of game would entice us to stay, and then our resting-place gradually assumed a very comfortable appearance. A tent of boughs carpeted with skins, a a substantial fire, a well-stored larder, a pine slab table, and the Doctor, half reclining, smoking his pipe, and watching the frying joint, lest Wag should steal it, formed an agreeable picture of contentment in low life, and made one marvel how few are the necessaries in this world essential to our happiness.

Several times we had our domestic privacy intruded upon by our rustic neighbors during our absence, and once in a way that ruffled the Doctor's good humor very unusually. The camp had been left at early morning as usual, and from the ridgepole of our tent was suspended a sandhill crane, recently killed, and waiting for a cooking. In returning, toward the dusk of the evening, the negroes had separated to drive in the ponies, and the Doctor was leading the van, and talking of his bird, the sandhill crane, which at that season of the year was very fat and delicate. The fire had gone almost out as we came up to the tent, but by its light we could see the little matters around in their usual condition. The Doctor laid down his gun against a tree, and, stooping down, walked into the tent. At that instant there was a purring growl, Poke was hurled over on his back, amid a cloud of feathers, and a big wild-cat came dashing out over the Doctor's prostrate body.

"Oh! ah!" sputtered the Doctor. "Catch him! stop him! The wretch has eaten my crane!"

The dogs yelped; I fired a flying shot, and with two or three rapid bounds the cat leaped up into a huge magnolia tree growing hard by, and with a corkscrew motion was soon lost to sight in the dense foliage that extended far above the level of the surrounding trees.

On entering the cabin, I found Poke disconsolately sitting on his blanket, with the long bill of the crane in his hand, the sole relic the cat had left him for his supper.

It was a pleasant hour in the old woods, when our day's travel was ended, we had pitched our tent and drawn up around our gipsy camp while the huge fire flickered and crackled and lit up the green dome of the woods. The tree trunks, for a long distance around, were lighted into rugged distinctness, and behind them remained the wall of shadow. The evening meal was ended. The negroes had curled themselves up to sleep, and the rest of the hunters settling themselves down to the easiest positions they could invent, drew forth their pipes, the universal solace to the wanderer. The dogs still mumbled their bones, around the fire, with an occasional wrangle over some breach of canine etiquette, and the two ponies appeared once in a while, when the flame blazed brightly, munching the wild grass that grew around.

It was the hour for meditation, and my mind, blandly composed by the fatigues of the day, the glowing light, and the voluptuous climate, wandered back through misty years. I saw the blue crisp waves of distant lakes, and my hand held the tiller, and dear old faces looked up at me from the thwarts of a swiftly sailing boat. My cheek felt the free wind, my eyes filled with moisture, I heard voices that "murmured proud pleasure soft and low," and then I heard "zee-zee-zee-zip!" Ah, misery! what a mosquito! And there is another—has been sitting on my cheek for ten minutes, and I didn't see it.

And now that I am listening I hear them on every side zee-zee-zeeing all around me, and every moment taking a nip. Oh, I see how it is! I forgot to light my pipe. There are Poke and Mike in undisturbed dreams of tobacco and glory, smiling faintly at my convulsive slaps. Now my pipe is lighted—no more nips, blessed pipe. Why are mosquitoes created; and what do they feed on when they can't get blood? Please answer me an oft-repeated thought, sage frequenters in Southern swamps.

"Charlie, do you know what an alligator is?" drawled out the Doctor, after he saw me fairly roused to the comfort of the pipe.

"No, do you?" I replied.

"Not precisely, but I came very near knowing to-day. I was stooping to gather a strange flower on the bank of the river, when the earth caved in with me, and let me down with a fearful thump upon an old alligator that was sunning himself beneath. He gave a snort, and plunged into the river, and if he was half as frightened as I, he will never come ashore again."

"Pooh, man! why didn't you take him by the legs and lay him over on his back?"

"Oh, I hadn't the time; he wouldn't wait."

"Doctor Poke was up the bank before the alligator could see him," said Mike, in a low quizzical voice.

"Oh Poke! for shame, to decline a fair fight!" said I.

"Who wants to fight with such a huge dragon? Not you, I warrant!"

"Whar your pup alligators?" said Mike to the Doctor.

"Bless me, I forgot them!" exclaimed the Doctor, diving his hands up to his elbows in his capacious pockets; out came bits of thread, seeds of plants, little tin boxes, claws of birds, and finally two or three young alligators, about the size and shape of small daggers. They were of a mottled chocolate and yellow color, and feeling the genial effect of the fire, commenced scrambling around like tortoises. The Doctor, with a hand on each knee, regarded them with unfeigned delight, and Mike, between his puffs of tobacco, looked on the scene with a quirk in his cheek.

"Mammalia, oviparous, amphibious," enunciated the Doctor.

Just then one of the little animals inserted his nose under Cæsar's neck, as he lay snoring by the fire, and commenced wriggling himself into the woolly retreat.

"Bress de Lord!" shouted Cæsar, springing to his feet; "what am dat yer pizen little varmint—what fur you cum here, hey?"

Seeing our laughter, he shook himself, and going to the other side of the fire, rolled up again like a ball, pulling his blanket over his head, and went to sleep as soundly as before.

"Charlie, do you see that alligator's tail?" said the Doctor, as he pointed with the mouth-piece of his pipe at the caudal extremity of one of the little brutes, as it lay on the warm sand. I admitted that I did, first because it was true, and next because I saw the Doctor was in a humor to talk, and I did not want to contradict him.

"Now tell me why it is that this animal should have such a big tail, for so small a body, when any one knows he can't wag it with any pleasure?"

"Couldn't say, Poke."

"Can't you imagine, then?"

"Ornament," I blandly suggested.

"Ornament, indeed! Now, I have been studying these mammalia to-day. Mike and I went down Black Bayou after bear tracks, and I saw he was going further than I fancied, so I sat down to watch the alligators lying on the opposite bank. I then noticed that an alligator, when he came to the bank and heard the others grunting in the reeds, climbed up as far as he could go with his short legs, and then bending his tail under him, against the beach, by that means, with a single jerk, threw himself up on the bank. Now, therefore, as these animals live chiefly on streams with low perpendicular banks, as they, by this example, do mount the bank with the assistance of their tail, and as nothing was made for naught, ergo, their tails were made to climb banks with."

"As these animals frequently scratch themselves with their hind feet, and as nothing was made for naught, ergo, their hind feet were made to scratch themselves with."

"That is sheer malevolence," retorted Poke. "You try to take away my cane and don't offer another."

"I did. I consider the tail an ornament, of as much use as the tail of a mouse or a turkey gobbler."

"And why should so cruel a monster, hidden in these solitudes, have his person decorated?"

"And why should the flowers bloom in the everglades with the same glory of odor and color as they do in the Tuileries?"

"There you go again. You are never kept down to the practical bearings of nature."

"I warrant you that these negro boys would coincide with me, and give the true reason. Cæsar! Cæsar! you sleepy-head. Explain to us the use of the alligator's tail."

"Wha's dat, maussa?"

"What does the alligator do with his tail?"

"Suck um in de winter."

"You fool—you know better than that."

"Dat so fur true, maussa. Maussa Poke, nebber see little alligator in de egg, just gwine to hatch, hey? Den he see little alligator wid his tail in his mouf, and when he cum out de egg den he take him tail out of him mouf and eat hop-toads, and debil-bugs, and sich like, till winter cum on, and den he curl up in de mud and suck tail agin till hot time cum agin."

"Oh, Doctor, there you have it, an explanation by a child of nature. I hope you are content."

"Cæsar, you're a fool!" said the Doctor sententiously.

"Cæsar ain't fool nudder," interposed Scipio, raising his curly head from behind his comrade. "Ef he don't pickle young alligators, he sees 'em and knows suthin or nudder."

This retort was hailed with a volley of applause, and even Mike smiled at the Doctor's discomfiture.

Scip, evidently elated with his success, continued: "I knows alligator from time I picaninny. I knows alligator tail's good to eat. Course he sucks 'em. Alligator's science varmint, and when he roars in de spring-time he knows what he roarin' bout; ain't no fool, nudder, and makes speech wiser'n the judge in 'lection times."

"What does he say, Scip?"

"Maussa ask ole Aunty Foko what he say. She's got witch roots, and she knows how to talk alligator. She stay out all night in Oke'fnokee swamp, alligator neber so much as looks to her. She tell me what alligator say to his picaninnies."

"Don't, maussa, ketch me tellin' bout alligator and them little alligators layin' there wid ears wide open. 'Morrow mornin they'll be in the ribber, and ole alligators know all bout me."

"Well we will stop that, by carrying them away." So the little eavesdroppers were taken by the tails and dropped into the nearest watercourse, and the superstitious negro looked all about him with suspicious glance, rolled over to a more comfortable attitude, and commenced his story:

"You see Aunty Foko's Guinea nigger, cum ober from Cuba, but after her boy he gin out, she don't work any more, and tuck to de swamp. She be older'n Cæsar an me, boff togedder, and her hair a'mos' white. She

know de pizens, and she know all de woods, an' day an' **night is all de same to her; an' she** knows medicine to throw huntin' dogs off her track, an' nobody kin **ketch** her. An' she tell dis child all what alligator say, an' so I knows. Alligator lay he eggs in de sand, and den when dey hatch **out on some** blazin' hot day little alligators cut streeks fur de water right off; dat's **all** seen of em till night. Night cum, an' ole alligator dat keep **watch cum up on de** sand-bank, an' he find de little alligators all hatch out. Den he turn round and commence to croak little: nuflin come; he croak little louder, nuflin come; den he stand up on he toes and he roar like all natur. It makes de water shake; den young alligators cum, an' ole marm alligator cum, an' dey all stand dere togedder, an' **ef** de moon is shinen it's real savage fur to see 'em. An' de ole alligator he takes de chair, an' he tells em, and dis is jes what he tells em, I knows it's so, and so does Aunty Foko:

"'**You young** alligators, you great fools! you tink you sumthin an' you aint nuttin. You live half de time on land, t'other half de **time in** bayou, an' so you ben't smart in nudder. You be so loggish-like in de water you can't ketch fishes, and you got such little legs on land you can't come up to nuttin. Now you must larn, and when you've larnt then you'll know suthin. And I'll give you a teacher and he's de possum.'

"When de ole alligator says dis all de young ones larf, for dey knows what a possum is, for dey seed em a pokin' long the b'yous and dey's clined to de pinion dat possum's a fool. But de ole alligator growls em down an' den he say:

"'Possum, he great animal; not kase he fast, for he bery slow; not kase he strong and kin fight, for he bery weak; but kase he's sly. When he sees anythin' cumin he make b'lieve sleep an' ketch em. When he get ketched heself he make b'lieve dead, an' dey let him go. Now you all play possum.'

"Den ole alligator send all de picaninnies back in de water an' dey grow bery smart. An' dey learn to lay in de grass for sumthin to cum long nice, an' den gobble em up. An' dey roll in de mud till gets all covered, an' den cum up in de sun to get dry, an' nobody take him for alligator, an' would cum an' sit right down on em, an' den he grab em. An' after a while he gets so he lays side to de water, little piece back, an' when anyting cums along de bank, he hit him a slap wid his tail an' knock em in de water, and den he slide in after an' eat em up, an' de only ting he won't hurt 'tall is de possum. Possum nebber gits ketched 'tall, an' dat am a fac."

Before the negro's fable had ended, one by one his auditors' pipes had gone out. The fire had burned low, and shadows, not parlor shadows, but huge ghostly shadows, went and came among the forest aisles as the fire flickered high and low. In Scipio's legend I remembered my first experience with alligators, and as it is of a kin with the legend, and as Scip, immediately after his recital travelled away to the land of dreams, I will describe it:

I was visiting a friend some years ago who lived on

one of the many banks of Alabama on the Gulf coast, and whose plantation was intersected by several little creeks. One of these inlets was quite near the house, and the morning after my arrival, while dressing at my window, I saw a large alligator crawl out of the water and settle himself down on the grassy bank on the other side of this creek. Between the house and the creek was a rice field, and the rice bank built along this inlet intercepted all view except from the upper part of the house, so I would have an easy approach.

Immediately I seized my double-barrel shot gun, and loaded it with the heaviest size shot I could find in my room, descended the stairs, and made my way across the rice-field to the rice bank, and there lay my prize on the other side of the creek, wholly unconscious of his fate. He was a huge beast, with scales glistening in the rising sun, and his big yellow eye shining like a golden pippin. After a moment's survey and a mental congratulation that there was a creek separating me from the monster, I took aim at the largest part of his body and fired. I heard a splash in the water, and when the smoke cleared away the waves showed me the spot where my friend had disappeared, and after waiting some time to see if he would float ashore dead, I gave it up and went back discomfited. As I entered the house I saw a dozen grinning rows of teeth at the kitchen window, and was thus made aware that the negroes were enjoying the spectacle of my skill in hunting.

At breakfast my friends questioned me about my shot,

which they had evidently heard of from the servants, and I learned, for the first time, that I could only kill the alligator with a ball, and even with that it was no certain matter. I also was informed that this particular alligator had frequented that spot for several years, and was well known on the plantation by the name of John Bull.

The next morning as I rose I incontinently cast my eye over to the bayou, and there, in the full enjoyment of the glories of the sunrise, lay my yesterday's acquaintance. It did not take me three minutes to get into my clothes and down to the rice bank. I saw the grinning waiters at the door, but I did not care, for I was armed with a rifle and sure of my game. I took a rest on the high bank, and sighting for a big chocolate spot on his side, I fired away. A wheeze, like a plethoric alderman, came from across the creek, and with a mighty splash the animal slid into the river, and the dark waters closed over him. I knew I had not missed him, but, as he did not rise, I supposed him dead at the bottom.

"Well, Charlie, my boy, how's the shooting to-day?" was the hearty salutation of my host as I took my seat at breakfast. A suppressed giggle, behind me, informed me that the negroes were enjoying the joke, and I had to explain it as best I could, which I did, by assuring my friend that the alligator was dead at the bottom of the river.

"How's that, Johnson? Do you think you can find his body?" said my friend to his huntsman, as he came in to get his orders for the day.

"Find his body, sah? Yes, sah, easy nuff find his body, sah; de body crawled up on de bank before de genleman got quite in the house, sah."

Every one laughed at me, and I did not forget the mishap until I became engaged in shooting, in which we spent all the day. The next day was a repetition of precisely the same farce, except that the conduct of the servants became quite extraordinary, laughing outright, as I went across the rice-field, and the little nigs came out of the cabins in crowds, and crowed with delight.

"Well, Charlie, my boy, how's the shooting to-day?" became a stereotype question at the table, and "tough as an alligator, hey?" one of the commonest comparisons.

At last my patience and my visit were finished together, and as I was being pulled out to meet the Mobile steamer in my friend's canoe, manned by eight as good oarsmen as ever pulled a blade, in passing by the head of the creek a heavy splash was heard in the water, and my friend whispered to me, loud enough to create a chuckle among the boatmen, "There's your target, you have left behind."

CHAPTER III.

A BEAR IN THE CAMP.

I'll pitch my tent on dis camp ground
A few days, and a few days,
Till I give old Cuff annudder round,
A few days, and a few days.
Wake, snakes, day's a breaking.
NEGRO BALLADS.

AFTER one or two days of quiet southward travel, sometimes verging toward the seaside, sometimes turning into the back country, we came one day on the banks of the Wakassare River, a deep, black stream that empties into the Gulf. No fording place being discovered, we halted preparatory to crossing the river. As this is an everyday exploit in travelling a new country, as much traversed by sluggish streams as the Florida peninsula, a description will not be unimportant.

Picture to the eye of fancy a camp, with all its accessories of rustic comfort, its bright fire, its feeding ponies, dogs, and hunters under the pine woods. Before it a close hummock of tangled vines, and tall trees bordering the bank of the river, and the long vines pendent from the branches. Beyond this leafy barrier, turbid with the gleanings of swamps, with whirl and glassy eddy, the dark tide of the river moves onward to the sea, trailing with it the floating skirts of moss that still cling to the trees. On the far side a dense canebrake arises from the low bank, from whose fastnesses, as the shadows settled on the view, came forth the quacking of ducks and the booming of bittern.

On such a scene we looked one afternoon, and forthwith began our preparations for crossing. Selecting from the fallen pine trees one or two logs of medium size, we cut them in uniform lengths, and dragged them to the water's edge, where they were bound in couples with grape-vine wythes. After having having made several couples, they were gently launched over the drifting wood and tangled roots that cluttered up the side of the river, and were all connected together with a rope, and then tied to a tree. This was our ark, and on it were placed, first of all, the powder and other ammunition, and Mike, as captain, and the two negroes as crew, each armed with a long pole and a rude paddle, began the first trip. First fastening the end of a long rope to a tree on the shore from whence they started, they poled out until the depth of the water prevented them from touching bottom, and then with the paddle slowly worked their way to the opposite bank. Then commenced the difficulty. The tall canes grew down into the water, and presented a barrier to the entrance of so obtuse a vehicle as a raft; and though they might be pushed aside sufficiently to effect an entrance, they would spring up on every side, and hedge the pioneers in an inclosure as tight as a bird-cage. To meet this difficulty, Mike sat down on the bow of the raft, and with a hatchet cut away the reeds, as the negroes poled the raft, until a narrow lane was cut through to *terra firma*, and the men landed with the munitions. Here selecting a sturdy cabbage palmetto, they fastened the other end of the rope securely, thus making a taut line entirely across the river, and throwing away both poles and paddle, by means of the rope pulled back to the shore from which they started.

Next came the ponies' turn, and with much coaxing, and some pushing and pulling, one of their equine highnesses was brought on board the raft and pulled to the other shore, where, when he was loosened, he quickly disappeared in the reeds. Sometimes we made him swim by the side of the raft, but it was a dangerous attempt in large rivers on account of the alligators that were tempted to nibble at the legs so invitingly paddling above them.

The third trip brought the other pony, who, by his obstinacy, came near breaking up the raft; and, finally, I rode over with the balance of the camp equipage and the dogs, that had to be tied up at the beginning of the operations to prevent them swimming, which, had they attempted, they would certainly have been lost by the rapaciousness of the alligators, that even in the early fall were still very active in all the rivers.

Lastly the raft was sent back empty, with Scipio to unfasten the end of the rope. He, after casting off the rope, pulled himself leisurely ashore with the slack line, and taking off the rope that had been used in the construction of the raft, he followed us back from the river to where we had pitched our camp for the night.

While coming through the canebrake, Mike, with an indication of his finger, and a quiet smile, pointed out the track of a bear impressed in the soft mud; his huge paw and leg left a print as though a man had walked by on his knees. The Doctor stepped around his mark rather suspiciously, and, I noticed, looked back at it as though suspecting his bearship might retrace his steps. The dogs were still tied, and they threw up their noses and whined piteously, but it was too near night, and we would not let them loose. The marsh was alive with ducks, and the grey egret, with his long crest, would constantly rise around us with a whoop of surprise. Indeed, the whole bottom was trodden up with the tracks of deer, turkey, and the smaller game that find refuge in these close coverts.

After making our camp, and as the darkness drew its curtains around us, shutting in the bright firelight, and shutting out the void of darkness beyond, all the natives of the forest and river lifted up their voices in concert. Each bird or beast that dwelt in these heavy brakes uttered his individual note, and while smoking one's pipe, lying by the fire, the mind amused itself listening to the confused cries and distinguishing them one from the other. The ducks quacked and fluttered in the marsh, the raccoon's plaintive call sounded its decrescendo from the wood, the honk of the heron, the shrill clatter of the rail, the mournful howl of the wolf, ascended in turn, or in a confused medley, now low, now high, as the wind rose or fell, and all up and down the river the bellowing of the alligator domineered over every other sound, with its huge volume of noise. Then there were other sounds that played low accompaniments to the bass of the river. The occasional twitter of a bird, the drops of the chinquapen nut, the patter of the dew falling from the trees, and the rustle of the leaves, all joined in that nocturnal anthem that was swelling from every rood of ground on the great Peninsula, and entered into our souls by the Wakassare with the mysterious lulling influence with which nature's chorus affects the human mind, where it is left open to the whisperings of the wild creations of God.

The day dawned reluctantly, the morning after our crossing, and so slowly the light broke through the mist that environed the camp, that it was more like moonshine than daylight. Drip, drip, drip, pattered the gathering moisture from the cypress trees into the pools beneath. The osier-grass bent down, heavy with the dew, the ferns were matted to the earth, and the glassy leaves of the magnolia glinted with a double lustre of sheen and water. "Like a sea fog landward bound," the warm fog shut us in, as did a few hours before, the darkness. The voices of the night were hushed with the dawning, and all animal life was motionless, save where, now and then, from the invisible heights of the tree-tops, some moving animal would shake down showers of drops.

"Geon—en—tu—ent!" roared out all the dogs in chorus, and before any one could get to his feet, a huge black bear dashed through the camp. Page 45.

One by one the negroes came to life, and yawning and muttering gathered together the remains of the fire. The Doctor raised himself on his elbow, and benignantly surveyed the dull circuit of a dozen yards that the mist left open to his vision. The dogs snuffed the air wistfully, looked into the trees, and sauntered out into the mist, looming as large as the ponies as soon as they gained a little distance. In a moment a sharp yelp was heard from one of the smaller dogs. Again, after a pause, another, then a prolonged " yeough " from an old hound.

"Whas dat are!" said Scipio, raising his curly pate from the coals that he was vigorously trying to blow into a blaze.

"Nebber you attendsiate to the dogs, you lazy nigger; you cook," retorted his comrade, and Scipio renewed his puffing.

"Geow-ou-ou-ou!" roared out all the dogs in chorus, with a burst of clamor that awakened the sleepers, and before any one could get to his feet a huge black bear, that appeared as big as a bull, dashed out of the fog, followed by all the dogs in full cry, right through the camp, scattering the fire, overthrowing Scipio in the ashes, scaring the ponies from their tethers, and leaving the Doctor sprawling on his back.

"Bress de Lord!" shouted the negro, scrambling out of the coals; "did de Lord ebber see like o' dat?"

"Tally-ho!" echoed the Doctor, hurriedly snatching an axe.

"After him!" shouted Mike, and with cheer and cry every soul dashed out in pursuit, and the camp that stood so picturesquely still in its first awakening, after the one rude rush of the chase was left deserted, while we followed the wide trail and frantic cry of the hounds.

The game, immediately after crossing the camp, turned toward the river, and entered the dense canebrake that fringed the shore for some miles. The hounds bayed and yelled with excitement, and hunters and negroes followed helter-skelter, now over grassy holes, starting the duck from her covert, now over slippery trunks of fallen trees that had been floated by the water, and left to molder green in the damp. One moment held back by a vine, at another so crowded by the reeds as to be obliged to lean down and run like a rail. One moment the crashing of reeds and baying of the hounds were close to us; then again they would gain on us; but far or near, we went plunging and rushing forward with a sense of intentness that gave no thought to anything but the chase. Soon we became separated; one man, plunged into a slough to his waist, was left to extricate himself; another was turned here, another there, by intervening obstacles, and presently I was left alone, following always the fierce rush before me, that wound hither and thither among the reeds, now pausing as if at bay, and then rushing on to the right or the left, as the hunted animal was assailed by the dogs coming up from either side.

Shortly there was a pause, and the prolonged

"Oo-oo-o!" of the hounds proclaimed the bear was at bay, and hastening in the direction, I came into a close thicket of canes that had sprung up as thick as wheat from the rich bottom land.

I could hear the bear, before I came to him, snorting and grumbling with rage, and as I entered his covert, I saw him on his haunches, with his back against a bank, his eyes red, his mouth open, shedding foam in huge drops on the ground, and surveying the dogs that were ranged in a semicircle around him, panting with rage, and bearing marks of Bruin's claws that had evidently taught them discretion.

But the greatest mark of respect to the grim woodking was presented in the person of the Doctor. He sat directly in front of the bear, and scarcely six steps off; his feet were half buried in the mud, and he was seated on the same easy cushion. His coat and vest were wide open, his hat was gone, his curly flaxen hair hung matted with sweat and dew, and his axe, that great weapon of offence and defence to the forest knight, was held in both hands directly in front of him, the handle sticking in the ground, and the blade pointing directly to the bear. If the bear's tongue was lolling, so was the Doctor's; if the bear seemed out of breath with his chase, the Doctor was doubly so with his; if Bruin disliked his position, the Doctor appeared more than uncomfortable in his. In his hurry he had tumbled down over the bank directly in front of the quarry, and what with the chase, and what with the fright of this fearful juxtaposition, the bear was in the better position of the two. The Doctor with his axe presented, and the bear rampant, with his fore paws just touching the toes of his hind ones as they projected up in front of him, resembled much some old coat of arms I had seen, only the Doctor's position was somewhat new in heraldry.

"Hurrah!" I yelled; "have at him!"

"Eh—eh," said the Doctor, all out of breath, "shoot him—eh—eh—quick—eh!"

I levelled my gun, and the bear's quick eye glanced at me fiercely over the barrel. I pulled the trigger, and a dull snap followed; the bear shook his head. Another snap, and another—my gun was wet with the dew.

The bear thus insulted gave a low growl, and a quick toss to his sharp nose. The dogs, construing this a challenge, and emboldened by our presence, rushed forward, and the huge brute, with a skill that was incomprehensible, would box them off with his fore-paws. One would be sent with a slap a dozen paces in the air; another would get a long cut from the bear's sharp claws, as he sat up like a boxer knocking over children with a mischievous playfulness that seemed more like fun than malice. Wag was there, as pert as the best hound in the brake, yelping, running, biting, and making much noise, and yet keeping out of danger. At length his turn came; a well-directed blow of that big black paw sent him curled up like a kitten, and as senseless as a rag, into his master's arms.

Poor Doctor! this seemed to awaken him, and springing to his feet he aimed a blow at the bear's head, that, had it taken effect, would have cloven him in two, but a scarcely perceptible motion of the same black paw sent the axe flying away among the canes, while the Doctor, from the parrying of the blow, came over on his face, and the bear, with a growl and crash, rushed off again into the canes, followed by the whole yelling pack.

The Doctor, gathering himself together, picked up his axe, and listened with me to the lessening crash of the chase as it turned down the river, cry of dog, and crackle of brush, and now and then the whoop of the negroes, who had apparently come up with the chase. At length another pause, and then the peculiar notes of the hounds, and the calls of the negroes, told us the bear was again at bay, and, having recovered our breath, we started to overtake it.

As we came in view of the spot selected by Bruin for his fight, we saw all the dogs gathered about the base of a tree, the elder ones squatted on their haunches, and the younger ones jumping up and snapping their teeth at the bear, who was comfortably seated on a huge limb, balancing himself with the skill of a dancer and the burlesque gravity of a comedian. The most urbane simplicity marked his countenance; he seemed of a character that would not have harmed a child, and if I had not seen him a few minutes before boxing the dogs with such vindictive vigor, I would have been willing to have climbed the tree, and put my arms around his neck. He looked down at us condescendingly, now and then winking his eye blandly, and then with a dexterous use of his paw, he scratched his side, or rubbed his nose, when the flies tickled him.

Presently Mike came up, with his rifle on his arm. A glance up in the tree, and he quietly took his seat on a log, remarking, as he did so, "He bear."

"Oh! what a murderous animal!" said the Doctor. "Look at my dog there; how he has treated him."

Sure enough, the dog was a living witness to bad treatment. He could just move, and when he lay down he gave one or two short yelps of mingled pain and spite. Never was a dog more miserably punished; had he been heavier he would have been killed, but as it was, he was only bruised, and woefully frightened.

The Doctor looked grimly at the bear. "Shoot him, why don't you?" he continued to Mike; "just see him making fun of us all!"

Mike wiped his rifle with his coat sleeve and raised it to his shoulder. A pause, and the clear ring of the shot was followed by a convulsive leap of the hunted animal, and a short, fierce cry, and crashing through the intervening limbs he came with a heavy, dull sound to the ground. We ran up to him; he did not move. The ball had entered his eye, and the bear was dead.

I looked at Mike. With his still smile on his wrinkled face, he was carefully fitting a ball to his rifle. He didn't even glance at his prize.

CHAPTER IV.

THE DANGERS OF FIRE-HUNTING.

> "The pass was steep and rugged,
> The wolves they howled and whined;
> But he ran like a whirlwind up the pass
> And left the wolves behind."
>
> MACAULAY.

"Mike, what kind of night would this be for fire-shooting?" said the Doctor to that meditative Nimrod, who was busy sewing up a moccasin by the light of the camp-fire, after a week of travel.

"So, so," replied Mike, without looking up.

"I am going, I think."

No answer. Mike put on the mended moccasin, and drew off the other.

"Do you think we can kill anything?"

"S'pose," replied Mike.

"Come Charlie, let us try it for a little while."

This was all a ruse on the part of Poke, in order to make Mike think our great hunt was an unpremeditated affair, and thereby increase the glory of killing so much game. It had been arranged between us during the day, that we would try fire-hunting that night. It promised to be a cloudy night, which was of great advantage, as it prevented the game from seeing anything of the hunters, and at the same time rendered their eyes more reflective when exposed to the torchlight. We had even gone so far as to make our pitch-pine torches, and the whole preparation was complete. It was a party of two—the Doctor and myself. There would be rather more interest in getting the game alone; and beside that, Mike's opinion on fire-shooting was well-known, and we knew he would not go with us —so constant a hunter scorned so primitive a snare as the one we proposed. The negroes we did not want, for the fewer in a party the better. So, one of us taking a gun, and the other carrying a torch, we left the camp.

The boys were chuckling together as they watched us go, the dogs howled because they could not go with us, and Mike gave one of his expressive coughs, that said as plainly as words, "Now for it."

We were soon outside of the glare of the camp-fire, the little creek was crossed, and our torch flashed brightly on the taper trunks of the pine trees, the climbing-vines, and the broad-leafed plants that grew by the pools of water. There was no wind, and, walking in the pine woods, there was no sound. Once in a long while, a sand-hill crane, disturbed in his wanderings, would be seen stalking away, with his red head high in air, like a sentry on duty; or the sudden motion of the underbrush would tell us that some one of the many little harlequins of the wood, that gambol most when men do sleep, had fled from this unusual spectacle of a moving light. But no deer rewarded our search; no bear showed us his heavy coat.

"Faith," said the Doctor, "this romantic promenade is getting somewhat long."

"Think of the deer, one buck will well pay us."

"Fudge! if there was no one to laugh at us, I would have turned back long ago. Give me the gun, and you take the light."

Accordingly we changed positions—I going ahead, carrying the torch before me, in such a manner that it would throw the light ahead as much as possible, and none on our persons, and the Doctor received the gun, and took my place directly behind and shaded by my person. The night had become still darker, and a misty rain commenced falling. We had left the pine woods, after walking a couple of miles, and had come into a grove of lower timber. The long moss drooped in curtains, the odor of magnolias burdened the air, and every minute a denser copse would force us to turn aside from our route.

"Hush!" whispered the Doctor, suddenly, with a spasmodic pull at my coat tail, "there's a deer."

I was just wondering at this absence of deer, and could not account for it, as it was a rare thing to go a mile in Florida without seeing one.

"Where?" I whispered; "I don't see it."

"Hush! it has gone now; but we will see it in a moment again."

We advanced on tiptoe, both in body and expectation.

"There! there!" said the Doctor, pointing with his

finger a little distance to the left; but the luminous spot was gone before I hardly got my eye on it.

We were in the very place for deer. A heavy windfall lay ahead of us, and the mingled trunks and twisted branches looked like the *chevaux de frise* to some great encampment. The flickering light made the shadows move back and forth with a spectral effect, as though dancing, and the hush of the forest was unbroken by any sound. Every moment, I expected to see again the two phosphorescent stars that indicate the deer's eyes, and then the true shot would bring us the prize for our labor. It seemed a long time in coming again.

"That deer must be very shy," whispered the Doctor, just above his breath.

The next time, I saw it first. It was some distance ahead, and there were two; but before I could point them out to my comrade, they had disappeared. Presently, we saw it on one side of us.

"Charlie, that's a will-o'-the-wisp," said Poke, in rather a subdued tone, "or the devil; who ever heard of a deer going around so?"

"He is examining you to see what manner of man you are."

"Perchance it is some spirit of a departed buck, leading us a wild chase to destroy us."

"There it is, right behind me, as I live!" ejaculated the Doctor, in evident trepidation.

Sure enough, as I turned my head, I saw the two blue lights that indicate the reflecting lenses of the eye. The

Doctor was taking aim, but I noticed it was not very steady. He pulled the trigger—a dull snap announced a miss-fire. He pulled the other trigger—it snapped in the same way. The gun was wet with rain.

"Was anything ever so provoking!" said Poke, as the eyes vanished in the darkness.

"If it is the devil, he will have you now."

"How *can* you talk so," said the Doctor, with a strong accent on the "can."

"There is your deer, Poke, in the windfall," said I, as I caught sight of the eyes moving rapidly along over the mass of timber that lay heaped and knotted together.

"That's no deer," said Poke; "no cloven-foot could ever go over that windfall that way. I would rather see the night huntsman of the Hartz Mountains than see those eyes again." As he was speaking, I saw in the inky darkness ahead of us, another pair of eyes, and two or three pairs on the left. The truth flashed on me. The scarcity of the deer, the proximity of the windfall, the restlessness of those baleful eyes, all gave me the clue—the wolves were around us.

A word to Poke, and the affair was explained, and we stood still for consultation. We tried new caps on our gun; but it was of no use, the cones were saturated with water. We turned toward the camp, but in our confusion we forgot the direction. To heighten the misery of the scene, our torch was almost burnt out—let that die, and the rest could be easily divined.

We were standing, at the time, under a grove of small

pecan trees, and at that instant a low snort was heard from the shadow near us, like the cough of a dog.

Poke did not say a word; but, dropping the gun, and seizing a limb of one of the trees over his head, with an agility for which I had never given him the least credit, elevated himself to the crotch, about ten feet from the ground.

I did not want to do anything of the kind, of course not; I would rather have placed my back against a tree, and won a glorious death in battle against my numerous foes; but, alack! for a bad example, I dropped the torch, that broke in pieces in falling, and, clasping the nearest tree, which happened to be a medium-sized gum-tree, soon scrambled up to a place of safety. Lucky was it for me that I had that torch in my hand, for when it fell, it lay scattered around the base of the tree, still flickering and flashing in the darkness, and the animals that had surrounded us, as they saw their prey escaping, rushed forward with an angry noise; they saw the glowing embers, and held back just long enough to permit my escape. As I drew myself up on the first limb, a rush of gratitude passed over my soul, and my feelings were as warm as a child's. Nothing could be seen, for the sombre forest shut out the little light there was in the atmosphere, but I heard the pattering of feet beneath my fortress, like falling rain. Back and forward they came and went, and snorting sounds and champing teeth made the black night alive with imaginary shapes. I wondered how it fared with the Doctor, yet dared not call, for the uncertainty was less fearful than the reality might be. I pictured him fallen, dragged back from his half-attained refuge, and divided among the hungry pack; and the very noises below might be the mumbling of his bones,

> "While their white tusks crunched o'er his whiter skull,
> As it slipp'd through their jaws when their edge grew dull."

At length I summoned courage, and called "Poke!"

"Hulloa!" was the response—more grateful to my ear than any sound in the world.

"How are you, my boy?" I called again.

"Safe, thank the Lord!"

"What a disgraceful situation to be in, and how are we to get out of it?"

"I will be grateful if I can only keep in it; for this tree is so small, that the wolves can almost reach me when they jump; and, as I climbed up, one caught my coat-tail, and tore it entirely off."

"Climb up higher, then."

"I can't; the tree is so small that, when I get any higher, it bends over, and lets me down—oh dear!"

"Haven't you your pistol with you? Try and shoot one, and it may frighten them."

"Oh, dear, no; there are hundreds of them. Just look at them below!"

I looked down, and surely I could see a drove of them. They were evidently the grey wolf, for, in spite of the darkness, I could, once in a while, detect their motions from their light coats.

Poke suggested they were phantom wolves and declared they were all white.

All the fearful stories I had ever read, came coursing through my brain. I saw snow-buried huts snuffed out and ravished by these prowlers, and heard the shriek of the child, thrown from the sleigh by its fear-maddened mother, and many an old dream reshaped in my mind the terrors of nights of fever. Were we to be tired out by their devilish patience? Was one gang to relieve another, until we wearily fell into their hot tainted jaws, thus to be hurled into oblivion?

I shouted in the hope that some one might hear me; but what good to shout in that midnight forest? I heard a voice—it was Poke saying his prayers. I listened devoutly, but could offer none myself.

When he had finished, I called to him. He answered faintly—

"What is it? speak quickly; I can't hold on much longer."

"Fire your pistol; do try, it may bring some help, even if it does not kill."

"I will try," answered Poke.

"There was a momentary pause, and then the sharp crack of a pistol was followed by the singing of a bullet close by my ear. By the flash, I saw Poke, hatless, and almost coatless, hanging on to the topmost branch of a young pecan, that bent with him like an orange-tree under a heavy load of fruit. With the report of the pistol, there was a scramble among the voracious crew at our feet; but they did not go away permanently, and were back in a moment.

"Fire the other barrel, dear Poke, but try and fire it the other way—point it down."

Bang! sounded the pistol, and I heard a thump on the ground, as the poor fellow threw away the now useless weapon.

"Hold on, Poke; take heart, my dear boy."

"Oh, it is easy enough to say take heart, but when the tree bends a little more than usual, I am within a foot of these hell-hounds. Oh, dear!"

At this moment, I thought I saw a light flashing through the foliage. A moment more, I was sure of it.

"Poke, Poke, they are coming—some one is coming."

"Where—where! Oh, dear, I can't turn my head, lest I slip off."

"There they come; I see them—three torches, and men and dogs."

"God bless them!" I heard Poke say, faintly.

I was afraid he was fainting. "Hold on, Poke," I said, and screaming to the men, I called them to hurry. On they came, at a run. I recognized them as they came up with their torches flashing through the woods; they were Jackson and his men. He had been in our camp only the day previous, and told us he had a sheep farm in this neighborhood. "Quick, this way," I shouted—"the wolves! the wolves!" He answered me. How blessed a thing was the sound of a human voice in our necessity. They came under the trees we were in.

"Hulloa there! where are you? where are the wolves?" he shouted in his stentorian tones.

"Dare's de sheep I'm bin huntin' all dis bressed night," exclaimed a negro who accompanied Jackson on his search.

I looked around, and there was Jackson's big flock of sheep, staring blandly at us up in the trees, and at their master, by turn. It had been their eyes we had seen in the darkness.

And there was Jackson see-sawing on a fallen tree—hiccoughing, and laughing and crying by turns—and there were the negroes, and they called in the sheep, "Ho! ho! ho! Oh laws a maussy, did I ever—ho! ho! ho! ho!—wolves, oh laws a maussy!"

Poke slid down the tree he was in, picking up his coat-tail, that had been torn off by a broken limb in his hurried ascent, sighing:

"Oh! that I had the wings of a dove."

CHAPTER V.

THE PLANTATION HOUSE OF "FAR AWAY."

"Ofttimes, in travelling through the west,
The stranger finds a Hoosher's nest.
In other words, a Buck-eye cabin
Just big enough to hold Queen Mab in."

JACKSON, the sheep-raiser, whose timely arrival had driven away the phantom wolves, was a fair example of many a planter. He was tall in figure, sauntering in gait, wearing a black beard and moustache, and hair so long as to be confined behind his ears. His hazel eyes were large and expressive, flashing with excitement, or quizzical with mirth, his face was sallow, his lips thin and stained with tobacco, his dress loose, and extravagant in color when he was where he could select it. His manners were like his dress, and he seemed reckless of all appearances as to what he said or did. He was wealthy, after his kind; that is to say, he had dogs and horses without number, and "men-servants and maid-servants were born in his house," and he owned, by inheritance, acres of land enough to have made him a duke in Rhineland; and yet for ready money he was poor as Peter the Hermit. Debts he had many, but they did not depress him; friends by hundreds, who would every one of them have gone his security for a million, yet could not have loaned him a hundred dollars in a month. He lived in a low, badly-built, wind-cracked, fenceless, vineless, paintless mansion in the Pine Lands, yet the proudest chief of all the McGregors could not have equalled the courteous pride of manner with which he welcomed the stranger to his home, and made him his friend. No matter for the rickety table; he scorned to mend it, and no one saw its defects, it was so gracefully presided over. He never alluded to the food he asked you to eat, and you never saw it was only pork, sweet potatoes, and corn bread. He was bountiful with the choicest wine, lavish of command, and never by any possibility did any labor that could be either deferred or avoided. Yet, for all that, he was an ardent hunter. Strange to say, all lazy people love to fish or hunt, and Macpherson Andrew Jackson loved the latter. Nor bush, nor savannah, nor river, nor heat, nor rain deterred him. He would ride where mortal man could ride, just for the fun of the hunt. So we camped by the side of his house, in compliance with an invitation from the proprietor, to spend a few days with him in pursuit of the chase.

Jackson's palace was of one story and two wings, and the whole building was raised from the ground about three feet by means of wooden posts, which left a pleasant abiding-place beneath for whole broods of young negroes that constantly lay in this novel kennel, looking out like young puppies. The cyperus grass grew sparsely in the white, sandy soil around the house, and the few out-buildings that straggled hither and yon. Fences there were none, but the overshadowing live oaks, with their trailing moss, gave an air of grace to the establishment that man never attempted to improve.

"Hulloa!" cheered the lord of the manor, as we drew up to the house a few days after our misadventure with the sheep; "glad to see you at Far Away. The door is never shut, and the bottle never corked, and we will make you at home for a year and a day. You Tom! Cuff! You Cuff! Hannibal! here, run call the boys to take the horses and tie up the hounds. Run, all of you! Fine day, this, for hunting. Bring out some glasses, Melissa! Dogs can nose well to-day. Lively there! Well, bring some tin cups, if there are no glasses, you lazy huzzy!"

The negroes ran, our dogs howled acquaintance with the dogs of the place, the little nigs looked on from every out-of-the-way corner, and with shout, and laugh, and much confusion, we soon had our tent pitched by the spring, the ponies tethered, and everything well regulated about us. Then came a good dinner, cooked in one of those little disconnected kitchens so favored by your true darky cook, who, when not engaged in stirring the pepper pot, or turning the corn-bread, stands in her red bandana in the doorway with her arms akimbo, looming as large as the wonderful fat woman in the Museum. We brought game, and Jackson had cooks, and we all dined well, and then a glass of good old wine, whose parent stock shaded the gravelly banks of the Garonne, carried our minds to other lands, and sent our tongues travelling all around the world for adventures.

It was dark as we finished the bottle, and Jackson unlocked his closet for another. I believe that wine-closet was the only thing that was locked on the whole place. The negroes had crawled out of their curious retreats, and were lying around in groups. The sheep-drivers had come in from the folds, and the tinkling of tiny bells announced that the sheep were penned for the night. The camp-fire was lit, pipes were smoking, Jackson was sitting against one of the pack-saddles, and his daughter was reclining against his knees. His daughter was a brunette girl of sixteen years of age, and her mother was dead, it was said, many years ago.

"*He* was a gentleman," said Jackson, pursuing a description he had been giving of some one living on the coast. "He never took an insult, and never gave one; what more could be said of any man?"

"And he gave dis child a dollar Christmas day—course he's a gentleman," struck in Hoppin Lem, the planter's favorite servant, who, squatted on his haunches a few yards behind his master, drank in all the conversation, and joined in the laugh, with the low "yah-e—ah-ah-ee!" so peculiar to the negro.

"Hold your tongue, you black rascal!" said his master.

"Was it not he who shot young Travers in a duel at the Mobile races?" asked the Doctor.

"Of course it was, and did it as bravely as any man

ever did. Yet that duel ruined him; he has been a broken-down man ever since."

"How is that?"

"Why you see they had a dispute about the winning horse. He said that Centiped came in first, and Travers replied that if had not staked so much money on Centiped he would have seen straighter. This was a reflection on his honor that no one was expected to stand. He challenged Travers, and Travers fell at the first fire. It wouldn't have been so bad, but Travers' old mother got wind of the duel from some of those Puritan meddlers, and came riding down to the field with her grey hair all streaming, and when she saw her son dead she cursed him. I wasn't there, but those that were there said it was a hard thing to see. He never got over it. It was a windy afternoon, about sunset, when the duel occurred, and to the present time, when there comes up a hard wind about that time of day, the poor fellow rides off as if the devil was after him, and will not speak to man or beast."

"What a diseased mind a man must have to fight a duel!" said the Doctor.

"How can he help it—is he going to have his honor impugned, his character insulted? He would fall so low that no one would speak to him."

"But he does not mend his character by killing a friend, and haunting his conscience."

"That is an accident inseparable from society. There are certain wrongs which the pistol alone will redress, and the duel puts the feeble gentleman on an equality with the greatest bully."

"No," said the Doctor, his impassible nature gradually warming, "it lowers the gentleman to a bully. If he gets shot, his honor dies with him; if he kills, he is a broken man—either way the wrong is doubled; and it is, after all, the bully that supports the institution."

"No, sir; it is the gentleman that supports the system, and is supported by it. What else gives the navy and army its character, and holds it together—what protects the weak, and cowers the laboring poor whose strength would make him over-reaching—what gives a tone to the gallantry of the South but a power that punishes insult?"

"And murders its own children!" added the Doctor.

"Murder! do you call it murder? My own father was shot in a duel, but he died like a man. Where's the poltroon that don't resent an injury?—as he lives, I'd spit on him; every woman would despise him. There is not a girl in Florida that would dance with Alexander Pell after he got slapped in the face without killing the man that struck him. Is man a dog that he should suffer this?"

Jackson's manner was wild, and he gesticulated with his long arms like a phantom. The Doctor's blue eye was kindling in the fire-light. We looked for a war of words that might even amount to a specimen of the battle they were discussing, when the Doctor, with one of his usual strong transitions, cut off the discussion with a favorite couplet:

> "A wink to a blind horse is as good as a nod;
> Your faithful servant, Ollapod."

Jackson turned his flashing eyes on the Doctor, his lids slightly contracted like a man in doubt as to another's meaning; it was evident he was reading the Doctor, and the bland face turned toward him was like an open page with blue marginal illumination.

"Where do you reside, Doctor Pollock?" he asked, after a moment's pause, and in the indifferent tone assumed by the Doctor.

"I was born in Virginia, and inherited a plantation of a hundred negroes," replied the Doctor, answering the planter's thoughts, and not his question.

A long pause followed. We watched the light wood crackle, and the big particles of fire climbing up into the canopy of woods on the current of hot air, reflecting brief circles of light on the foliage above, and then going out in blackness. The Doctor resumed his pipe. Mike pondered, cross-legged, puffing at his cigarettes, and the boys talked among themselves in under tones.

"This won't do, gentlemen! Mike, hand me that bottle," called out Jackson, rousing himself. "One drink all around, and now for to-morrow's hunt. What shall it be, deer or turkey?"

"Or sheep?"

"That's a shame, Mike!" laughed Jackson.

"Don't let him quiz you that on mishap, gentlemen, older hunters than you have fared as badly. Did you ever hear of my blunder in fire hunting?"

Of course we had not.

"Then I'll tell it to you."

JACKSON'S STORY OF A FIRE HUNT.*

"It came about this way. I was up country looking around for a good two-year-old to run at Charleston races, when I met my old comrade, Stockton. We had been chums together at Princeton, as thick as two cats in a bag, sometimes studying, sometimes courting, and then we were good friends. When we had nothing else to do we quarrelled; it is a sure sign of a good friend when he loves you enough to quarrel with you. Strangers don't care a picayune, and won't quarrel about you any way. Stockton had settled down to a sober life, owned a pew in the church, and as many little carroty-haired tokens as you could stand up endwise in a ten acre lot. *I* was—well about the same sort of fellow as when a boy, only the devil had covered me up with his wicked ways.

"The first thing after seeing Stockton, that was proposed, was a fire hunt, and a fire hunt it was. Dark still night—you could hear a peeper squeak a mile off, and run your nose against a cotton bale without seeing it. 'Just the night,' said Stockton; 'Just the night,' says I.

---

* For this tale, I am indebted to the graceful pen of my friend, Guillermo.

'Come Jake,' says he to his son, a boy about sixteen, long and lank like his father, and always ready to poke away from home. Accordingly, all things ready, we trailed off into the woods and took a course along the sea-side, thinking to find more deer.

"I led the way with the frying pan on my shoulder, keeping the fire in it well up with pitch pine knots, Stockton right behind with his rifle, and Jake keeping within sight in the rear. We had gone about a mile or so and the pan began to grow heavy, when I suddenly felt Stockton's hand on my shoulder, compelling me to stop, and then the crack of his rifle from under my arm told me that he had fired at a deer that I had not seen. 'That deer shone up bright any how,' he said, in a low self-satisfied tone, as he proceeded to load his gun, 'only to get blown out.'

"'Hadn't you better secure your game before loading?'

"'Ha! ha!' said he, 'that fellow will not leave there until there is another set of legs under him. But come, I'm ready.'

"So saying, we started in the direction of our prize; when to our no little joy and surprise, we beheld another blue light apparently just beyond the spot where lay our fallen deer. Stockton again fired, and out went the light.

"'I first shot the doe,' he remarked, while deliberately loading his rifle, 'and the buck would not leave her.'

"Again we started, but had not taken a dozen steps, when lo! and behold, another eye appeared.

"'It's deuced strange,' said Stockton, quickly, as he raised his gun to his shoulder, 'that I have seen *but one eye* each time.'

"'Perhaps they have all accidentally been standing sidewise to you,' I replied.

"'Side or front,' he answered, 'I'll black that fellow's eye for him.' Crack went the rifle, and down went the eye. We had now arrived at the place where we supposed the first deer to have fallen, and made search for it, but nowhere was the game to be found.

"Turning from the place, imagine our surprise at again beholding that single fiery ball glaring upon us with the same identical motion of the others. Stockton mechanically raised his rifle, but paused as he did so. As for me, nothing prevented my throwing down the fire-pan and giving 'leg bail' but the disagreeable certainty of not being able to retrace my steps. I ran back in memory to childhood's hours, and recalled the old nursery tales I had heard of bears, lions, and hobgoblins, until I was satisfied beyond a doubt that Stockton had been shooting at the devil! I was, however, aroused from my revery by his exclaiming, 'Ha! I am a pretty fool. Something is the matter with my rifle, and I've been shooting all this time at the same deer! Here, give me yours.' I did so, but could not help thinking that the deer was a greater fool by far if he had stood to so many shots.

"The eye was now hid behind some bushes, but soon appeared again, when Stockton, after a long and deliberate aim, discharged his piece. The eye immediately disappeared, and he turned toward me, triumphantly nodding his head and exclaiming:

"'He'll not show that infernal eye of his again, I guess, for I put that ball square into it.'

"I made no reply, but the term '*infernal eye*' seemed to me to be very appropriate indeed. I had now placed the 'pan' upon the ground, and was arranging the fire, when Stockton uttered a suppressed exclamation of surprise and disappointment, which caused me to look up. Down went the fire, gun, and everything else; my mouth gradually opened until my dinner was perceptible, and I felt satisfied, from the progress my hair was making, that I should soon be relieved of my hat, for there was that little ball of fire moving very slowly toward the ground, with the same singular motions of the others.

"'Stockton,' whispered I, as soon as my feelings would permit me, 'we are a set of jackasses, for as certain as fate, we have been chasing the devil to-night.'

"He turned toward me with a half comical, half inquisitive look, and finally remarked:

"'Well, hang me if you're not complimentary, very. No, that is not the devil, but I am very well satisfied the devil is in me. Here, take this rifle, and when he again shows his eye do *you* let him have it. I'll hold the light.'

"I could not refuse, and so I took the gun, and was slowly and reluctantly raising it to my shoulder, when a noise behind me attracted my attention, and looking around, I perceived Jake conducting in a most discreditable manner, twisting and squirming and holding on to his stomach as if he had the colic, and all the while making a noise like choking.

"I wish you would be kind enough to stop that infernal clatter!" said Stockton sharply, and adding immediately, "There he is—now give it to him—right in the eye."

I was again raising the rifle to my shoulder, but was a second time deterred from my purpose by a peal or yell of laughter, from Jake, sufficient to have frightened every deer withing ten miles of us. For Stockton and myself, however, there was no such thing as laugh, but, on the contrary, we were both rather inclined to raise a row than be laughed at, and Stockton, grasping his son by the shoulder, in a passion exclaimed:

"What the devil is all this tomfoolery about? Say? Tell me this instant, sir, or I'll 'boot' you clear home."

"Ha! ha! Oh Lordy! ha! ha! *Amelia Lighthouse!* O, Lordy! Did I ever? Five miles—ough—my poor sides!"

My curiosity was now excited to the utmost, and I turned to Stockton for an explanation. I shall not attempt to describe the expression of his countenance. Mirth and anger were never so well mingled before.

"Jackson," said he, finally, "we are a pair of jackasses, and have been shooting at the *revolving light* on *the Amelia Lighthouse, five miles off!*"

Then suddenly dropping the fire-pan, he ran to where

THE PLANTATION HOUSE OF "FAR AWAY."

his son was kicking and screaming about on the ground. He picked him up by the coat collar, shaking him into silence, and then said, "now look here, if you say one word about this at home, as sure as I'm your father, you shall never fire a gun as long as you live."

As the laughter and comments on Jackson's story subsided, one of the negro boys said :

"Wish maussa hunt dat are varmint what's takin' off de lambs so ; 'spees as him hab no lamb 'tall soon."

"Lost any to-day ?"

"'Spec a los' two, and two afore yesterday, and gwine to lose two to-night, kase all sheep come in airly, bein' wild : sure sign dat."

"What is it, do you think ?"

"Painter, for true ! I'se seen his tracks !"

"Why don't you let your boys sleep by the sheep-pen ?" I asked of Jackson.

"I am afraid I would have to pen them in," he replied ; "and then, if it was a panther, he might take the negro, and he is worth more than the sheep."

"Then why don't you shoot the beast ?"

"I have hunted her till I am tired, and it only ends in her killing my dogs, and keeping out of shot herself. She will get tired here by and by, and then will go further down the coast. She has raised a young one here this season, for in the summer one of the boys, while coming up the river in a canoe, saw her swimming across with her kitten in her mouth. He could have come up with her then, but she growled so fiercely that he was afraid, and made a fool of himself."

"'Spects anybody make a fool of hisself, when painter want to climb in his boat!" replied a self-conscious voice in the background.

"We had Mike here last year to hunt the same panther, I think, but I believe he got whipped; at all events, he went out one day, and didn't come back since."

"Mike smiled his peculiar smile, which meant, like the German 'Yah wohl,' anything according to the speaker's intent, but said not a word.

"Tell us of that hunt, old father of Dinah," said the Doctor.

"Where is my panther skin you promised?" said Jackson.

"Painter is an oncommon onsartin varmint," was Mike's musing rely, as he put his brawny arms around his knees, and rocked himself backward and forward like a China Mandarin.

"I should think that he was *onkimin sartin*, for he comes here regularly once a year."

"Wall, you see, Colonel, this war the way I was done for that time, and when yer heern it, you'll say that it was skeery, and no mistake."

"A story—a story!" exclaimed Miss Jackson. I leaned forward to see the speaker, and he began his tale.

CHAPTER VI.

THE PANTHER'S CUB.

"He who fights and runs away
May live to fight another day."

"Well, it was airly mornin' when I started out after that air painter. Small sign I had to steer by, only the hearin' tell that there was a painter 'bout. But it had been showering o'ernight, and so trailin' was easy enough, and yer could see every stalk of grass that had been shook, let alone the tracks a varmint the size of a painter would leave. I tuck down to Spring Creek, and followed it e'enmost to the barrens that stretch toward the salt water; then I fetched a turn north, and struck inter the big swamp that comes out of the Suwanee. Here I saw an all-fired big bar's track, and slathers of deer, and a show of gobblers, but no painter whatsumever. Got a gobbler and tuck breakfast, and then kept on. Struck the branches of the St. John that arternoon. Good painter ground here, tearin' big swamp, and all-fired high cottonwoods and sycamores. No signs, and my dog was gin out, so we shantied under a grape-vine waitin' for daylight. Heered a painter holler in the night, but knowed it was a young one by the voice, and it was off the wrong way. Mornin' come, and I got around through little Ammauinac Swamp, and by night time had come purty near whar I fust started from, having made a purty tolerable circle, and nairy a painter. Sez I, 'Those cusses at the sheep-farm have been foolin' me, and tuck wild-cat for painter.'

"So arter soundin' around to see where the buildin's lay, and whar the sheep-pen was, Yowler and I lay down together, and were doin' some tall sleepin', when I heerd a soft kind o' crying down the woods. I knowed it in a minnit; it war the same painter—he hadn't been outside of my circle at all, the dratted cuss! He had just been a layin'-to for another haul on the sheep-pen, and so I hadn't struck his trail. I kept quiet, thinkin' he would come up toward the improvements, and I could tickle him, but he reether seemed to move off. Arter a while I heerd him purrin' like, and then I knew he had something to eat—fawn, like 'nough, or some small animal. This guv me a mean opinion of this painter, for your rael snortin' big fellars don't stoop to small fry, but live on deer, sheep, hogs, or sich like. Wall, mornin' come on, and when it bruck enough to see a meetin'-house, I pushed on, but the painter had moved off. I found a sheepskin all rolled up, and I knew then why he had been purring. The painter had caught a sheep on the range some time in the day, and not eaten it, so he didn't have need for more fodder all night. I found the trail, and then sez I, 'Now, Mr. Painter, we'll see who's best at walkin'.' Yowler tuck the trail, and along we bowled for about an hour, when all of a sudden I heerd Yowler, who was some ways ahead, stop his yelpin', and back he come, with somethin' arter him, tight as he could buckle. As they come up I let drive at what was arter him kind o' promiscuously, for it wasn't fairly dawn yet. The shot hit, I knew, for the varmint held up, and then run off.

"'Now,' says I ter myself, 'isn't a painter a mighty onsartin varmint? Here is one that gets wounded, and yet don't pitch inter a fellar. Who'd ha' looked for sich a coward in a painter?' Then, after loadin', I put on Yowler again, and we bowled along, not quite so lively as afore, for Yowler was a leetle kind o' shy, but still we did some pretty loud goin'.

"'Whar's that air painter?' sez I to myself; 'did any painter ever run so far before?' It come on to be light, and I could see the trail, and it was an all-fired big trail. Presently it got into a cane-brake, and then tuck a turn. Yowler guv tongue. I could hear the canes rattle as he jumped, but the painter broke out of this on the fur side, and made a bee-line agin right straight for the Ouithlacouchee River.

"When we got to the river it was noon. I looked down the bank, and saw the tracks along in the mud where the varmint had been lookin' for a good place to cross. Presently I could see where he had laid down in the mud, and then for the fust time I saw it was a she painter with sucking young ones. As near as I could make out by the marks in the mud she had two cubs lugging at her, the rest of her tits being of no account.

Then the track went in a little further under some alders, and there she had laid down agin, this time on her side, and, Jehosaphat! thar by her side, as clare as daylight, was a dozen little tracks of a cub she had been a-carryin' in her mouth all that way. She had tuck to these bushes to give it some milk, and was goin' with it into the big swamps t'other side of the river. It was all as clare as if a schoolmaster had written it. That war the reason why the she painter didn't come on to fight when I fired at her; she wanted to git her pups clare from the dog; that's the natur of a painter, and an oncommin considerin' natur it is, too. My 'pinion of that painter rose some. Arter the trail left the alder bushes, it went right into the river.

"I soon found a log big enough for me and Yowler, and, puttin' the dog on one eend on't, so as to save him from the alligators, I slung my rifle on my back, and paddled across. I soon found the trail, and went jogging along pretty slow, for it was a tough kind of swamp, when in a minute or so I heerd Yowler burst out in a clear yell. I knowed he seed the painter, and I hurried on as well as I could, but, Jimminy Peters! that painter, when he made a jump across the fallen logs, went as fur in one minute as I in ten. I soon come to where I heerd the dog break out so, and I seed somethin' kind o' curious. The old tracks went straight on south, but there were a set of new tracks that came right back on top the old ones, and just where the dog had come up they had turned off to the east.

"Wall, that's queer!' sez I to myself. 'If that's the same varmint, she's what I'm arter, and if she aint she's just as good, for I calkelate that one painter is just as good as another, providin' allers she's as big.' So I cheered on Yowler, and we went on the side track. Now over logs, then in a mucky place, and now through the water, that dog and I stuck to that painter like two wood-ticks. Arter going a little to the east the track went back to the river, and went across about a mile above where it had crossed before. 'Wall, that's queer,' sez I to myself. 'There's somethin' onnateral in that painter. She won't tree, and she goes in a straight line to t'other eend of creation, and now she's going back agin. Wall, here goes,' sez I, and I took another log and ferried back agin to the north shore. There was the trail as clare as mud, and big as an alligator's. Up the bank and away inter the woods we went. There's no sucking of cubs now. Yowler is a hurryin' her along a leetle too fast for any sich family doin's. So on we went right north. 'Jerusalem!' sez I to myself, ' keep on this way, old steamboat, much longer, and you'll be back where you started from, and I'll drive you into Colonel Jackson's pen, and shut the door on you!'

"'Bout by the Black Mud Creek there's a flat of land that had been overflowed and had dried off, and as we come here I seed the painter had jumped through, and every time she had jumped she had come up to her belly in the mud, and once or twice had come so low that her neck and chin had sunk in the mud. Thinks I, that must put the cub under in the mud, yet I don't see the marks of the little rat.

"Jist then we got through the creek, and I seed whare the old painter had lain down on the bank with her side to the river.

"Thar were her tracks as clare as Gospel, but whar was the cub? The cub was gone! Whar had it gwine to? It was clare it hadn't gwine anywhare that Yowler and I had been; it had been left on the fur side of the Ouithlacouchee. It tuck just a minute of thinkin', and it was all clare. The bee line she had made, the two full tits, the bee-line back agin; what a cursed fool I was not to have seen through it afore I had come so fur!

"The painter had littered two cubs somewhar near whar I had seen her in the mornin'; she had been chased, and knew the parts was ousafe; she had made up her mind to carry her cubs into the Ouithlacouchee swamp, and had started with one when Yowler struck her trail. That was the reason she sent Yowler back; that was the reason she wouldn't tree; and jist keepin' in sound of the dog's yelp, had gone right to the swamp, hid her cub, come back on her back track to ketch the dog and lead him away, till she could go back fur t'other cub, bein' sartin that the hound and his fool of a master were away from her cub, and were chasin' her about.

"Soon as I had reasoned this out I called Yowler in, and turnin' about, struck for that ere swamp straight. Yowler come on behind, and about two hours afore sunset I struck the river, ferried across, took up the old trail in the swamp, and was busy pickin' it out over logs and under vines whar the moss grew so thick it didn't leave room for a track. The scent was cold, and Yowler could jist ketch it, but what with puttin' our two noses together we fetched up in a big windfall, and jist in the snarl of trees, whar the splinters and branches, and growin' vines was the wickedest, there was a little bed of strips of bark and leaves, and the young painter cub was curled up, dreamin' of supper-time. He was about as big as two tomcats tied together by the tails, and his natur', when I come to prick him up, was not quite so sweet. He meowed, and sneezed, and about chawed up my coat-sleeve afore I could bag him, which I did by takin' off my huntin' coat, jammin' his head into one of the sleeves, and buttonin' and tyin' him in bag like.

"When I got all this done, I thought of the old painter, and what she would say to me when she come home with her t'other young 'un. The more I calkelated, the more it seemed onpleasant, for though the varmint was so perlite when she was outwittin' me, I reckoned that she wouldn't be so much so when the boot got on t'other leg. Fust I thought I would get out of that air windfall, and wait for the old lady on the bank of the river, whar we could have a clare field, fur I knew it was sartin she would be arter me, and I'd a leetle reether the fight wouldn't be fit out in that swamp. So I put out for the river, and when I got thar took a clare spot, and puttin' the cub down for the stakes, sat down to wait fur the other party.

"The wind was still, and I could hear around a considerable distance. A few big frogs, and once in a while an alligator, let on for music in the river. Now and then an owl hooted in the bottom land, and the cranes goin' out to sea were honkin' away overhead, but I couldn't hear any painter, and accordin' to my calculations there would be some howlin' when she cum home and found her pappoose bagged. Yowler began to get restless, and watched the swamp as if he knowed what was comin'. The woods begun to get blacker, the sun had gone down, and some black clouds bellowed overhead. It looked like a squall.

"'Why don't she cum?' sez I to myself; 'or maybe she's sich a knowin' varmint she's waitin' for night, to chaw me up completely.' Once I thought I seen her eyes in the edge of the bushes, but it turned out to be some rotten fire-wood. 'Jerusalem!' sez I, 'why don't she cum!' It got to be so dark I couldn't see the sights on my rifle, and I thought it all over to myself. I own up I felt kind a mean like. This stealin' young cubs out of their nests is onnateral, any way. It is good enough for an Injun, but's not Christian-like. I could see that old painter comin' home, with her second cub in her mouth. I could tell jist how she felt. I could see her big nostril open when she smelt my tracks about her nest, and when she saw her cub was gone, Lord! what a cry she would give. I'd given a bearskin to put that cub back, and then have fit it out with a clare conscience. But 'twas no use a talkin'; it couldn't be done, no how. All that's left when the deal is made is to stand up to yer hand. 'But,' thinks I to myself, 'ef it's right to shoot the old painter, it is right to ketch her kitten.' That's the natur of man; ef they do anything wrong they reason to themselves to make it right.

"'Jerusalem!' sez I, as it got blacker and the fire-flies cum about, 'why don't she cum?' Jist then, in lookin' around me, I sees a light shine on the other shore a little way below. I knew right off it was an Injin camp, and reckoned it was part of Tiger Tail's band, that had cum up from below. Nasty varmints that band was—worse en painters any day. Howsumever, Injins or no Injins, they will help fight the painter; so I rolled a drift-log into the water, and once more paddled over the river. I looked behind once or twice to see if the painter wasn't a comin' over, too, and climbin' on the log behind me, but it was only the mullet jumpin' in the river, and so I got over with the cub all right, and put right down the bank for the camp. Yer better believe I didn't let grass grow under me. As I cum up to the fire-light, I saw who the Injins were; they were friendly enough that summer, but mighty mean cusses, and had served me many a dirty trick. Their camp was just in the edge of the timber, and the squaws were cooking supper in a pot, while about a dozen men sat around in a ring, lookin' on and suckin' their thumbs, wrapped up in their blankets, just as if it was cold. As I cum up, I looked back on my track, and whar the sandy bank lay agin the water, whar it war brightened up by the sunset, I see the she-painter cumin' like greased lightnin'.

"I walked composed-like and slow into the Injin camp, and right through the ring, puttin' the painter cub all rolled up in the coat down in the middle, and then goin' to the fur side, set down as far off as convenient.

"'Injin Mike is welcome,' said a young man, who I made out by his paint to be Tiger Tail's son, waivin' his hand like to me, and keepin' his eye inquirin' like on my coat, that was a wrigglin' about on the ground.

"'Injin Mike is a hunter, and he brings a hunter's gift,' sez I, slow-like, and speakin' Injin; 'he was afeerd his Injin brother would be in want of some game.'

"I knew this would rile 'em some, for Tiger Tail was allers a big hunter, and he didn't like me, for I could take the feather out of his hair any day. I war goin' on to say more, but I didn't have time, fur jist then I heard a thump in the bushes, and the she-painter cum in as ef she was flyin'; ears back, eyes like candles—she was some. She tuck the young chief before she landed with a sort o flyin' box with her paw, and he never riz hair arterwards, for she tuck scalp and all.

"The lousy devils rolled over like prairie dogs—the pot upsot, the coals flew around, the squaws yelled, the dogs pitched in, and afore any one could get out his knife, that painter did some tall tearin'. They rolled over and over, yellin', bitin' swearin; some got hit fur the painter, fur they couldn't see whar to strike, and thar was no room for shootin'. Lord, Colonel, it would hur done you good to have seen that air scrimmage. I got behind a tree and larfed so it hurt me, and when I

Just then I heard a thump in the bushes, and the she-painter cum in as ef she was flyin'. — PAGE 84.

see they had well-nigh fit out, Yowler and me, thinkin' they might blame us, stepped out, and I hain't seen them Injins, nur that air painter since, though I've heer'en tell that Tiger Tail ware lookin' for me about the Mccaco this summer."

"And if he catches you, you will not be able to raise hair either," said Jackson.

"*Ef* he does," answered Mike, laughing.

"But what became of the other sucking cub after the Indians had killed its mother and brother?"

"I went back arter it that very same night, and found it jist whar the she-painter had left it when she tuck my trail. It was a meowin' away in the woods all alone, and I felt kind a sorry for it, and carried it into the Fort at Tampa Bay and guv it to the Colonel thar, whar it growed up, and got so big and saucy that it licked the hull fort one day and then cleared."

CHAPTER VII

THE DEER HUNT.

"A hundred hounds bayed deep and strong
Clattered an hundred steeds along."
SCOTT.

The light broke early on the planter's house, and the smoldering brands of our camp-fire the morning after Mike's panther story. It may not have been early, though our late hours of the evening before made it seem so to me, and I silently banned the sleepless hound that bayed at the early day. Then "the cock's shrill clarion, and the echoing horn," ushered in the fuller light, and drew us to our feet, yawning and drinking in the misty sights and sounds.

The sheep were crowding out of the pens, and spreading over the open woods. Their constant bleating drowned the cries of their negro drivers. The horses were whinnying for their food. Our boys were lighting a fire, and preparing meat, singing and laughing away. There were calls to negroes with fancy names, and shouting answers; guns were discharged, and saddles examined; a dozen things were wanted that could not be found, or when found were not in a condition to be used. The little nigs were running to the spring for water, or to the shed for corn, or all around the grounds, merely for the fun of running and shouting. They were dressed alike, in long, brown cotton shirts, and one sex could not be distinguished from the other. Aunty Blaze, after seeing the table was spread, and the meat cooked, brought out an immense corn-cake, on a wooden turner, and with a commendable feeling of pride threw it down on the table, right side up, steaming hot, and brown as rosewood. Turning to go, she stumbles against a little nig girl coming with the sugar-bowl; a smart slap applied with the cake-turner propels the little nig forward a yard, and elicits a yell of disapprobation from the clumsy child, who drops the sugar-bowl to the floor, and then runs off.

The Doctor loads his double-barrelled gun, and explains its new-fashioned lock to Miss Jackson, who comes out arrayed in a tight-fitting cap and bodice, and her eyes lit up with the anticipation of the chase. Mike slowly and methodically wipes out his rifle with dry flax, and every moment is seen eating some hidden remains of last night's meal, which he has stowed away on his person, and which are to form more than half his breakfast. We eat our hurried meal—it might be called a passover, as no one takes time to sit—and then ride off down the woods.

Jackson and Mike are leading the van, Lou and the Doctor still side by side, and there goes a negro on a marsh tackey, and there a neighbor that has come over for the hunt, mounted on a vicious mare as thin as a crane. The hounds, of a dozen different colors and sizes, go along in couples, led by the negroes on foot, and on ahead to a given rendezvous shuffles Pompey Duffield Sah, the oldest negro on the place, driving a mule laden with two baskets of provisions intended for the dinner of the party, and the mist comes up from the river in golden clouds, for the sun is just rising. Down along the bank we went with call and laughter, and the bittern arose from the sedge with a guttural cry, and the alligator sank into the water with a heavy splash, as our cavalcade moved onward to the lower pine lands that skirted the big swamp. The trees were all white pine; there was no underbrush, and we could see down the long arcades they formed for nearly a mile. Now and then a flaunting flower would rear its crimson cheek to the wind, or a vine could be seen clasping a trunk, and drooping from branch to branch in long festoons, but generally the ground was covered only with the yellow siftings of the pine, and free from all vegetation. The horses trod without a sound, and, save now and then a squirrel, we met no animal life, until we came to the hummocks, and drew together to give general directions for commencing the chase, the manner of which is necessary to explain.

A hummock is a thicket often covering but an acre or two of land, and sometimes presenting an extent of several miles. The one now in view covered about thirty acres, and half a mile further down the woods, we could see another. It lay in a low swale of land, and in it the haw, the alder, and willow, grew into a tangled copse, studded with the red leaves of the pinckneya, while above them all, a hundred feet or more, the ash, the magnolia, and gum-trees, reared their long arms, and opened their blossoms to the upper air. It was an admirable spot for game, with succulent grass and flags, and a dusky shade that was never penetrated by the sun.

"You stay here, Doctor Pollock," said Jackson, as we rode up; "and mind your eyes."

The Doctor drew himself up with a doubtful air, as if uncertain whether minding his eyes referred to the uses he had just been putting those organs to in watching Miss Jackson's face, or whether it referred to watchfulness in the future; so he answered at random, "All right, sir!"

"And you," he continued, turning to me, "take your place two gun-shots off on that side, keeping always within five or six rods of the swamp. And you," turning to the neighbor that had joined us, "go on next; and you, Lou, come with Mike and me."

And away they cantered, with the dogs, around the other side of the swamp, dropping one or two negroes, as they passed, to guard some particular point of the hummock, and in this way we inclosed two sides of the swamp with a cordon of hunters stationed just so far apart that if a deer came out, one or the other of the hunters in waiting was certain of a shot. On the further side, and the only portion of the swamp that we were unable to surround, the driver was to enter with the hounds, and the deer would not be likely to make his escape in that direction.

The last I saw of Jackson he was winding around the swamp with Mike, having left his daughter on a little knoll that commanded a fair view of the hummock, and where her bright bay horse and little figure stood out in relief against the dark pines beyond. She caught sight of me and waved her hand. I could see, from her attitude, that she was intently watching the swamp, and her short double-barrelled gun hung from her arm with all the ease that it would have been carried by a stronger hunter. The doctor I could not see, but my negro, Scipio, armed only with a knife, stood between us, and only a short distance from me. I looked for the other members of the hunt, but they had gone, and perfect stillness reigned over the pine woods and hummock. Moment after moment slipped away; I listened for every sound, but could hear nothing, save the impatient champing of my horse. Away down the woods a fox-squirrel flirted his broad tail as he chased his comrade up a tree, or a painted woodpecker passed by in undulating sweeps as silently as a moth. At length I heard a distant call; it was so faint it just reached me, but I recognized it as the driver cheering the hounds as he cast them off. Now for it. Another pause. The cry was repeated, and with it the low yelp of a dog, then another, and then a ringing shot away down the woods. My horse pricked his ears, and Scipio mounted a fallen tree the better to survey the scene. No cheering shout announced the death of the deer, though the dogs stopped yelping.

At this moment I heard in the bushes the rapid bound of some animal; it came nearer and nearer. From the higher ground where I stood I could see over the bushes a pair of antlers, and I supposed it to be the same deer that had been fired at down the swamp. I dismounted to take surer aim. How my heart beat in unison with the bounding of his feet, while every sense converged into the coming of his presence! But, alas! he did not come out by me, but between me and the Doctor, and very near to him. Bang! bang! I heard his gun explode, and immediately the deer turned in again, just keeping the edge of the bushes, and showing his back at every jump. As he passed me, I took deliberate aim, and when his flag showed over the grass, I fired. A better aim never was taken, but the deer only seemed to move with an accelerated speed down past the next stand, and receiving a shot there, and two from Miss Jackson, then rushed back into the swamp from whence he came. The dogs, with the firing, broke out into a louder chorus; the negro drivers were coming on, thrashing the bushes and shouting away. I heard Jackson's horn winding its clear notes nearer and nearer; he was following up the dogs, keeping in the open woods, while Mike was doing the same on the other side. All at once the hounds broke out with a louder yell, and at the same moment the buck broke cover again in front of me, accompanied by two does, one on either side. I had just loaded, and had my foot in the stirrup, when, without changing position, I fired at the stag's shoulder. I missed my mark, but shot one of the does, that tumbled down in the grass. The buck and the other doe once more turned back, and, wild with fright, coursed down the edge of the hummock toward Poke, who fired his barrel again, and this time, with some correctness, for the buck dropped his tail for an instant with an uneasy motion, when raising it again, he turned back, followed by Poke, on horseback, directly past my stand. I fired my second barrel without effect, and then, not able to resist the contagion of the chase, spurred my horse after the flying animals. Away they went down the little swale that led toward Lou Jackson's stand. One hound after another, as he came out of the rushes, caught sight of the deer, and joined in the chase with a double note. Bang! came a shot from my left, missed clear, and the hunter, not stopping to load, joined the chase. Now for it, Miss Jackson! I saw her raise her gun, her father was close behind, riding hard to get to her, and away down the woods I could see Mike trying to head off the chase, his long hair streaming behind him like a woman's. A puff of smoke, and a report—the buck staggered; another shot and he seemed to renew his courage, drawing in behind him, in one yelling, shouting, crashing train, every man, horse, and dog, in the woods.

"You hit him, Lou. Tally-ho! Hi on! hi! Hurrah! Faster! There's Tip, and there's Slasher! Go it, Music! Golly! maussa, gib him fits!" were the cries that were intelligible in the medley of sound, until the yelling of the dogs, and the trampling of the horses drowned all words. The horses, as wild in their ardor as their riders, needed no rein. The buck led the way directly for another hummock that was situated about three miles away, and which was now within sight; his flight was straight and well sustained, though now and then a spot of blood on the leaves showed that he was wounded. The dogs were toiling on behind, not two yards away, and close behind the dogs came all the hunters, the Doctor, riding the fastest horse, taking the lead. As we approached the hummock, the pine trees grew closer together, and while going between two of them the Doctor was caught by his gun, which he held crosswise before him on the saddle, and was swept off his horse to the ground. "There's a ten strike!" called out Jackson, as we rushed by. Closer still we came to the deer, every dog stretched to his utmost length, every rider bending to his horse's mane; Mike was just raising his rifle to his shoulder to shoot, when without a sign the big buck fell head first to the ground, and rolled over and over with the impetus of the chase. His heart had broken in the desperate burst just within reach of his lair, in whose close covert the doe, with one long bound, was lost. Up came the dogs and horses so fast they ran over the game, and crowded and jostled together as they pulled up. So rolls and bubbles a wave that meets a rock on the sandy beach. Then there was dismounting, and whipping off the dogs, and a search for the wounds in our quarry. Two buck-shot, in the thick part of the neck from behind, came from the Doctor's second barrel.

"Where is the Doctor? here is his horse. Oh! there he comes limping along rather sore with his fall." A laugh and a sly joke were all the consolation we had to offer him. Two more buck-shot in the right side, close together; that is Lou Jackson's shot. They were the only ones of the party using shot guns. None of the shots were heavy enough to kill the deer, though altogether they had broken him down in the chase. We wound a horn to tell the drivers we left behind our whereabouts, and putting the buck on one of the negroes' horses, and coupling the dogs to keep them from entering the swamp, we turned back the way we came.

"Now for the does we left behind," said Jackson. "How many were there!"

"I saw two bucks and four does," said the Doctor.

"Fudge! those were the same deer we have been chasing, only your people turned them back into the hummock two or three times without killing them."

"I killed one," said I.

"Where is it?"

"It fell in the bushes."

"Reckon you did not hit her."

"You had better believe it; I can show you the place where she fell."

"That isn't what we want. Where is the place that she is now, can you tell that? I fired at a doe, too, but a long way off, and she probably is where yours is."

"Doctor, how's your back?"

"He he! golly mighty! he quit saddle smart dat time!" remarked Cæsar.

As we rode up to the hummock where we had started the game, I found the place where I had shot the doe, but she was not there, though the negroes said she had fallen.

"Throw off a dog, then," said Jackson.

"Let Music try," said his daughter; and accordingly Music was loosened and sent in the grass. Music was a young hound, spotted white and black, like a coach-dog, and with such silky ears they felt like a satin robe in your hand. She was led to the place where the deer had fallen, and taking its track with a plaintive whimper, commenced unwinding it from among the bushes and reeds. Presently a louder effort warned us to beware, and cantering apart a little, so as to be able to see all around the hummock, Mike's grey eye caught a sight of the doe trying to steal out of the bushes. A clear ringing shot was followed by a quick leap, and she fell dead.

We laid them side by side, the stately buck and his gentle consort. The dew of the morning was still glittering on their hides—their eyes were as bright and as full as in life. I wondered if Miss Jackson felt any pity for them, as she saw the dogs licking the blood that flowed from their throats.

One of the negroes dismounting from his pony, we substituted the two deer in place, and tying their feet beneath the belly of the struggling horse, had them sent to the place where we were to meet for dinner.

"Now one more hunt before dinner. Where shall we go, boys?"

"Saw de ole white buck fur sartin, dis day, maussa!" said the planter's head negro, coming up.

"Where did you see him?"

"Down by de run, ober dere," said the negro, pointing with his finger; "his tracks fresh as dis niggah's."

"You mean you saw his tracks?"

"Yes a maussa."

"How does he know that it is a buck?" I asked.

"How fur to know he's a buck? Haint chased dat air deers' often fur nuthin'; 'spect I be'ent a fool!" replied Jumping Lem, with some asperity.

"Wall, if that ere is the buck that run in this range last winter, I kinder guess ye'll all have to rub your legs with bar's grease to ketch him," added Mike.

"Don't you think we can shoot him, Mike?" asked Lou Jackson.

"No, young woman, I don't; thar are too many here to make certain of any deer. When a man wants a deer bad, he goes alone and keeps his mouth shut."

As we rode over to inspect the tracks, I learned, partly from the exclamations of the negroes, and partly from Jackson's account, that this buck passed the winters in the pine woods, retiring when the mosquitoes become thick in the spring, to the cool swamps of the Ouithlacouchee. It has been so often hunted, and was so successful in escaping, that it become well known at the Jackson plantation, and was the object of a covert superstition to all the negroes, which mysterious fear rather aided his escape, for when the boys saw it coming they became so frightened, they could not hit forty paces off.

On reaching the run that Lem had mentioned, we readily found the tracks, and all drew up to examine them. The presentation of some unknown bone to a company of *savans*, or the appearance of a new bonnet at a country sewing society, occasions not more curiosity and sage comment than does the discovery of a new track in the woods. One mentions its size, another recognizes old peculiarities or marks, another says it was the foot of a male animal, another that it was fat in flesh, and another that it was going on an easy trot, and not disturbed, and what is stranger still, from the small data of four marks in the damp soil, all these facts arrived at are the results of careful observation, and seldom incorrect.

According to the congress now assembled, this buck was the old white buck, so called from an unusually white coat, and had gone at a gentle gait into the Black Jack hummock, which lay two miles further on, and before which we presently arrived. It was about a half mile in length by three quarters broad, and was filled, like the other swamp holes, with long grass, bushes, and vines, from which rose several tall trees of those species that spring in swamps and savannahs, and at its upper end there grew a close thicket of black jack trees.

5

Once more the members of the chase separated to take commanding positions, overlooking the edges of the thicket. We were cautioned against shooting at anything that might come out, until we were certain the white buck was not there. Once more Mike and Jackson disappeared, and with them the hounds, already snuffing the air from the swamp, and tugging at their leashes to get away. Once more the forest was still, save the throbbings of our hearts, that counted the anxious seconds.

In a short time I could hear the cheers of the negroes, and the thrashing of the bushes as they struggled forward in the tangled underbrush. At this instant a doe, followed by a fawn almost grown, came to the edge of the bushes. She looked up and down for an instant, her large ears turning this way and that, when not seeing any one, she came out on a lope, and passing close by me, ran down the woods, making for the river. I had my gun to my shoulder, but remembering the white buck, withheld my fire, lest the bigger game should follow the course of the doe and find me with an empty gun. Yeow-ow-ow came from the hummock; that was Music's voice—her tone was like a bugle's. Then two or three whimpering notes from other hounds.

"Wha's dat air a bobbin' in ee bushes?" asked Scipio, standing near me and eagerly trying to overlook the grassy valley. "A cat—a cat!" he shouted, "sure as gun," and a handsome specimen of the feline genius sprung out of the bushes, and then seeing Scipio, darted back again to cover. "Golly mighty, wouln't dat cat get shook up—yah—ha, yah—ha—he!"

Now the hounds broke out in chorus, with a multitudinous cry that babbled in the bushes and wailed in the air, as though the echoes caught the sound and mellowed it down to a continuous accord. Scipio felt the contagion, and dancing up and down, relieved himself as follows:

"Dar dey come! dar dey come! Bress de Lord! don't dey skin 'em—dat beats dis child; hy ah ha, hy ah ha!—go it Music!"

The dogs had come half way down the cover, when a buck and doe broke out together. He did not appear to be of unusual size; but I could not wait any longer, and fired. He fell and rose again, running over the brow of a little hill with his tail down; here he drew the fire of my neighbor on the right, and fell to rise no more. The doe halted a moment where her comrade fell, as if waiting for him to rise, when away down the woods a rifle rung its sharp crack and she fell like a clod almost on the body of her mate. I knew Mike's rifle by the effect, even if I did not know its sound.

The hounds came closer; we could see the grass and bushes moving where they were winding about, and now and then their sickle-shaped tails above the weeds. The clamor increased, the dogs were almost through, and yet no white buck to correspond with the negro's description of the big buck they had so often hunted.

At this instant I saw rise up from the very edge of the bushes, a buck, that from his stately size I at once recognized to be the big buck. He had evidently been watching the preparations for the hunt, and selecting the very time our guns were discharged, he rushed out between me and one of the negroes, and without regarding either, flew down the open pine woods at a flying gallop. Hardly had he cleared the valley, when I heard Jackson shouting, and saw him riding hard toward my stand; but the dogs coming out and taking the deer's track with loud clamor, prevented my hearing. I sprang into my saddle, and went flying alongside of the hounds, with the air soughing through my hair, and the deer in view a hundred yards ahead. In a moment or two Lou Jackson and the Doctor were in sight, their horses skimming the open woods like birds. Then came the sorrel mare, and next Scipio on the pony, and then in the distance Jackson and Mike, with all the negroes that were mounted. Faster, still faster, heart and sense fixed on that flying buck, and the trees merged together in a mass as we swept among them. Whoop! why cannot a man cheer louder; why cannot a horse fly faster when a deer is in view. There is a crash and a flash of dirt and sticks; the sorrel has gone down, and her rider rolled over and over, and far ahead of his steed. There is no time to see if he can get up again. Hurrah! there is a hummock! See Tiger and Bess turn to the left! They know the buck will not run through it, and they turn aside to cut the radius of the arc he is about to make.

He sees the plan and accelerates his speed. His horns are lying on his back; he is stretching away at his highest speed, and whenever a bush intercepts his flight, he leaps it with a bound that must give him a bird's-eye view of his pursuers.

Far ahead of the deer grew a close swamp, and from the straight line the deer was making we knew he was looking to it for refuge. Behind, I heard Jackson shouting at us, but who could stop to listen with such a buck in view? On we went, the dogs still nearer the deer, and Tiger almost within reach of his haunches. Lou Jackson held one rein in each hand, her eyes fixed on the chase, and her hair flying loose behind her. There goes the deer in the bushes; he touched a log here and a bog there, and along he went like a rope dancer. Tally ho! On went the dogs, when, to my surprise, Tiger disappeared from view, and in a second of time the whole pack were floundering in the morass. "Hold hard!" I heard again from behind. "Hold hard, Miss Jackson!" I screamed, as the truth flashed on me. "The quicksands!" Too late; her horse was wild with the chase, and she could not hold him. He made one or two desperate leaps as he found himself floundering, and in a second of time was half ingulfed in the mud. His rider still held the reins and kept her seat on the struggling horse. The Doctor was in equal plight, while his frightened beast pawed the air in its attempts to regain a footing. My horse, more used to such ground, turned short around when he felt it quaking, throwing me in the edge of the mud like a clown in a circus. Up came Mike as fast as he could ride, and Jackson behind him.

Mike threw himself from his horse, and while the others were cutting sticks to throw to the ingulfed riders, ran out by quick jumps to the log over which the deer had run, and then cutting off with his knife a grapevine that had climbed a neighboring tree, he wound it around his arm and swung himself out toward Miss Jackson. The first swing did not send him far enough, but putting his foot against the trunk, as his rope oscillated, he swung out to where the young girl lay up to her arm-pits, and rapidly sinking in the sands. He said something in a low voice to her that we could not hear, and putting his hand under her arm began slowly to draw her from her perilous position. When she was entirely above the surface, he swung the vine sufficiently to carry his charge to the root of the tree, from whence it was comparatively easy to reach the shore. I would have given a year of life to get such a look of thanks from a lady I know as the breathless girl gave Mike—the ugly scamp! The Doctor's turn came next, and then the horses, until finally, after two or three hours of hard work, we were all once more in the saddle, and some of us bearing more resemblance to scavengers than gallant hunters under the greenwood tree.

"S'pose you tink dat white buck is de debbil for true now, hey?" said Scipio, as he was tightening my girths.

"No, I don't; why do you ask?"

Cutting off with his knife a grape-vine that had climbed a neighboring tree, he wound it round his arm, and swung himself out toward Miss Jackson. - PAGE 102.

"Kase I'se not sartin the niggahs here'bouts knows heaps, and dey sez dey ain't a gwine to hunt dat buck no how, and I guess as how I wouldn't nudder. 'Spec as how sumthin' wuss en what we've seen will come out a' that eer chase yit. I'se not scared, but dat is very 'plexing."

The day was wearing away fast, and, sending one of the boys for the two deer last killed, we all turned toward the place appointed for our meeting, where after a few minutes' riding a blue smoke column arose among the trees, and the distant gleam of water announced a dinner and a rest—two pleasant things, whose worth is only known to those who have labored well. From our dining-place, a bend of the river showed us two vistas down the ancient woods, and the broad sheet of water, half in shadow half in sunshine, was broken by the flocks of ducks that were coasting along its banks. The trees that fringed the shore were covered with immense creeping vines, that clasped the trunks and suspended themselves from the branches. Down by the water's edge, the golden-rod reared its yellow head, and the love-vine wove its orange thread like a net over many a rank grove of water plants. The opposite shore was lower than the bank on which we were standing, and the eye took in miles of cane-brake and forest, unbroken by any sign of human labor.

"Look at those turkey buzzards, Doctor," said Miss Jackson, pointing to two birds that, with matchless grace, were floating in slow circles high in the air. "I would like to see the view they are taking in at this moment."

"So would I; they are eagles in the air, and crows on the ground," replied the Doctor. "They seem never to move their wings, and yet how powerfully they fly, while they watch every motion that is going on in the woods below them."

"Do you want one of 'em?" said Mike, raising his rifle from the ground.

"No, no, Mike; when God makes anything so beautiful, let it live."

"Dinnah's ready, gemens *and* ladies," called out Pompey Duffield Sah, with a marked accent on the *and*, while Jackson's horn played the stave of a march that made the dogs howl, and we turned away from the bank to the dinner that was spread out on the grass. There was cold wild turkey, and ham, and sherry wine, some excellent hot coffee, and corn-bread and bacon. It wouldn't have been a Florida dinner without the corn-bread and bacon. Oh, what a blessed thing is hunger, when one has the means to allay it, and how contented and beneficent one is when the dinner is ended, and how pleasant when seated, after a day of rough toil, at a rude meal, to have the gentle presence of a woman making the beauty to the rugged scene! Did it ever occur to you, fair reader, that if that gentler grace that wins and governs man's young love should accompany him to his scenes of pleasure, his out-of-door pursuits, and natural studies, it would always exercise the influence over him that it did when he was a boy? Do you not believe that each would gain, the one a wider field of opportunity, and a more experienced taste, the other the restraint of a presence whose absence is never for good?

After dinner came the pipes and a long talk, and then as the sun went down, tracking the woods with his sanguine trail, we packed up our game, one deer to each pony, and with **Pompey Duffield Sah** taking the lead, filed off through the shadowy woods for the plantation.

CHAPTER VIII.

THE FIRESIDE AT FAR AWAY.

"'Tis home where'er the heart is."

Lou Jackson was not a beautiful girl—much less did she deserve the title of pretty. Her eyes and hair were both good, though the coarse and irregular eyebrow gave a masculine cast to her regard. Her nose was short, her mouth almost a line, and her complexion, naturally dark, was further injured by a roughness of skin that made it resemble a laboring woman's. The prevailing *pose* of her features was thoughtful, at times almost stern, yet once in a long while the lines of her mouth would curve, her cheek slightly dimple, and her eye would flash out a look of joy, recognition, and sympathy, the more gentle for being rare. So, at the close of a murky day, the western sky flashes out the sunshine of the morrow, and darkens again into twilight.

She had received the ordinary course of education as practised among American girls. A little geography, a little history, a little of the natural sciences, a little of two or three modern languages, and a little of two or three dead ones; a little music, painting, **polite literature, mathematics, crocheting,** moral philosophy, and **dancing**—all in homœopathic courses; and then **was launched out into** that practical world where one true **lesson learned in life's** school counterbalanced the teachings of **years.**

From the fashionable school **she stepped to the monotony of an interior plantation life. No musical instruments to play** on, no foreign friends to talk **to, no foreign books to read, even could she read them, where everything was simple in action, and** the bare **bosom of the world, with its** vegetation, minerals, and **animal** abundance, **was budding and throbbing** all around **her, and** the springs of domestic life, **its great needs and** small **attainments, its social loves and hates, were** open before **her. Then came the question, "What is my** place, and **can I fill it? If I claim to be a** flattered lady and a wife **of high rank, I have no beauty and** cannot attain it. **If I am to be a literary woman, and** make my **position by** my thoughts, **I have no** education **to** invent or model them. **If a mere waif floating on the stream of** life, the **very** animals **on the** banks **are better than I."** She reached out for anything she **could do, and** turned **in** every way **for some recourse** against that nothingness **that swallowed her up—that** dreaminess that all the day **filmed her** eye, and all the evening upbraided **her.**

At length, one day, the first time coming abroad after a severe illness, her mind drank in that confused blending **of sound,** color, motion, and fragrance, that is so pervading in the early spring, and which affects the nerves after a severe illness with so acute a pain. The buds seemed expanding with an inherent instinct, the birds seemed arranging their social affairs with a high intelligence, which had never struck her before. There was a relation of one to another, a connection to herself, and an apparentness of creation by that Higher Relative, that had just raised her from her feeble bed, that seemed never so plain or so beautiful as now. The more she pondered and examined, the greater seemed the field of thought. She was not idle now. Body and mind grew strong together. No one slighted her homely face in the fields, and with what aid from books that could be had, she wandered forth a thinking, happy, laboring, achieving, student. At last a field was before her; how strange, it had been under her eyes from childhood!

The fire was kindled in the planter's house, for it was a chilly night; the rain commenced to fall immediately after our return from the hunt, and from the pitch-pine branches "the light fell off in hoary flakes," painting bright the heavy furniture of the room, and belching from the chimney above the house, as from a smelting furnace. The room was adorned with implements of the chase, antlers, and rude stores of goods, and yet there were marks of a gentler taste in the engraving primitively framed, stuffed birds, and gracefully-disposed Indian weapons, decorated the walls. The interior of the mansion was more comfortable than its rough and dismantled exterior promised; and from its lonely situation, over sixty miles from any town and more than a dozen from any house, it had been appropriately named Far Away. The door stood open, the negroes sat on the sill, drinking in the conversation and laughing at every joke, while within, Lou Jackson, her father, and all his guests, sat or reclined around the room as best they could find places.

"Golly, Maussa, dat air buck's a grave-digger! Da's de same deer for sartin dat Blossom fired at two year ago Christmas comin', when his gun bus'. Das de same deer dat ripped up Snorter and Grip, de best dogs in dis county, and now wha's dat air he's gone dun dis day? He run Miss Lou's horse whare we like not see 'em till day o' judgment."

"Lem, you fool," called out Jackson, "hold your tongue; you will get all the boys on the place to be as great cowards as you are."

"I'se no coward, you knows dat's well's anybody, Maussa Jackson. Ef de Lord want a brave man, de Lord gonter call Lem; but I'se seen a buck run o' nights in de range, and he feet struck fire, and when I sees dat I comes in, and so'd you, Maussa Jackson."

"What for gwine contrariwise to de Lord?" said an old negress, whose white head was obtruding in at the doorway.

"De Lord send de debil and de debil come. Dare's Maussa Wilson's Ebo Jane, a rael little drum-cuss of a nigger woman; no genouwine religion 'bout her, and jist afore she die dere, by de door dat look toward de piney wood, an old buck—oh, golly, Maussa! look in at her! She guv one call and die, and de buck go away into de dark woods. I seed dat wid mine own eyes, an' it make dis eer hair of mine stan' straight up

On looking at the crisp, curling locks alluded to, no surer proof of a miracle was required than the fact that they could be made straight, for they were kinked into little cocoons of yellow white over the big, black face and staring eyes. As this inspired fact was related, the negroes, with their credulous susceptibility, edged closer in the open doorway to be fully within the circle of firelight, and even Lem had pulled in his legs from the outside of the open window, where he was sitting, and turned his body fireward.

As I looked at the bank of faces at the door, I saw a feeling of horror dash over their countenances that was singular to behold; following their dilated eyes, I saw them all fixed on Jumping Lem as he sat in the window, though from my position I could see nothing about him to excite the feeling. Mike kicked my foot, and I saw his eye, with a laugh in the corner of it, turned to where Lem was sitting. I leaned forward, and could see in the darkness beyond, only partially lighted up by the fire, the head and antlers of a large deer.

Lem had not seen the apparition, but continued: "Down on de Waccassasee dare's a deer-path made by dat air same buck, and when de dogs cum dere, dey down tail an' take de back track, howlin' all de time as if dey"——

At this instant one of the protruding tines of the deer's horns touched the earnest story-teller on the shoulder. He looked around, and caught sight of the spectre at his side. He gave a wild shriek, and darted toward the door; the negroes, frightened more by his fears than what they saw, came crowding in and blocked up the door, when Lem jumped into the middle of the circle by the fire, crouching at his master's feet, and crying, "Oh, Golly! Maussa! Lord a massy, dare h'is! dare h'is!"

The spectre head continued to advance into the room, when one of the horns, touching the side of the window, it fell down from the pole on which it was stuck, and lay on the floor. It was the head of the buck we had shot that morning.

"That is my deer's head," said Miss Jackson. "I was having it stuffed."

"That's that are boy Scip's doin's; he's a queer critter," laughed Mike.

"Get up, Lem, and tell us something more about that buck," said Jackson.

Lem sprung to his feet, and, amid the jeers of his comrades—who laughed at him all the harder because they were frightened themselves—he rushed out of the cabin, and we heard him running around the house in pursuit of the mischievous inventor of the ghost, and giving vent, as he ran, to divers threats of punishment, which had the effect of rendering Scipio invisible for the rest of the night.

Mike picked up the fallen deer's head and examined it closely.

"Why, Lou, child, I never heard of your dressing animals," said Jackson.

"Nor I, father, until to-day."

"What are you going to do with it?"

"Make it as correct as I can, and then hang it over the front door until I can make a better one. The ornament is the Doctor's idea."

"The head is as correctly dressed as it can be," said the Doctor. "Don't you think so, Mike?"

"Wall—no, I don't," answered the literal hunter.

"What is it that is wrong, Mike? It must be in the setting it up, for you cleaned it for me yourself."

"It moit be one, and it moit be the t'other; but I guess it's some of both. Yer see the hair ain't over slick—that's *my* fault. Wall, arter that yer've got the eyes a lookin' for'ard, and the head well up, ain't that so?"

"Yes," said Miss Jackson, leaning forward.

"Wall, then," continued her instructor, taking the deer's head on his knee and illustrating his position with his fingers, "he's a makin' out somethin' ahead of him, and he'll have his ears for'ard to help him, one on 'em anyhow."

"That's true," replied the pupil, with a glance of pleasure, taking the deer's head in her hand and pulling out the wires by which the ears were supported.

"That's the natur' of a deer. I one'st went to Charleston and seed more lies than you could shake a stick at, and one was a stuffed deer a-feedin' with his flag straight up. Wall, ef that didn't make me sick. Sez I to the show-man, 'Mister, I'd jist like to tie you to a deer's tail in Floridy to show you how they carry their tails; dod rot me if I wouldn't!'"

"Ha ha! that is not as bad as my friend the Doctor," I said.

"You had better stop before you go any further, I warn you," interrupted the Doctor.

"You must know," I continued, "the Doctor, early one morning in Pensacola, saw two deer feeding in the garrison garden on the old Commodore's pea vines. So he ran down, and imagining that they had come in through the open gate and could not surmount the high picket that surrounded the garden, carefully closed the gate. Then, with his gun in hand, he ran in to call the Commodore to inquire whether he preferred them dead or alive; but when he returned the deer were half way to the Perdido River."

"Oh, that is too bad, Doctor!" cried Jackson, as the negroes shouted with fun.

"No, no," said the Doctor, laughing away, "that is not all of the story. My friend here was there, too, peeping through the palisades over his rifle, when I shut the gate. It was his proposition that I should go in for the Commodore, and as I came back, I heard a cap snap, his gun had missed fire while endeavoring to kill one of the deer, while I was gone."

The mirth that followed this apocryphal story was like nothing but the laughter that hails some unusual feat of the Polichinelle, before the gaping circle of children and nurses in the gardens of Paris, and it gradually subsided, lingering longest furthest from the door, where the negro boys could roll over on their backs without restraint, and laugh themselves to smiles, and then to return for a fresh draught of fun.

"To come back to your deer's head," I said to Miss Jackson, after the laugh had subsided, "where did you procure the glass eyes?"

"Oh, father supplies them with his broken bottles; the shoulder of the bottle makes an eye, only a little too flat."

"And the birds on the wall are dressed by you?"

"Yes, all of them."

"And they are truer to natur' 'an a picter," added Mike, approvingly.

"Where did you get your taste for such matters, Miss Jackson?"

"I think I must have got it from associating with them, to the exclusion of most other society. We lead a lonely life here in the pine woods, sometimes, and I believe that when one has many gifts he does not gain from them all as much as he does from one well studied."

"Where did you get your original plan, your first lesson in taxidermy?" said the Doctor; "for I have studied the art, and it seems to me that I have never dressed a bird as well as some you have here."

"I never had any lesson, save what I have read. Once, when first attempting it, I sent to Savannah and bought a stuffed bird which I pulled in pieces to find the secret. But the true teacher is patience. Try again every time you fail."

"They have kept well for so warm a climate."

"That's a woman's secret," said Jackson. "Lou bakes her birds in the oven."

"I'll tell you a joke," said Miss Jackson, "about baking birds. One day there was a bird pie in the oven, the pride of our new cook, and on looking at it, I found it done, and the fire low enough to dry some birds I had just set up. Accordingly, I stood them in the oven all covered with white strings, in front of the pie. When dinner was ready, Dinah went for the pie, but presently came running back, calling out, 'As sure as I's 'live, missus, dem birds is out ob de pie, or else dere ghosts am standin' dere in dere grave close. Oh Lor' help us!'"

"Your birds were correctly set up, then, if they deceived even a cook. What do you do when you are where you cannot have the use of an oven?"

"Oh, I do the best I can; use pepper-grass, dry them in the sun, and then let them slide."

"How pleasant it is to have a copy of nature's works by your side, so well prepared that it reminds you of the original bird," remarked the Doctor, laying back on a wooden bench, looking at the hawks over head and swinging his feet back and forward under his lounge.

"Yes," answered Miss Jackson, "and to study the positions, and manners of the birds and quadrupeds, so that you can copy in your subject the true position and figure, and not burlesque them. So, sometimes, what would be thrown from father's game-bag to the cook to be plucked, or, more likely still, cast away as worthless, with a little care and study resumes its old shape, takes again its natural *pose*, flashes its eye, and remains 'a joy forever.'"

"Do you not believe," said the Doctor, "that beautiful associations, because beautiful, make the mind, by exciting it in that direction, beautiful and gentle likewise?"

"No, not altogether. Why, if so, should not the Indian be the most beautiful minded of us all?"

"Because he has no beautiful moral or mental bases, but, on the contrary, *they* are bad. The soul and the mind are greater than the senses, and their associations counterbalance. But let the soul and mind lie idle, or present no counterbalancing force, and then the natural lesson elevates by assimilation."

"Oh no, Doctor; nature is more of an active teacher than a mere assimilator. She not only teaches by her unseen influence, but she preaches by word, and sound, and sight. For what is the unfolding year?—for what the garnered grain, and sapless winter? It has more than a productive use. Who tells the young Brent Goose, at Vancouver's Island, that he will find no winter at Tampa

Bay? And what teaches the saracena plant to shut its fingers and gather in its leaves all nourishing insects? Thus, when you see these things day and night, you are led to reason of them, and your thought makes you better by a positive judgment. It is no mere assimilation, but a refined study."

"I will propose a question to you," retorted the Doctor: "why, then, should not the Indians be better men, as they see these things day and night?"

"Simply because the Indian never had mind enough to think or reason at all of such things. You commit an error by assuming that, because all these things are visible and constant, therefore men of no mind will read them aright; but I think that it is, on the contrary, the greatest minds that are the best students of nature, and until a mind has received some education, it cannot appreciate nature to any extent. Listen to the monstrous errors the rustic repeats of what he sees in the fields, and then, as the world culminates in a highly religious and educated society, see how it gathers, as in London, all the birds of the air and beasts of the field, together, to 'consider their ways and be wise.'"

As Miss Jackson talked, her grey eye kindled, and a blush brightened either cheek. The Doctor raised himself gradually to a sitting position, then to his feet, and then he walked across the floor, saying, in his clear, hearty tone: "Give me your hand, Lou Jackson! who cares which comes first, the love of nature or the mind, to appreciate her, the one is sure to produce the other."

"Wall, that's so," said Mike.

The evening promised a rainy day for the morrow, and therefore it was arranged that Mike and I should have a still hunt while Jackson would ride down to the coast to see to some stores that had been promised to be landed at a given point by a boat from St. Mark's.

"I think I will stay home to-morrow and set up some birds," said the Doctor.

"You had better *let 'em slide*, Poke," I remarked in a low tone.

"Never you mind," answered the Doctor, with a low laugh. "A man's a man for a' that and a' that."

The negroes were turned out of the cabin, the fire was covered, and in three minutes, oblivious of rain or deer, all were in the "land o' dreams."

CHAPTER IX.

THE STILL HUNT.

L'Aurore paraissait à peine,
Quand dans la brume à l'horizon
Je l'ai vu rentrant de la plaine
Tout chargé de sa venaison.
Redressant sa large empaumure
Il s'est arrêté par trois fois
Puis il a longé la bordure
Ecoutant l'eau tomber sous bois.

As the first light struggled through the clouds and the tassels of the pines overhead, Mike and I alone, with our breakfasts in our hands, were winding our way through the forest.

We trudged on as best we might over the rolling knolls of sand, laced by the long, tough roots of the palmetto, across hollows choked with grass and vines, and down and up the quaggy sloughs that the waters had made while seeking their level in the Ouithlacouchee. The tough little ponies scampered along on the level land, and where it was muddy Mike would slide to his feet and cheer them on with whoop and hulloa, until they ran up the banks as fast as they jumped down. The rain had ceased, yet it was not clear, and the drops hung on all the bushes, or showered down on us from above as we struck the young timber.

Having reached a point of land in the bend of the river, the ponies were unsaddled, their halters were tied to their knees so that they could not run, though giving them ample liberty to graze, and left behind with an injunction to "Stay thar, yer sarcy critters."

Again the word was forward. Mike led the way on a long stride, his rifle lying in the hollow of his left arm, and his body bending and oscillating to conform to the inequalities of the ground. As he walked he turned hither and thither, taking in with his eye everything in the forest. At times, he would pick up a leaf here and there, giving it a glance, and cast it down again. Where the river bent, and we came where we could see around the elbow, his walk was slow, and his foot came down like a cat's; when he was in the hollow he ran, and almost halted as he rose the succeeding knoll, and could take a view beyond.

As we walked, he pointed to a place in the sod, looking at me with that communicative glance that said, "There is something pleasant." On looking carefully, I could just see a mark where the grass was thin, but a mark it was, and nothing more; it might be a natural discoloration, or the result of one of the thousand motions constantly occurring in a forest.

"What is it?" I asked.

Mike picked up a broad leaf, one of those growing in

a dank place, and handed it to me. The leaf was cut almost in the shape of the letter V.

"What does that mean—a deer's track?"

Mike nodded.

"How long ago was that track made?"

"Two minutes—'bout."

My looks must have expressed doubt, for Mike replied: "Look here, now, leaves don't tell lies in the piney woods, though I've heern tell they do in books. D'ye see that juice comin' out of that leaf thar jist whar the the deer's huff cut it?"

"Well?"

"D'yer think them air leetle drops has been more 'an a week formin' when they're growin' bigger as ye look, and haint run together yet? Tear another leaf, don't it come jist as fast? Ain't that as plain as a bar up a gum tree? He's a sockdologer of a buck, too!"

"Now, Mike, look here. I will believe what you say about the time, but don't say what you don't know. You can have everything your own way here, but there are no means in the world of telling this deer to have been a buck, so you need not say so till we see it."

"Wall, now," said Mike, setting down the breech of his heavy rifle on the ground, and leaning his chin on the muzzle, while he looked at me with an expression of pity; "wall, now, ef I had a young 'un, and he couldn't tell that he was a scandalous big buck, walking alone slowly like out to the feedin' grounds, ef I wouldn't claw his back with a wildcat, I would.

Now jist look a here, there's one track by the lance leaf."

"Yes."

"Here's the t'other on the same side, and here's the t'other, and here's the t'other. Wall, that shows he's a walkin', don't it?"

"Ye-e-s."

"Thar he's nibbled off that young tree, haint he?"

A small birch sprout, of about a foot in height, was stripped of its leaves and bark.

"Ye-e-s."

"Wall, that shows he was feedin' slowly, and warn't the leastwise anxious, and by the way the tracks pint I calkerlate he's off for the meadows."

"Well, but how do you know it was not a doe?"

"Cause he writ it up on that pine tree on ahead, where the tracks are thick at the bottom. Now look on the bark about six feet up, and tell me what rubbed that bark off ef it warn't that buck's horns—and you better believe it was a whopper; no small buck kin scratch up thar."

I thought a moment, and then the only wonder to me seemed why it needed an explanation at all, it was so clear.

"Whare has he gone? Thare's a meadow across here chock full of sweet grass and lily pads, and I reckon he's thar, and slathers more."

A few minutes' walk, and we came on to the verge of a natural meadow, bounded on every side by the forest, and yet smooth and waving as a field of grain, or a level prairie. Here and there a water-oak reared itself from the grass, twisting its great limbs on every side, shading the sward below, and supporting wreaths of mistletoe vines covered with waxen berries. But all else was one free rustling field, grazed by the deer alone, and mowed only by the winter fires or the hurricane. Over the grass could be seen the marsh hawk wheeling along the level in long slanting curves, while in the distance, where a tall tree leaned over the eddies of the river, a solitary eagle watched his primeval realm, where

> Unheeded spreads the blossomed bud
> Its milky bosom to the bee,
> Unheeded falls along the flood
> The desolate and aged tree.

This was a great pasture for the deer, and ever since the creation thousands had spent the nights here, retiring with the heat of the sun to the closer cover of the pines.

"I haint seen that air buck's tracks agin," said Mike; "I rather think he haint got in yet. We'll go a leetle further on to this ridge; he will likely come down that way, I reckon. Come, Yowler?" and taking the long ear of his dog in his hand to prevent him taking to the meadow, we ran on to the ridge. By the side of the ridge we found quite a well-beaten deer path leading through an opening in the fringe of trees that surrounded the meadow, and through this, from time immemorial, doubtless, the great horned herds had wound their way in and out at their pleasure. Here, too, were found tracks of wild hogs, and Mike pointed out to me a broad foot-print of the cougar or panther that had been made only the night before.

It was agreed that I should lie here concealed behind some branches with my eye on the path leading from the woods, while Mike should go around in the woods and see what had become of the buck. In a moment he was gone, and I was left lying on my breast, with my rifle ready cocked before me, watching the lonely path that led into the forest.

As soon as Mike was out of sight I began to feel that intense loneliness and shadowy presence that is often with one when in a great forest, particularly if unaccustomed to its solitude. The stillness, the majesty of the woods, the strange insects crawling about, the flickering light that complexes the eye, the heart counting the time with heavy throbs, the apprehension of making a noise, all press on the senses with a bewildering power. I felt this sensation, and longed for the deer or Mike, I cared but little which. I sighted my rifle, and tried to determine from which way the deer would first come, feeling certain he was mine if he appeared.

As I thus lay putting propositions to myself, I heard a loud snort or whistle directly behind me. I turned hastily, and away bounded a buck that had been standing apparently within ten feet of me. How I apostrophized my carelessness, and watched the waving grass as he wound among the meadow paths far away on the plains!

Again I watched, and this time more successfully, for over the knoll I could see a pair of horns coming slowly forward, though the deer was still out of sight. They advanced like a rower in a boat, with measured but irregular speed, and once in a while stopped altogether. Then my heart beat like a drum, but when the horns advanced again I felt more composed. At length the head appeared above the brow of the hill, then the shoulders, then the full length and height of the animal; there was no more doubt—it was *the sockdologer of a buck* described by Mike. When it reached the hill it seemed to halt for a survey, and viewed the whole extent of the woods and savannah. Trees, and waters, and waving grass, the cool retreats of low hanging bushes, all appeared to his eye like the pleasant meadows to the monarch bull, when released from his winter's stall, he looks over the farm in the spring. All kinds of nervous apprehensions arose in my mind. I feared lest he might turn back, and almost called out in my anxiety. I dreaded lest he should see me, and crouched to the earth to prevent it. Presently, apparently satisfied with his examination, he marched down the hill to where I lay in ambush. His head high up, his great horns back, his step like the step of a race-horse, he looked like a marching king. I could not see any part of his body but his breast, and did not like to take a front shot, but waited until he should present some other view. But the stag did not intend to turn aside; he saw his feeding ground beyond, green with the succulent herbage of the lowlands, where his mates had awaited him all the night, and he walked right onward. Now he was too near to shoot. What should I do? If he sees me, he will dash off, giving me the worst possible shot. My heart beat so I could not lay on my side, but raising my gun gently on my left elbow, I depressed the breech, and without taking sight, when the deer was almost over me, pulled the trigger. With the report of my gun the frightened animal sprang into the air as though he had been blown up by a mine, and then dashed off into the woods. He flew over the hills, and just as I had given him up for lost I heard the clear ring of a rifle in the direction he had gone. It was Mike's; I knew its voice. What a load fell off my mind—the deer was ours!

On reaching the place from whence the shot came, I found Mike loading his rifle, and the deer with his antlers ploughed into the ground by the force of his running fall, and his throat cut. On looking for my shot I readily found it in the breast, and the ball had gone through the thick part of the neck without doing much damage. Mike's had struck him in the head.

Selecting two small trees that grew from the same root, we lifted our quarry up until his horns caught in the angle, and his body hung down with his back to the tree. Mike then cut the skin in a line from the throat to the tail, and also a transverse line down each foreleg. Then loosening the neck from the skin, he cut it off from the head at the first joint, and then pulled the fore shoulders **directly out of** the skin, which, with the hind **quarters,** was left hanging by the horns. When the body of the deer was skinned **as far** down as the loins, it was cut off there and thrown aside, while the hindquarters were neatly rolled in the skin with the branching horns, and hung **on a sapling to await the time of** our return at night.

Our original plan had been to drive the deer from off the meadows with the dog, we standing at the run**ways, thus getting very fair** shots on the open plain, but by reason of **the advanced** hour of the day it seemed doubtful if this plan would succeed; **however, we** resolved to try it. Therefore we selected two paths, apparently much frequented by the deer, and in some **places worn** into channels, and sent Yowler off to hunt. The old dog seemed to know his duty well, for he hied away with a look at his master, and we could occasionally see him, where the grass was thin, making long casts, and occasionally his mellow voice would be borne in faint from the distance.

Mike was standing not far away, and looking across the **grass I** could see him leaning against a tree surveying the scene before **us.** Afar down in the horizon I saw a gang of deer headed by two bucks going out of the meadow by some other path on a long lope; I pointed them out with my arm, and a nod from Mike showed me he saw the game and understood my gesture. There go two herons, blue and grey, flapping up from the grass, and turning their heads first on one side and then on the other; the dog must be in that neighborhood and have sprung them, though we cannot see him for the grass.

There comes a deer; he is close by before one can see he is started—a young buck with spike horns. How fast he comes! once in a while jumping high above the grass to view his pursuer. Mike has disappeared behind the tree against which he was leaning. I wonder which path the deer will take. I raise my rifle; no he is running for Mike. He comes now fast, and close behind him is yelping the hound! he is within shot of Mike, running right for his stand. Spang! rings the rifle; the deer jumps, staggers, halts, and falls. Well done, old Red Beard! next to shooting game one's self, the best thing is to see it well shot by some one else.

Yowler is caught by his master, and sent back on the meadows. Hardly had he gone out of sight before I heard his yelp again, and a great rustle and shaking of some reeds that grew a hundred rods in front of me. There it is! one, two, three deer—and there goes another—and here comes a third party! The firing has alarmed them, and they are off with a snort and a whistle, each his own way. One has turned this way; no, he has gone toward the river. There is another; he is coming this way, surely; yes, here he comes, head up, horns back—a noble fellow. "Dear me!" I ejaculated, "this is like shooting deer in a park." As I crouched low in the narrow pass I was occupying, with a dense thorn thicket on either hand, and the grass growing in front of me sufficiently high to conceal me from view, I heard the grass rattle furiously, and out dashed an old boar, seeming in a desperate hurry; he ran close by me, giving a malicious lunge with his snout, at me in passing; I sprung aside in time to avoid the compliment, and gazed after his retreating form with feelings of great indignation. The Spaniards of the coast had turned out some hogs in this neighborhood in previous years, and their offspring, increasing with great prolificness, had become as savage as the boars of the Black Forest.

Before I had recovered my composure, another hog came rushing past, grunting and tearing along, followed by a whole herd of smaller animals, that thrashed down the grass, and jammed past me in the wildest fright; as the last one came, I lost all patience, and fired. The crowd was too thick to miss, and I had the satisfaction of seeing one tumble over on its back. But my satisfaction was short-lived when there swept by me a beautiful deer on a long lope, and running as if playing with its pursuer. He came so near me I could have hit him with my gun, and did not see me until directly abreast; he then rushed onward with a terrified leap, and was immediately lost to view. At this instant I heard Mike fire a shot, but could not see what he had killed.

When the dog came in, which he did in a moment, on the trail of the deer that had passed me, he seemed much worried, and laid down close at my feet and refused to go out again. I could not account for his singular behavior, but, not seeing any more deer on the meadow,

I took him by the ear and walked around to where Mike had taken his stand, and where he was busy taking off the skins of the two deer he had shot.

" What did you shoot at ?" he inquired, as I came up.

" A young hog !" and then I told him how the drove had rushed upon me, led by the vicious old boar, until in desperation I had made bacon of one, and so lost my chance at the deer.

" Some takes kindly to pork," replied Mike, " and when hard up I can worry down a leetle roast pig myself —but I don't keer to have 'em too often. Howsumever, they like 'em at the house."

So taking up the two saddles of venison, we hung them in the woods by the side of the other, and went down to get my porker, but, alas! like the old lady in the nursery rhymes, when I came back my porker was gone.

" I am sure he was dead," I replied to Mike's quizzical smile. " He lay there at that spot, and I had my feet on him while I loaded my rifle. There's the blood on the grass now."

" What druv the hogs out so fast—was Yowler arter 'em ?"

" No, they seemed to come alone, and Yowler skulked down, trembling, just as he is doing now."

Mike glanced at the dog, and then leaned down until his face almost came against the sod, when, drawing himself partially up, he said, " We'd better make tracks out of this corner; there ain't room enough for a free fight heyur."

"To fight what?"

"Painter," he replied.

I looked at the speaker, but there was not the least bit of joking in his face.

"How do you know that it is a panther?" said I, in a half whisper, the skin on my head contracting in spite of myself at the idea of the animal having been there where I stood only five minutes before in such fancied security.

"Wall, I know it in two ways," said Mike, in his natural hearty tone, but without raising himself from his stooping posture, and slowly bringing his rifle to a level, "and one's 'bout's good as the tother. In the fust place, thar's the mark of his foot on the grass; and in the next place, thar's the old sarpent himself under them are bushes."

I leaned down and followed the direction of Mike's eye under the bushes, and truly there was the panther crouched under some wild plum-trees not forty feet off from where we stood. He was in a sitting posture, and one arm was stretched out and placed on the body of the hog that laid beside him. There was something handsome in that position of easy grace, with the careless claim of ownership that he extended over his prize. I caught his yellow eye, and could scarcely remove my own from the fascination of its glance. He had the air of a sentinel challenging us strangers, and I, for one, felt like an intruder, and had a mental desire of apologizing and retiring.

"Jist keep steady-like," said Mike, in his usual slow

tone, "Don't move fast, but step a leetle away from me, and ef I miss him he will come out, and then you try."

As he finished speaking, his rifle was at his shoulder, and the clear report of the piece was followed by a rushing bound as the animal came out. Mike drew his knife, but it was useless; the panther spent his life in that prodigious leap, and lay dead on the grass. The rifle ball had gone through his brain.

"Ha!" said Mike, with a prolonged accent and strong out-breathing that showed the force of his feelings. Then, leaning down and laying his hand on the tawny face of his fallen foe, he caressed him as he would have done a child, smoothing his cheek and lifting his paw, and speaking to him in the proud yet tender way he would have spoken to his sweetheart. "And ye be a purty critter; yer eyes has babies in 'em. My beauty, didn't you know me when you squatted thar? I've knowed you, pet, I reckon, when yer were quite a youngster. I've seen you sleepin' on my coat like any cat. I've watched you almost ever since, and heerd of all yer doin's. Yer forgot me, but I didn't forgit you, no how at all, little yaller back, and now yer dead, poor thing. Wall, wall, we'll all come to that soon, only let's have our traps all ready. I wish Lou Jackson could see you where you're layin'."

When this funeral address was ended, we dragged the body out of the bushes into a more open place, to take off the skin. The shooting of deer was an every-day work, and they were skinned in a minute; but the death of a panther, and the taking off his robe, is an incident that calls forth the liveliest feelings of pleasure in those who participate in it, and only the hunter can understand the accent of pride with which Mike at length held up in both hands the huge tawny skin, with its pendent claws and cat-like head, saying, "Ain't that a bed for a king?" When we had completed this work, noon had long since passed away, and we looked around for a spot to dine.

Near where we had hung our first deer, on the sloping side of a clay bank, a spring of water rose from the earth, "and a clearer one never was seen," which filling a natural basin among the roots of the trees that overhung it, poured down the hill in a trickling rivulet, and joined by other smaller springs, sought its level on the great savannah, where its course could be traced by the eye for a mile or more by the line of joint grass and flags that took root in its waters. By this spring we carried our three saddles of venison, our hog, and our panther skin, and sat ourselves down to dinner. Not a grand dinner of cold fowl and claret, sandwiches and cakes, with which in more favored places hunters in the woods regale their inner man, but a dinner that consisted simply of a large square of corn-bread, and an equally large square of venison steak, but so hungry were we that no rich repast, even though spread at Verey's, at Paris, would have been more highly honored, and surely no table, even on the Santa Lucia, with the broad bay of Naples, and the flaming spire of Vesuvius before the door, could have been spread in a more graceful place, or with a more characteristic view. The deep well spring with its seething sands at the bottom churned into a constant motion, the trees that for ages had guarded that source, the rippling murmur of the brook, the soughing of the pine leaves, the broad perspective of meadow, with the distant belt of river beyond, so far away that its gleam was like the horizon, the nearer scamper of the squirrel, or the flap of the heron's wing as disturbed by our presence he rose from the flags, all gave a landscape to the eye, or a sense of solitude to the mind, and occupied us in contemplation for an hour or more after the dinner was ended.

"Do you think you ever saw that panther before to-day?" I asked of Mike, as I tossed him over the tobacco pouch.

"I'm not over sartin, but I reether spect. Yer see thar ain't many on 'em heyar bout, and it was jist two years ago when that ere painter cub I guv Colonel Brown, at Tampa, vamosed, and then he was two years old. This one, you see, would be nigh on to three, and that would jist make it." A long puff or two followed from his short pipe, when he said in a musing manner, "That air cub left bekase of a fight he got in with a soldier at the fort. Yer see he guv the soldier a slap, when the soldier struck him with his bay'nit, and then the painter jist chawed him up and sloped. Wall, now look a heyar, do you see that mark on his cheek?" There was a triangular scar on the animal's cheek, just under the eye. "That, I calkelate, is that ere bay'nit dig. This is the last o' that settlement. Grey Wolf's band got the old painter, and the cub I left thar in my coat, so I've heern; the t' other cub, the one I toted to Tampa Bay, is this heyar, and that's all the painters thar is round these diggins."

Without precisely understanding the reasoning by which Mike arrived at this last affirmation concerning a wood that apparently might contain a thousand such animals without any one being aware of it, I could not help smiling at the particularity of his genealogical knowledge of this family.

"Thar's somewhar here about another varmint, and a partier one yet, though tain't of much account as a fighter. I've seen his tracks and have promised his skin to Lou Jackson, and ef he ain't a ghost I'll git him some day, though I've been a month tryin' to find him."

"What is the animal?"

"Tiger cat; a rael likely little critter; yaller with black dabs. I reckon he's 'bout the size of a small hound."

"You were in a hurry to make your promises. How do you know you can get it?"

"Because Lou Jackson wants it."

"Could you get anything Lou Jackson wanted?"

"I reckon," replied Mike, with the assurance of a man that had never failed in any thing he desired with his whole mind.

"How long have you known Lou Jackson?"

"Goin' on to three years."

"Where did they come from?"

"Oh, Jackson had a big plantation on the upper coast somewhere nor'east; but I've heern say he lost his crops and got in debt, and fit a duel, and then cum heyar, and built this house, and called it 'Far Away.'"

"I thought you had known his family longer, you seem such a friend of Miss Lou."

"I have known them only three years; and some folks you know soon, and Lou Jackson is one of them kind."

"She is a pleasant girl."

"Yes, I can say that. Thar's nobody in Floridy that can say so much, and be so sparin' of words. She's always the same; she makes it light all about the Ouithlacouchee when it's black dark everywhere else, she's so happy like. Even the Injins, when they come there, draw in their claws and act genteel, and that's oncommin for an Injin."

"They are very much exposed, living here so far from protection, and bands of these Indians rovirg about, and sometimes Jackson himself away."

"No; he don't leave often unless she goes with him; but many a night I've kept round that house when nobody knowed it, jist to know that she was sleepin', when these cusses has been about."

"What did she say to you when she heard of your watchfulness?"

"How would she know? Do you think *I* would tell

her sich like **stuff? It's** natural enough that I should watch fur **her.** Wall—wall—thar are piles o' painters in **this** State purty as this one, but there aint no woman **that** is as handsome as Lou Jackson. That's so?"

"Do you know anything about the duel that Col. Jackson fought?"

"I've heern tell that it was a hard go; they **fired one at the t'other till the** Colonel bored his man, and then he larnt it was all **a mistake,** and they needn't have fit at **all;** but who the man was, or what they fit about, I don't **know. Whar's the** terbacker?"

I passed the pouch **of** squirrel-skin over to the hunter, and filling his pipe again, he relapsed into a musing silence, while I watched the lengthening shadows, and **thought over the strange life at Far Away,** the moody, **reckless, hearty, proud** planter, and **the** gentle though strange tastes of the daughter. What a wasting, sensitive, weary heart **he seemed** to carry, joyous only by **turns, and then boisterously gay!** What a cheering controlling presence hers, so earnest and frank, yet all the while so lively and self-willed! And the house itself was a perfect mixture of roughness and grace, the life within contrasting with its appearance, as did the fancy of its name with the rudeness of its exterior. No news of the world, no society, no lover, no music, the literature **of the most** meagre kind, and yet the whole family instinct was graceful and thoughtful, and like to no western farm that ever yet was seen.

As I thus ran on, I noticed the sun was low in the west.

"It will be dark soon."

"I reckon," said Mike, in his usual manner.

"But we can't stay out here all night."

"I've lain by this spring right often, but I s'pose we may as well go now; you go ketch the ponies, and I'll get their pelter ready."

I accordingly went after the ponies, which were found near where we had hoppled them. As I rode back I saw a single buck feeding in the open woods, but stopping to attempt a shot, he ran off in the direction that we had come in the morning. On returning to the spring, Mike had the game already bound, and balanced so as to hang over the ponies. The hog balanced two saddles of venison, and the panther's skin another saddle. After loading the ponies we started toward home, Mike promising to get the buck I had seen when I went for the ponies. I showed him the place where the deer had been feeding when I first saw him, and the direction he had taken.

"Wall, that'll do," he said; "he's so much nigher home."

In a few minutes after, as we mounted a hill, we saw the deer in the distance again, and as we came in view he looked at us for a moment, and then gently trotted on, and some small galls or swamp holes intervening, was soon lost to sight.

"Thar, he'll do now. Take your pony by the bridle, and follow fast right for that gall."

We came within a hundred yards of the brake, and

then hoppling the ponies, ran on to the edge of the bushes, that afforded a good cover. Having reached this, we passed carefully through, looking out toward the open land beyond in hopes to see the buck within shot, but, alas! he was too wise for that, and had only stopped when fully beyond the **reach of harm** from the thicket close behind. Near by, a turkey-hen was leading a large brood of young ones, nearly full grown, clucking and hopping along, and running hither and thither in the pursuit of spiders and other insects, that showed she was utterly unconscious of her dangerous neighbors.

"**Now** we'll have to crawl for it," said Mike.

"Then the sooner we begin, the sooner we get within shot," said I, moving forward.

"Stop," whispered Mike; "wait till those turkeys get **away. If the** deer sees them run away in a hurry he'll make tracks too, for he knows thar is something wrong hereabout, and having seen us **once, he'll** know it's us."

So we waited patiently until the turkey brood had sauntered down the woods, and then emerged from our place of concealment. Mike ran ahead in a stooping posture, and I followed close behind, running when he ran, and halting when he stopped. The first run we made was comparatively easy, for an immense pine tree, made doubly large by a large grape-vine that wound around it **and** hung in clusters by its trunk, fully concealed our approach. Here we took another survey of the ground and the game, and then, when a tree intervened between us and the head of the deer, which stood with his side toward us, we ran forward again until the deer wagged his tail, when we halted, in whatever position we might be.

It may be necessary to explain, for the benefit of those who have never learned the fact from deer-stalking, that a deer feeds and watches at irregular intervals, and that always, two or three seconds before raising his head, either to walk forward, or to cast a glance of watchfulness around him, he gives his white tail a quick whisk or two. The knowledge of this simple and peculiar habit is of immense use to the still-hunter, who is thus forewarned when to advance, and when to lie still.

Thus by quick and short advances we approached to within a very long shot of our deer. My heart was beating thick and fast, and the sweat of great mental excitement stood in drops on my face, and rolled in my eyes, causing me to wipe them with my sleeve every minute.

"Now," whispered Mike, "ef yer want to try him, yer must crawl alone while I wait; we can't get any nearer together, but mind his tail."

So Mike laid still behind the weeds that were sheltering us, while I went on alone. Horatius advancing before the Roman army to defend the bridge, could not have felt more keenly the prominence of his position under the eyes of all Rome, than I did as I stalked forward, under the keen eye of Mike the Spook, to shoot that deer. First I had a little shrub between me and the buck, and about twenty feet ahead; to this I advanced safely. As I arrived, the deer whisked his tail and looked round. Waiting a moment, to my great discomfiture he turned his face toward me, and then commenced eating again. This was a state of affairs that I had not anticipated, for it shut me out from a view of that barometer tail. However, I calculated the time during which he would probably feed, and made a short advance. The deer now turned quarteringly toward me, and, taking advantage of this change, with my eye fixed upon him, I was hastily advancing, when something disturbed the animal before his usual time. I laid down flat on the grass, with my rifle before me, as the buck, now within shot, raised his crowned head, and took a long and deliberate survey of the ground. There seemed to be some latent suspicion in his mind, for, though not seeing me, he yet looked all around him several times, and then over me, and finally commenced walking directly toward me. I slowly elevated my rifle on my left hand, my elbow all the while on the ground. The piece reached its level—my heart beat as though it was tugging with the blood that flowed through it—the deer was at a close shot, and all the time coming nearer, yet I could not aim correctly. Still on he came toward me, his ears turned back and forth, his head stretching forward, his nose dilating as he snuffed the air, and his eyes seeming to look me through. I summoned my courage, and held my breath; every sense seemed to pause while I sighted for the white breast not forty yards off. Dear me! the gun was not cocked. A pause was required for this, and I became more nervous than ever. I aimed again. A brief instant—it seemed an age between my pulling the trigger and the discharge of the piece—when the clear crack of the rifle sounded, and the deer, wheeling around, flew away " as if the wolves of the Apennines were all upon his track."

I looked around for Mike; there he lay in the weeds, and on the end of his ramrod he had been waving a little red flag that had attracted the attention of the buck, and lured him on to his dangerous position. I saw the deer for a mile down the open woods flitting past the trees, and I knew I had made a clear miss. On coming up to Mike his dry smile glowed in the corners of his eye as he asked me, " Did you hit him?"

Without answering the question, I asked him why *he* did not shoot, as the buck was clearly within shot for him as well as myself.

" We've got our pile of deer's meat, and 'nuff is 'nuff, and what's the use a wastin'?"

So we went back for our ponies, and again started for home, where we arrived safely late in the evening, to find the big fires blazing, and a supper kept all ready for our coming. How pleasant the cabin looked, from the damp darkness without!

> " And sweet the music of the step
> That meets us at the door."

CHAPTER X.

THE FLORIDA POCAHONTAS.

> "Their memory liveth on your hills,
>   Their baptism on your shore,
>   Your everlasting rivers speak
>   Their dialect of yore."
>
> SIGOURNEY.

THE evening meal was ended; the planter's family and the hunters were circled around the fire, weary with the day's fatigues and enjoying rest as none but the weary may. Pipes and cigars were lit, and the negroes crowded the door-way, while, as in many a hunting-lodge before,

> "The stag-hounds, weary with the chase,
>   Lay stretched upon the rushy floor,
>   And urged in dreams the forest race
>   From Teviot Stone to Eskdale Moor."

"Now for a story, Mike," said Miss Jackson.

"No, taint my turn. Doctor, slide along with a yarn."

"No, no; stories are dealt like cards, always to the left. It is your turn, Jackson."

"Well, what shall it be—anything from a fight to a foot-race?"

"Let Miss Jackson name the subject," I suggested.

"Then it will be love," said Poke, with his blandest bow to the lady in question.

"More likely hate," said the planter's daughter, her dark skin flushing at the Doctor's speech. "Tell us a tale of woman; we have the chase in reality every day."

"As you will—woman forever. Throw on another log, boys."

The fire belched up a million sparks to the deep sky. The flames started out afresh, and Jackson, putting his pipe in its buckskin cover, and drawing himself up by his elbows to the convenient support of a log, where he could face the whole of his auditors, in a rough, though deep, voice, and with occasional gesture, as he warmed with his theme, spoke in the following romantic and poetical style:

"Three times, since the Spaniard came to this country, has a century rolled its wheel over the Floridas, each time burying a generation of oaks, that mature and fall once in a hundred years, each time obliterating two generations of man—more transient than the trees of the hummocks.

"*Now*, the land is a common, every-day reality. The planter eats his corn-bread in his cabin; the negro toils at his daily task; the Indian hunts in the pine-land, at peace with the settler; and if there is anything of the poetry or romance of life in the land, it is to be found in the tropical luxuriance of vegetation, and the beautiful life of the everglade, and not in the noble daring of man.

"*Then*, in the Floridas, there was romance in thought

and action—romance in history and in fiction, in dress, in races, and the love of man and woman, and all the world was tame when compared with this El Dorado. Here was the warrior's field; here the adventurer's goal, and hither came the poet to sing of Eden. Here landed the courtly and refined cavaliers of the most chivalrous nation of the earth. In an age of discovery, when all the world was intoxicated by those vistas of wealth and novelty that the Genoese opened to the ardent, no one Arcadian land loomed from the waters of the Occident, so clad in purple, so vocal with music, so voluptuous with beauty, as this so-called Island of Florida.

"Its discovery was wrought by, and illustrates the romance of the age. Ponce de Leon was a hidalgo of Spain—noble, accomplished, and renowned. With grey hairs had come honors and high command in the Indian Islands, when the tales of his mistress, a Carib girl, told him of a spring whose waters would bring back the fire of youth, and renew his wasted years. This fountain was situated on the coast of the great Mexican Gulf, where the oak, when dropping into the sea, is transformed into coral groves, its pendent moss waves beneath the waters changed into sea-fans, while, mirrored in the sea, the scarlet flamingoes reflect the colors of Paradise.

"The old knight sailed with his cavaliers in search of this fountain, and landed among the mangrove bowers and painted birds of the western coast, on Easter-day or day of flowers of the year 1512, and thence baptized the newly-discovered land by the name of Florida. Not finding the fabled waters, the Quixotic knight and his visionary followers succumbed to those years they sought to reverse, leaving a heritage of poetry and fiction to the coast they discovered, as rich as the tales of Genii to Araby the Blest. They died by shipwreck and wars; or, if the legends of those seas may be believed, they still live among the coral reefs and keys that girdle the coast, and there, having found that long-sought fountain of perpetual youth, wander where the coral bowers make forests of beauty—where the sands are strewed with gems, and the summer never wanes. It is said to be a comely sight to the diver there, when the waters are clear, to see the Castilian knights, with their costly armor and their trailing plumes, loitering with the Indian girls of long ago under the pink shadow of the coral."

"What a ripper!" ejaculated Mike.

"An untimely remark," replied Jackson, turning to the hunter, with a solemn wave of the hand, "and it savors of unbelief."

"Wall! the Gulf is a mighty safe place to yarn about —for nobody knows enough to know nothin' about it— that's sartin. Pile on."

Thus enjoined, Jackson, after a glance at his daughter Louisa's wondering eyes, opened his mouth, and continued as follows:

"Following fast in the wake of the explorer, came noble and vassal, for fame, or greed, or heroic quest. Velasquez, De Guerray, Narvaez, succeeded each other as conquerors or visitors to the newly-discovered land.

"Pamphilo de Narvaez was no mere adventurer. To family honors and name he added the higher title of a fame won on the battle-field, and wealth and love added their charms to bind him to ease. But he also had heard of that fabled spring, and from the esplanade of his princely home in Cuba had seen the evening sky refulgent with what was said to be the reflection of the gold of the Floridas; and so, when the wind came fresh from the eastward, the morning-star saw his black-eyed lady watching from her balcony the lessening galleys that were bearing away her chief and four hundred men.

"After seven days of favoring winds, Narvaez landed on the western shore of the peninsula, near where the Mecaco River empties into Charlotte Bay, and forthwith the bands of armed men, with their standards and their horses, landed on the beach, and took possession of the land in the name of Spain. A curious spectacle did the adventurers present. There were the chiefs, with their haughty mien, and Moorish war-horses, the soldier with his pike and lance—the blue-steel cuirass, the chain shirt, and Toledo blade—all contrasted with that tropical country of birds and flowers, and the gentle mien of the Indians that welcomed them. Around their leader were gathered chiefs of noble name: Cobecca de Vacca, the treasurer; Quesada, from his stately house in Cordova; and La Manca, the most gallant gentleman of Navarre. There came, also, priests to cure the souls of the benighted—hooded priests, whose convent stood high on the hills of Sierra de Diego, and little boys to swing the incense at the altars; and hounds in couples nosing the scented air with their tawny muzzles. All the paraphernalia of glorious war, and the emblems of an ostentatious religion, or wild sports, swept by Gaspiralla Island, and with the sound of the trumpet and the horn landed on the main land.

"But a short history remains to be told. Treachery to the natives aroused revenge. The arrow soughed on every wind, hostile bands disputed every stream. One battle followed another. The troops were divided in different bodies, under different leaders, and fought their way northward, until all but fifteen of that hopeful army found a grave, either on the field of battle or the quicksand swamps. Fifteen, under the command of De Vacca, coasted the Gulf, and gained a shelter in the Mexican colonies. But one man, a common soldier named Ortez, escaped the others' doom. Being left wounded on a battle-field, he watched his opportunity, and, as night covered the shattered dead and trodden field, he crept down to the water's edge, guided by the splash of the sea. Here, finding a canoe of the natives, he hastily gathered some fruit to support him on his voyage, and setting a sail, was soon beyond pursuit. He coasted down the shore, only landing at night to gather the turtle's and bird's eggs that were abundant on all the islands, until he reached Cuba, and saw once more the towers of a Spanish town.

"A sad day it was in St. Jago de Cuba, when Ortez came back with that Indian boat, and the grim tale of disaster. Solemn-moving men, cloaked to the chin, in spite of the tropical air, clustered together in the Plaza. Lustrous eyes were dim with tears, and duennas hurried hither and yonder to gather some scrap of hope for mistresses, whose first young love was buried in the buzzard's maw.

"Ortez was summoned to the presence of Narvaez's widow. In a few moments he had entered the quadrangular stone court, and stood in a room where the light came in through canopied windows, and the air was cool with the splash of waters, whose music brought back to his memories the houses of Seville. The stately dame of the lost knight sat on a cushion by the window. Her eyes were hollow with watching and grief, and her voice was solemnly deep and low. Behind her sat her daughter, with a black veil shrouding her face. The soldier, leaning on his sword, at her word of command, told the story of their cruise, of their landing and bitter war, he narrated how, one by one, the leaders found inglorious deaths by disease, by heat, by arrows, or flood or quicksand, and how presently they had none to command but De Vacca.

"'But your chief—your chief, man! Where did he fall—how did he die—did you kill the foeman that struck him, and honor his corpse as a king's?' demanded the proud woman.

"'De Narvaez did not die by my side, or I would have revenged him; nor was his body buried by our band.'

"'Where did he die—how—when? Speak faster, man.'

"'I don't know how he died. They say he died like a hero; and when attacking a fort at Appalachi, with his good sword cleared a road so far into the stockade, that his men could not get to him, and there he remained and fell.'

"'And where were you, did you leave your chief, heathen Moor?'

"'No; would I come back to Cuba had I done that? I was not with Narvaez's band; they had separated before into five parties.'

"'Who was with my husband?'

"'They are all dead that saw him fall, or prisoners among the Indians.'

"'There were Spanish prisoners among the Indians, then?'

"'Yes, they seized three or four; but we counted them dead, for they never kept Spanish prisoners.'

"'What then did they do with them?'

"The soldier replied not in words, but taking his unkempt locks in one hand, with the edge of the other he made a circle around his head, and then with the first hand gave a twist, and a wave that was horribly significant of the scalping process, that had then but just come to the ears of the Spaniard, and possessed, to his mind, the double terror of mystery.

"A groan and a long pause followed this pantomime.

"'Soldier,' said the lady, 'he was your chief, you left him in a hostile country; you do not know his fate—will not honor, a soldier's name, tempt you to return, and seek to bring some tidings of his death?'

"'Ha! where is the honor to all my comrades who are buried in those woods? There is no honor there, my lady.'

"'Where is your religion man? You swore on the cross in our Holy Mother Church to defend your liege and propagate your faith.'

"'By My Lady, I kept my oath; but where there is no standard, and even the priest is slaughtered by the savages, there is no piety in staying.'

"'Have you ever loved since you left the Tagus?'

"The soldier's eye glanced quick at the lady's, but he did not answer, and the young girl peered from her veil beside her mother, on the comely form of the soldier.

"'Ortez, I will give you the fairest girl in all the colonies if you will do this one thing for me.'

"'I can't. What is love worth if you cannot enjoy it? I have been been a true soldier in many a war; but this is no war. We have lost our ship, our lives, our horses, our chief, everything is gone of that array, and never a real have we won to repay us all. What, then, could *I* do alone?'

"'Soldier, you are a poor man now, are you not?'

"'As poor as a muleteer.'

"Do this for me and I will make you rich.'

"The lady's eye was on the adventurer, and noted his look.

"'Do this for me. I will send you with a pinnace, I will name you a lieutenant before you go, and when you return, I will pay you here in this chamber two hundred ounces of gold. Stay here now as you are, and you remain the bankrupt soldier, pointed out as the man who left Narvaez in Florida.'

"Steadily Ortez weighed in his mind his chances of life, and the golden sum that was as sure to him on the promise of that woman as though belted at his waist. His eye looked at the soft light that came in at the window, and the spattering fountain in the court below, vacantly, while one could count two score; and then, turning to the widow, he said:

"'I will go,' adding, with Spanish grace, 'and may our Lady Mother keep you well till my return.'

"In a few days the adventurous soldier was again in the Mexican Gulf, steering for the battle-fields where he had left his chief. He sailed among islands covered with mangroves, and pillared on coral, touching at every prominent point, and threading the broad lagoons where the sea-ferns spread their palms to the light of the upper air. When opportunities offered, he landed on the shore, and tried, by presents and gentle words, to gain from the natives the information he desired, but they remembered the fierce forays of Velasquez and Narvaez, and only treated with the adventurer to betray. He was induced one day by the Apalaches to visit the shore, and was at once seized; and being recognized as one of Narvaez's band, was condemned to death. His frightened comrades having lost their guide, made haste to weigh anchor, and sailed away to Cuba, glad to escape from the terrors of that Stygian shore.

"Ortez was a true Spaniard. His haughty mien, dark hair and eye, his active strength and bronzed face, all spoke the soldier of fortune, and impressed the feebler natives with a respect in spite of their hatred. His dress, in the fashion of the day, of embroidered velvet and lace, gave him the appearance, to their eyes, of a chief of rank, and they rejoiced that they could punish their Spanish foes by the sacrifice of one of their great men, and led him, bound, to the village of the Appalachean Cacique. This town was situated, as near as the old histories of those days can inform us, on one of the many islands that crowd the mouth of the Appalachicola river. It is the more difficult to designate the spot, because, from the currents of the river, new islands are formed and the old ones are buried in the lapse of time, and the whole character of the timber has been changed. Where now groves of stunted pine surmount the sandy ridges, and the swamp poplar and the rank titi cover the piles of drift-wood that lodge on the upper end of the islands, there formerly stood the life-oak, the gum, the maple, and the pawpaw, while the deer grass beneath was purple with its fragile flowers, and the blossoms of the running gourds that the natives loved to cultivate.

"Ortez was rowed in a canoe among many an island

7*

covered with this rich vegetation, and dotted by the rush-thatched cottages of the people. He saw stockade forts built of reeds frowning down in mimic pomp on the waters that had never bristled with more dangerous arms than the tomahawk and the arrow. He heard the shrill sound of clarionets and horns, and saw waving standards of gaudy feathers. The women that rowed the boat in which he was bound were dressed in the simple robe that befitted the summer land. Their linen, or sea-grass kilts, were trimmed with feathers or furs, and sea-shells ornamented their hair and ankles. Their olive colored limbs, unshackled by dress, were as graceful in form as the children that played on the sand; and the men in the stern of the barge, though warriors, all had that gentle manner and expression that belongs to the natives of every southern clime.

"On arriving at the village, the prisoner was led to the Indian chief and his council, before the public lodge of the village. There was short discussion as to the punishment, and no remarks were made by the prisoner at the bar why sentence should not be passed, for, in sooth, he could not say a word in any tongue they could understand. An Indian communicated to him, by a symbolic motion of shooting with an arrow, that his death was appointed; and then, pointing to the setting sun, and describing a semi-circle with his hand, assigned the time for the morrow morning at sunrise. The prisoner was led away, little noting the laugh of the Indian child that pointed him out to his comrade at play, little heeding the wondering eyes of the Indian girls that followed his steps; for his **thoughts** were where the Alcanadra River **was leaping his native** hills of Arragon, and the castanets **clacked to** the dancer's tread unner the walls of his home **in Huesca.**

"But there were others at the **village** who did not join in the verdict of the **chiefs.** Those simple **hearts, whose love and faith in the forest, or the** town, all **the wide world over, makes** the sunshine to man's gloom, the hope **to passion's rigor, had** seen **the stranger,** had sorrowed **for him, and had longed to save him.** First among them **all was the daughter of the chief.** Availing herself of her rank, she had stood without the ring when Ortez was **under examination. She had seen** his melancholy atti**tude, and met** the fiery glance of his Spanish eye. She **had marked his slashed doublet, and** the graceful em**broideries of his vest.** His heavy moustache was different from the smooth-faced warriors of her tribe, and **his** form, by their lithe figures, towered like King Richard's at Askelon. Her uncovered bosom throbbed beneath **the** necklace of coral, her deep **eyes were** vacant with thought; Yahchilane was in love; **and** the object of her love was the Spanish soldier that was to die at sunrise."

"That's **not natteral** at all, an Injin woman is a leetle wuss nor **an** Injin man, and is allers down on a prisoner."

"You Mike!" said Louisa Jackson, with a hushing gesture of her hand; and the hunter relapsed into silence, and sat as before, listening to the story, and rolling backward and forward, with his arms clasped around his knee.

"It was the old story of Pocahontas anticipated among a gentler people, and Yahchilane did not need to throw herself under the war-club to gain the prisoner's pardon. She came, when the moon was up, to her father's house, and with her came one of the young girls of the tribe, the friend of the chieftain's daughter. They brought a roll of cloth, finely woven from the inner bark of trees; they brought tatooed gourds, filled with the precious stones that Indians prize so well, and wampum belts of amber-colored shells; they brought their gayest kirtles of the skins of the merganser and wood-duck; and the moccasin, deftly sewed with the porcupine's quills; and when the old man, the chief of the Apalaches, sat at his door sill, and the next eldest chief beside him, Yachilane and her maiden threw all these things at his feet. Then stripping from her head the long white feathers of the egret that shaded her neck, and unwinding from her waist the cocoa-fibred skirt, she tossed them on the pile and sat down in the sand, saying:

"'Yahchilane is sick, and will need these things no more—she is ready to go with the dead that go to-morrow morning.'

"The old chief sat silently looking at his daughter; but he understood her not.

"'Where will the Young Swan go to-morrow morn; and why is she ill?'

"'She sees a great man, with eyes like an eagle's, and

hair like a bear's—with a mantle of moleskin and gold, and a silent tongue—he is alone and a stranger—and tomorrow he dies; and Yahchilane would rather hunt with him in the Happy Land than stay here alone.'

"When the old chief heard this, he knew what the offering meant; for it was all of his daughter's goods, and all that she and her maidens had woven through the year. He knew how fast love comes under a tropical sky, where the blood is hot, and how far the wild feeling would carry an Indian girl. He remembered the days when Yahchilane's mother was a maiden; and he turned away to his brother chieftains, and left his daughter still bent on the sands.

"At a summons hastily sent, the warriors came again together, and sat as before around the door of their chief. They kindled a fire, and the flames flashed red over many a reed-covered house—over the pickets and lagoons, and the still bowed figure of girl. None looked at the chief's daughter, though all saw her sitting, and wist why she remained; and then they talked long and slowly, and from mouth to mouth passed the pipe, fringed with eagle feathers and the long beard of the turkey-cock. Hardly would it have fared with the Spaniard if they had confined themselves to his deserts—for the cruel wars of Narvaez were fresh in their minds, and they remembered Anta, and how their kinsmen had fallen there under the arquebus and the long Spanish blade; but when they frowned and looked down, they still saw the young girl in her beseeching posture, divested of her robes, with her face in her hands; and their hearts failed them, and they consented. The council again broke up, and the old chief, raising his daughter there under the palm trees, gave her the life of her captive.

"When the morrow's sun glinted athwart the persimmons and sycamores, Ortez was again brought before the council. But how different the scene! His eye was bright and hopeful—his step as proud as a Don; and in every corner and on every face, fell his glance in pleasure and in love. How had he learned the change in his fate? Who could tell him that he had been pardoned, when none in all the land spoke a word of his tongue? When he was led before the council, Yahchilane stood beside her father arrayed in her brightest dress. Ortez walked to her, and raising her hand to his lips with the dignity of a cavalier, kissed it and drew her to his side—she was already his wife. And all the chiefs, the women and children, understood that mute ceremony; and they clapped their hands and shouted unintelligible words, and Ortez and his young bride were the fairest and bravest for many years of all the Appalachians.

CHAPTER XI.

THE FLORIDA POCAHONTAS CONTINUED.

" Pray how comes love?
It comes unsought, unsent.
Pray how goes love?
That was not love that went."

"Among races but little advanced from a state of nature, no human quality excites greater reverence than **personal bravery, and** Ortez inheriting this power as a natural birthright, soon sat in the first ranks among his adopted people. He had to throw aside his arquebus for lack of powder; but acquired the art of shooting the bow, and flinging the metal ball, with as much accuracy as his instructors. He still retained his basket-hilted sword, and his shirt of link mail; and in the different wars of the tribe, there **was none** who could strike a surer blow, or stand longer **in the** breach, or was greater **feared for his** prowess than the adopted Spaniard, who **rose to the position of second chief of** the nation, passing those who were immeasurably above **him when he began his race. Some were proud of** his young renown; **but** others, as in every land, imputed **their** own subordinate position to the just honors showered **on his** head, and were proportionately jealous. But honor or jealousy made no difference in the love of his wife—the same gentle, passionate kiss greeted the soldier if he came back honored or suspected. It was a woman's love, and it flickered not; and when angry voices told of Spanish aggressions and coming wars, and pointed to him, she merely said: 'He is not a Spaniard, he is my love.'

"There had been a fierce battle fought between the Yupaha tribes and the Apalaches, in which the latter had returned with not their usual success, bringing home with them the bodies of many of their warriors. They came to the village with all the insignia of woe, beating of drums, formed of the sections of hollow trees covered with deer skins, and the mournful blast of their conch-shell trumpets.

"Wealuste, the great black water chief, had been killed, and they placed him on the shore, with his arrows and his quiver, his knife and his eagles' plumes, and a goodly store of chinquapin nuts and maize, to support him on that long journey to the happy Hunting-ground that he was to make in darkness and alone. His body was sewed in deerskins, pictured with the scenes of his life, and then placed in a wooden canoe formed from a cypress log. This canoe was fixed on upright posts, and the warrior was left to float away, as a chief should go, to that silent realm that lies beyond our ken. But for forty days and forty nights, or for one whole moon, the corpse was to be watched by comrades of equal rank with the deceased, so that neither beast nor bird disturbed the dead. This is a part of the simple faith of the tribe; and they affirm that after decay has taken the body, the departed chief is safe beyond earthly harm.

"Ortez was the first in order that had assigned to him this honorable duty, and in the early part of a summer eve he took his post by the dead man. The sun laid down in his golden bed in the western waters, and the stars one by one stepped to their places in the sky, as the watcher paced to and fro by the side of the scaffolding where the dead chief slept. He heard the distant wailing of music from the village, and the nearer hooting of the owls, and the honking of the herons from the wood. He saw the pawpaw wave its purple bells between him and the sky, and the green balls of the buttonwood looked liked the olives on the hills of his native land. But it was not of the storied peaks of Spain the soldier was then thinking—nor was he listening to the twittering of the birds in the reeds. He was watching the path that led toward the village, and his heart was beating thick and heavy with the anticipation of meeting some one that was fairer than the pawpaw bell, and dearer than the towers of his native town. He listens on his beat with one foot raised—he turns his ear aside, and his thin nostril quivers like that of a horse. He hears a splash in the water—it was not the grey duck. A canoe touches the shore, and a girl steps out on the strand. Her luminous eye is half veiled by its lashes—her limbs are trembling with delight. She falls into the arms of Ortez, and after an instant of fainting embrace, they turn aside into the Ilex groves that fringe the bank of the lagoon.

"'Ortez, does not honor call thee to the dead man's side? Ortez, does not thy wife's low voice, that saved thee once, beseech thee now?'

"Ha! who hears voices pleading in the mad tumultuous hours of night—thought comes with the bare-faced morn. The glare of the torrid day is for rest, and penance, and prayers; and the tropical night is passion's own holiday, when love and hate roll like the sea."

"Hold there, and turn down a leaf," called out the Doctor. "That's pure error. It is the day that is made for action, ambition and hope—far reaching pride, and quick deeds come with the sunshine. Then man does his works for good or evil; but when the day is gone, the grey of twilight, the chill hush of voice, and emblematic sleep, bring thought and repentance. His good spirit comes to him then, and whispers of errors done, and cools his ambition; and, if he is a true man, he says his prayers, and "——

"Goes to bed," laughed Jackson. "That's all very nice for a man who lives in a land where water freezes after dark, and nobody but a bear can keep out at nights without the ague. That is not the way the hot blood rolls in the Creole veins; nor was it the way that the Spanish soldier reasoned with the Indian girl. Where was I?"

"Ortez had just met the Indian girl."

"Ah! yes; Jumper-boy, give me a light."

Taking the stick from the hand of his negro, he lit his pipe, and resumed the story.

"That young Indian girl had left the village, as quietly as the dew, her moccasin had made no foot-fall on the path, and her paddle scarce splashed the lagoon. When she met her lover, their voices were as low as the eddy of the wave in the river; and when she parted, and took her course back to the village, though her speed was slow, and her stroke was languid and uneven, yet still, her boat passed like a shadow beneath the low, arching titi boughs, and the hanging folds of the Spanish moss. But, for all this, an eye was on her in the darkness, and an ear heard her very breathings, and when she landed, and her bark canoe was hidden in the joint-grass, she passed so near Yahchilane that the tails of fox-squirrels, that fringed her kirtle, touched the shoulder of the young wife.

"The girl, once in the path toward the village, walked swifter still, now and then pausing to listen, when in the deeper shadows. On her route, she crossed a dense grove of wild plum trees, where the scarlet fruit covered the ground, and the low-reaching branches made a shadow as dark as a stormy night. When in the centre of the grove she started, uttering a quick, aspirated sound, for a hand was laid on her shoulder, from behind. She turned quickly, but could not see who it was, the grove was so obscure.

"'Who is it?' she demanded, in a low voice.

"'An eagle who had a mate,' said Yahchilane, in a voice so quick and fierce that the young girl could not recognize it, though she cowered from the threatening shadow and rasping voice that continued. 'And who are you? The wild cat that killed him.'

"Nothing more was said, though the mocking-birds that roosted in the grove flew frightened away. If any more, there was, the lamentations from the town, and the hollow drum, prevented it from being heard. And then, down among the mourners, with her proud head at its uttermost height, and her black eye flashing fire, strode the chieftain's daughter. Old chiefs lay there with their lips in the dust, but hers were as proud as a conqueror's; the women of the tribe were there, with distorted faces, beating with hollow canes the war-drums or the Apalaches; the conch shells uttered their loudest wail, and the fairest maidens sat, in their shame, uncovered in the sand; but with no semblance of sorrow on her sovereign face, Yahchilane walked among the bonfires that lighted all the town, and across the council-lawn, and went into her father's house.

"The next morning, when the young girls of the village, in laughing troops, with palmetto baskets, wound down the path to gather fruit for their simple meal, they found one of their number dead in the grove. A knife of fish-bone, with a beautifully carved handle, was driven in her breast, so deep that the point came out behind, between her shoulders.

"Hardly had the news been told, before a young warrior came rushing into town with a tale, whose horror exceeded even the crime of murder.

"It appeared that the relief-guard that went out early in the morning to take the place of Ortez, at the tomb of the dead chieftain, found the Spaniard absent from his post. On coming to the scaffolding they discovered the canoe overturned, and the body of Wealuste dragged out and mutilated by some wild beast. Depth of all disgrace! the face that had fronted a hundred battles had been mutilated by a carrion wolf. Where was now the soul of the chieftain in the shadowy land? What great doom was hovering over his people for this neglect?

"As the warriors wondered and mourned, and hastily gathered up the body of their dead, Ortez was seen coming back from woods, dragging the body of a huge grey wolf. The animal, while making off with its prey, had been pursued by the soldier, wounded with an arrow, and killed with a dagger, after severely tearing the arm of his antagonist. Ortez could give no explanation of how the animal had succeeded in mounting the scaffold, unobserved, or what he was doing during the scene of sacrilege. The fault was fearful, and the Spaniard was bound and dragged back to the village. Again he was the outcast criminal, chained and reviled. Now, all the suspicious spirits that mistrusted his prosperity gloated over his fall, and reviled his situation. They called up every misdeed that had come to their knowledge. They cited his Spanish origin; and reasoned, that because he was one of their natural enemies, the comrade of Narvaez, and the countryman of Velasquez, therefore he had permitted this unpardonable sin, and brought down the anger of the Great Spirit on the tribe.

" Justice is not slow of foot among simple people, and that very evening, while the young mistress of the soldier was wrapped in fawn skins, and sewed in palmetto leaves for her long sleep, her lover was brought to trial before the chiefs of the village.

" The great fire of loblolly pine climbed up in the air, and lit the scene with the whiteness of noon. The bamboo and grass cottages; the overshadowing cabbage palms, with their colossal trunks and spike leafed crowns; the solemn circle of chiefs, and the background of women and young boys, formed a great picture glowing with the colors of Rubens.

" Ortez stood in the centre, bound to a stake. He appeared the same man as three years before, when he stood in the self-same place. He wore the same steel shirt, the same fierce look of pride; and from his ragged arm, the blood, unnoticed, dropped slowly on the ground.

" The warriors smoked long and doubtfully; and when they had done, and the pipe had been lain down before the cacique, they spoke their views with the gravity and sententious eloquence of Roman Fathers.

" When all had finished, Ortez replied. His words— in the Appalachian tongue—were broken, though his voice was deep and clear. He recounted his deeds, and alluded to his offence in comparison; but the oldest men shook their heads, for the soldier never gave any reason for his neglect, or told whether he was absent or asleep, or how that shameful fate came to pass.

"He alluded to his wife, calling her by name, when a step without the ring drew all eyes in that direction. Yahchilane stood in front of her husband, as beautiful as a panther. She tore off from her shoulder an embroidered sash, which is worn by the married women of the tribe to support their infants at their back, and which is the distinguishing badge of the matron among the Appalachians, and tossing it in the circle, it fell at the feet of her husband. She never said a word, but her steady eye was on the Spaniard, and it did not fail in its effect, for a tremor passed over his frame, so that the links in his mail rattled together; and all the chiefs, and all the women of the tribe knew that Yahchilane renounced her husband.

"There was no more doubt in the council. Ortez was condemned to death at daylight, and was led away to confinement.

"The council fire had burned low in the Apalache village, and the few smoldering brands gleamed among the ashes, or sputtered brief jets of flame and smoke, like the smoldering passions that tossed the sleepers strewn around in the open cabins, still dreaming of the stirring events of the day. The sentinels by the fort walked backward and forward, or leaned on their thin lances tipped with the spikes of deer's horn, tasting in anticipation the savage pleasures of the execution of the coming morn. The young moon had set, and millions of frogs and peepers in the marsh filled the air with their shrill calls, and forewarned the rain that was coming up with the easterly wind. Heavy masses of damp fog rolled in from the sea, and left the palisades of the fort, and the zizanea grass that grew from the water at its side, wet with their soggy **breath**. It was drawing toward morning.

"Within the adobe cell of the fort, the condemned man sat on the ground; and if a man's mind is ever occupied with his coming destiny, his must have pictured the approaching execution, of which he was to be the victim. The stake and the fagot, the red-hot brand, the pricking reed, the scalping-knife, the gauntlet, the jeer and the death-song, had all been familiar to him in his short episode of Indian life. If the southern savage was of gentler mien and comelier appearance; if his women were fairer in face, and more lustrous in eye, than their more northern tribes, they were in no wise inferior in their ferocity of punishment to their prisoners. Even the Spanish inquisition was not more refined in cruelty. Well might Ortez ponder his death, and mumble long-forgotten fragments of Latin prayers.

"There was another in the Indian town, who kept vigil that night.

"Yahchilane, the young, the beautiful daughter of the cacique, who had been loved by many in her tribe before the hated name of Spain was heard—she who had saved the prisoner's life—who had taken him from death to be her lord and chief in the land—who had cradled his head on her bosom—who had borne him sons—who had been deceived and slighted—who had risen in her wrongs, and condemned to death the mistress and the husband—she, the fierce, proud, vindictive heart, and woman withal, through the moonlight and the fog, roamed and wrestled with her inner self. There was no prouder blood from **Natchez** to Honda Keys; and for four and twenty hours it had coursed through her veins like rivers of fire. Had she met her husband and the native girl together, she would have slain them both. When she saw his blood flowing from his wounded arm in the council ring, she sorrowed only that she had not made the wound from which it flowed. Had the council acquitted the prisoner she would have tracked him like a hound; and now her wild delight made her fevered step carry her to and fro, like the panther that sweeps his tail while watching to leap. Down by the fort she went, and away on the point, wading into the water-grass, until she seemed like the Naiad that lives under the sea. Then she walked back again with a long, elastic step, eyeing the palisades and the sentinels, her kirtle draggled by the dew, the long plumes in her hair broken on her shoulders, and her symmetrical limbs cut by the sword grass. Another turn would take her to the lagoon, where she had watched her husband's trysting, and then again she flitted through the plum-trees, where still a dark stain lay on the grass. So back and forth stalks a tiger-cat, when the spring water intrudes on the island where she has dropped her young. Thus along the bald cliff dashes back and forth the mother eagle, when from below she sees the hunter patiently climbing.

"The night gradually passed away. The big wave that the Southern tribe declares comes landward when the god of night turns to go back in the sea, had broken along the shore with a hollow roar, and the marsh rosemary had turned its petals to the east to await the rising sun.

"Yachilane noted these tokens of the hours. She had taught them all to Ortez, and they had heeded them many a night when fishing in the lagoons. He had narrated for her the legends of Spain, and the wild Moorish pranks that haunted the old towers of his native town, when the chimes tolled midnight. She had plumed for him his arrows, and softened his tongue to the liquid accents of her language; and he in exchange had sung her fairy tales, and drawn on the sand the outlines of great houses and sailing ships. He was a handsome man. How his great moustache curled over his chain mail! How he took the arrows and gave the blows in battle! How proud she had been at village galas! How sad at distant forays! How her heart had yearned to him in that second love, when his child had tugged at her breast, and they three had laughed together!

"Sad thoughts these to the bitter woman, and she stopped in her walk, and leaned against the palm-trees.

"Yell, and curse, and seething iron probed in the

quivering muscles, while the naked wretch feels the licking flame.

"Ha! had he not slept in her arms many a night and day? And up and on dashes the tortured wife, balancing her hate, that was of her race, with her heart, that was of her common motherhood. And the hours waned, and sick and hot the wind came in, and the odor of the honeysuckle and the water-lily were oppressive to the senses.

"Chatte Echo, the Red Deer, was a young chief of the Apalaches, of a noble name and tried courage. In Chatte Echo's cabin hung the skins of ten panthers, and behind his house stretched a field of maize and melons that was smaller in size than none but the cacique's. This warrior had loved Yahchikane; but when Ortez came to Apalache, his suit was discarded; and ever since then he had remained unmarried. He had always been an enemy to Ortez, and was now one of the sentinels that watched over him in prison. Posted on the side toward the sea, from the low rampart where he stood he could look out on the water and down into the inner fort where Ortez sat. A proud man was Chatte Echo that night, and none in all the band would guard the prisoner surer. As he was leaning on his spear and thinking of his revenge, a brown canoe floated up from the water, and among the bending reeds. It came so whist the sentinel did not hear it, and the fog was so heavy he did not see it until it touched the wall, and an Indian woman stepped on to the parapet. Chatte Echo would have struck at her with his spear, but she seized his arm, and, bringing her face close to his, he recognized Yahchilane.

"A moment's pause followed this strange interview. She seemed to be studying him; and he was wondering at her. Had she attempted force, he would have called; but her pleading look kept him silent. A little of the old love seemed softening his eye, and the touch of her hand thrilled his arm.

"'Chatte Echo, you have my husband here, let him go.' Her voice was low and inquiring.

"'Sooner a wild cat when I had my arrow drawn to shoot,' replied the warrior, in a bitter tone.

"'He shall flee us, and will trouble you no more.'

"'He can trouble me no more than a few hours if he stays.'

"'You refuse me this, and you will be my enemy.'

"'I am your enemy now,' said the warrior, gloomily.

"'No, Chatte Echo; you are my friend,' whispered the Indian woman, in her lowest tone, laying her arm on his shoulder.

"The chief's voice trembled, as he replied: 'Where will be your friendship when you get your lover back?'

"'Ha! he is no lover to me!' said the woman, in her quick, fierce mood. 'Listen boy! that brave is a wolf—yet he must not die—I do not love him—he is no more of mine—let him go, and he will flee, and—Chatte Echo, I will love you. Refuse me this, and I will hate you. No one will know it—he will take that canoe and go without a trace, and the dawn will find him leagues away.

Say it quickly, chief; for the air is grey, and the gulls are going seaward.'

"There was a hesitation in the warrior's eye, and doubt, and hope, love and hate, chased each other over his tawny face like the fog-clouds that were scudding by.

"'How will I know your face will be the same to-morrow?' he inquired, doubtingly; 'the doe may flee with the buck.'

"'Keep me here—take me now—I am yours, Chatte Echo!'

"The wild light lit up the coal-black eyes of the brave, and the prisoner was free. Ortez silently hurried out of his cell, and stepped on the low rampart, saved once more. He saw his wife, and recognized her as the means of his deliverance, and, with the quick perception of a reckless adventurer, accepted the chance without a word. He stood in the canoe, with the paddle in his hand, and awaited, as for his wife to enter with him, while the young chief stood by her side at the water's edge. She leaned down to speak to her husband, and her voice, necessarily low, was so distinct that not a word was lost.

"'Sail south to Macaco's land in the Great Bay—stop not for your life, and tell Macaco who sent you.' Then, in a lower and a harsher tone, she continued: 'The canoe you are in carried your mistress to see you at the grave last night. She is dead now—stabbed while her lips were yet wet with your kisses. Go, hound of a Spaniard, or I may stab you, too.' The last words were fairly hissed by the woman, the old tide of hate welling high and fast as she saw the Spaniard safe again. Ortez's countenance blanched under the swarth of years. Chatte Echo gave the light canoe an impetus with his foot, and shoved it out into the lagoon. Her eyes followed the spot where it disappeared, her outstretched arm trembled, she staggered and fell into the arms of the young chief who carried her into the fort. He had won her."

"I don't like that story, father; it gives a low ideal of woman."

"But, child, remember it is savage woman that I tell of; you can't paint a crow green."

"How much is true?" asked the literal Doctor.

"Is it not all written," answered the narrator, "in the faithful annals of Garcilasso de la Vega?"

CHAPTER XII.

THE BATTLE ON BONDA KEY.

"The stout Earl of Northumberland
A vow to **God did make,**
His pleasure **in the Scottish woods**
Three summer days to take."

CHEVY CHASE.

As the Ouithlacouchee River emerges from the bayous, lakes, swamps, and drowned lands, which it has drained for many **a** square league, and reaches the salt water, it **widens its** bed, and harassed by the heavy beat of the **sea, deposits its** accumulation of vegetable matter with **the sands of the ocean** in little islands, that are presently covered **with the rankest** vegetation. There grows the cane like **a gigantic grass,** and **the** cabbage palmetto there **rears its** huge, **twisting, bayonet** bristling trunk-like the fanciful verdure **of** Utopian **land.** Sometimes these islands are based on **the sand, and** are as stable as **the main** land, but again they are the mere accumulations **of floating vegetable matter, rank weeds,** and decaying rafts of trees, **lashed** together by sea-weeds and clamping **vines, and** resembling those floating gardens that the ingenious Celestials moor in the great rivers of China. The aquatic plants and nameless vines cover them with festoons, and a large shoot striking down in the water anchors the raft, which will float hither and thither by the wind, closing or opening some water passage, to the great discomfiture of the bewildered explorer.

Beyond these ranker islets, and acting as outer piers or breakwaters to the still inner bays, lie other islands in long reefs, covered by sea grass and a smaller growth of trees, and washed on their outer sides by the surf of the Gulf. All of them abound in game of every kind, the fame of which led our party of hunters with our hosts for a few days' hunting and sporting, bringing tents, dogs, and servants enough to beat up all the woods on the Gulf Coast. These species of hunts are frequent in the Southern States, where time is not regarded with the monetary eye to value with which it is measured in Doctor Franklin's proverbs, and where an ample range of unclaimed ground is open to all that choose to come and enjoy it. Such hunts are called marrooning, and we were marrooners as soon at we had reached the low sandy shore of Bonda Key, and pitched the two white tents that formed our travelling homes.

One hut was occupied by Poke, Jackson and myself, the other by Lou Jackson and her girl Rosa, a bright negress of the same age as her mistress, and around the big fire a large row of screens of blankets or evergreen branches sheltered the dozen negroes that constituted our party. As to Mike, he always preferred to carry up his canoe, and elevating the side next the fire on a stick, would crawl under it and sleep like an alligator.

In many respects our camp was more orderly than the

plantation house we had left. There were no sheep to tinkle and bleat away the hours of the night, reminding you of your bed in the Tyrolean chalet, with all the herds stabled beneath you. There were no young negroes constantly disputing or tumbling under your feet; there was no old Aunty Blase tyrannizing over your culinary department, and ordering around all the boys within reach. But we still had one nuisance, in the shape of dogs—

"Both mongrel puppy, whelp and hound,
And curs of low degree "—

melodious hounds that bayed at the moon; sullen dogs that snapped at your heels; insinuating dogs that crept under your tent and into your arms when half asleep; spiteful dogs, with their voices attuned to the sharpest chords, and that came under Shakspeare's definition of being "fit for treason, stratagems, and spoils." All this mongrel herd had been kept in peace at home; some were quartered away from the house, some were chained, and others meditative or sleepy. But here, as sure as pleasant harmonies came over your soul, and the hush of sleep fell on the camp, and the loudest sound abroad was the flitting bat and droning sea, some canine tyrant would infringe the etiquette of the brotherhood, and immediately there would break out a most fiendish turmoil of snarls, yells, bays, howls, growls, and yelps, intermingled with the babble of the negroes' voices and the whacking of sticks, and when you were fully awake, and had seized your gun, or a paddle, determined on deeds of revenge, peace would be declared in a loud voice; in some such phrase as

"Ketch you yowlin' again. Tink Ise got a stick here for nuthin', eh?"

Bonda Key was perchance half a mile in width at its widest part, and three miles in length, where we were encamped. The thickest growth of trees and shrubbery stood at our end, and near the outer side was a long pool of water, formed by the sea throwing up a bank of sand and leaving this isolated pond. The nearest land adjoining this island was at the two ends, the sides being bounded without by the open ocean, and within by the sheltered bay, which, dotted with islands of different sizes, extended up the broad mouth of the river and to the mainland.

Thus much for the geography of our temporary home; as to its geology, it might be said to be, in the words of Mike, "sand-some;" its botany was represented by swordgrass, palmetto, sea-wrack, some wild plums, and a few water-oaks and pines; by the pond the reeds and jointgrass grew very closely, and in the centre we could see a close tangle of vegetation, that would defy the best hunter in the land to crawl through. As to its conchology, I can only say it produced excellent clams, and a kind of conch shell, that Scipio manufactured into a species of annoyance he called a dinner-horn, and which when blown made all the dogs on the island set up a prolonged howl. As to its zoology, man seemed absent, and every other created thing had its representative, particularly those classes that preyed on man, which seemed the more voracious from being so seldom gratified by visitors.

I am thus particular as to the peculiarities of this place, that my readers may well understand the process of hunting which we adopted the morning after our arrival, and the success of which I will always remember. It was Jackson's idea, and he styled it the battue. On our arrival in the evening, the hounds had all been tied to prevent them coursing over the island, and the negroes had been restricted to a very narrow range in the collection of firewood and fish, so that nothing should be done to disturb the game that might be on the island.

The next morning, as we came out from our tents with the first grey light, the cool wind was still coming in from the sea, laden with the salt flavor; the negroes were poking together the half-burned brands, and preparing the breakfast in haste, or rather all the haste a negro ever assumes, and I plunged into the sea with the happy anticipation of a grand hunt, and all a-glow to hear the first cry and ringing shot of our grand battue.

"Good morning to you, Miss Jackson; you look like Diana this morning in your canvas jacket and gown."

"And you like a shipwrecked mariner, with your dripping locks, and jacket on your arm."

"Where's Mike?"

"Maussa Mike's gone off with he shell on he back, like a gopher," said Scipio.

"There he comes; he has been around the head."

"How are you, Poke?"

"O—ho—hum—oh—ho—heo-o—hum!" yawned the Doctor, rubbing his eyes, as he staggered out of the tent.

"How are you?" I reiterated.

"Oh, ho!—there's one of those dogs named Music, I believe. I'd have his name changed after to-night. I didn't get a wink o' sleep."

"Hulloa, gentlemen, a pleasant day to you," said Jackson, just protruding his head from the canvas. "You boys, hurry there with breakfast!" and with this general order, the head disappeared.

"Oh, ho! dear me! Break—breakfast—on thy cold, grey stone, oh! oh! sea—and I would that my tongue could utter the thoughts that arise in me."

"Pete, you boy! pour some water on the Doctor to wake him up!"

"You, Sam! tie up that Black Bess; she will be clean gone presently. Where is Sumpter?"

"Maussa Jackson, Pomp say you a-goin' to leff him shoot a gun to-day?"

"Go along with you!"

"Yah! yah! yah! I knowed de niggah lie!"

As the noise and hurry progressed, breakfast began to smoke on the fire, the boats were launched, and in a few minutes everything was ready for the chase, while a hearty breakfast of venison and fish was spread before us and the sun arose in the woods on the shore, and his level beams trailed the smoking water, and painted the tops of the taller island trees with golden tassels.

The hunt was arranged by Mike as follows: The dogs were to be led to the extreme end of the island, not far from where we were camped, and all the party was to **follow,** either on foot or in boats. One boat was to keep on each side of the island, close enough in shore to shoot any game that might take to the beach; the rest of the hunters, with all the negroes, were to follow the dogs, and, keeping at equal distances apart, beat down **the** island shouting and thrashing in the bushes, and thus drive before them everything that would run. As the chase progressed, it would come to the narrower portion of the island, and thus the men would come closer together just at the time when the game would be most anxious **to** turn back, so that they could form a complete barrier, through which nothing could return.

After all had reached the point appointed for the meet, and taken their stations, Mike harangued them, telling what **should be** done. Lou Jackson was in one boat, with Rosa to paddle; the Doctor in another, to guard the two sides, and all **the** rest were to follow the hounds. Scipio had been sent at starting to the other end of the island, in a canoe, to lie close to the nearest shore, to head off anything that should attempt to cross to the main.

"Now remember!" said Poke to Jackson, just as the hounds were being loosened.

"What?"

"Thirty centuries look down upon you from those gum-trees."

"Shough! Go ahead all!" shouted Jackson.

The hounds were cast off, and with their noses high in air coursed into the underbrush, and with yelp and cry the boisterous crew of coon-dogs and half-breeds rushed in their wake, while the negroes, each armed with a big cudgel and a heavy knife, with which to clear the vines, dashed off, yelping very much after the manner of their dogs, cheering on their particular favorites with endearing cries, and all were soon scattered out of sight in the dense undergrowth that succeeded the sandy ridges and level grass of the coast. From time to time, we could hear their shouting, and the crashing that was caused by their progress, and when within sound, many a rough joke and laugh came down the line.

I was nearest the inner channel, and within sight of the beach. Jackson was next to me, then Mike and the negroes all beyond. At first we could not see each other except at intervals where the woods opened, but as we advanced we came into a less tangled ground, and we could maintain a connected vision entirely across from one to another.

"Thar's deer," said Jackson, as we crossed the fresh tracks of one. "And thar's Beauty," continued he; "do you hear her?"

"No, I cannot tell one from another; they are all yelping, each on a different track."

A loud burst of voices from the negroes proclaimed something started.

"What's that, Mike?"

"Coon," answered Mike.

"No—thunder! it's a cat; see it come."

Grimalkin, **however,** did not like such a multitude of **foes as presented themselves, and turning to** the right, **shot in under the underbush ahead of us,** while two of **the** younger dogs came full cry **on her** heels.

"There's a coon—two of them!" **I** shouted.

"Out of the frying-pan into the fire I think," said Jackson, as they ran into the same thicket the cat had taken to.

Here **the** bushes became so thick that I had to **take** my hunting-knife to cut my way and free my legs from **the** close binding of **tenacious** green vines that seemed stronger than packthread. We could hear **the** dogs **ahead of us and on either side** yelping **and** scudding hither and **yon, and I at once** saw the advantage of the mongrel pack we were using. They wound in and out **of every corner, and** under every fallen leaf where a hare could **lie, yelping as poor** puss started from her form, **and** only following her a few steps to pursue their researches in another cover.

Slowly we progressed ahead, and after about two hours of labor we had come down one half of the island, and had drawn so near together we could see each other. **On calling down the line we had** reported two deer as **having** been seen, and "some coon," with such a strong **accent on the some,** that we were inclined to think that this particular game was very plentiful. Indeed, Scipio **was** seen with **two** hanging **to his** girdle. I could see, from time to time, Miss Lou's boat paddled by Rosa, and **the young lady seated in the bow.**

"What's that ahead?" shouted Jackson.

"Can't say, though it looks black," I replied, as some indistinct body rushed out from under some grape-vines, shaking down the ripe fruit in showers.

"Yeow! yeow!—oohow!" chimed in two or three dogs in chorus, on some new and fresh scent, and Wag, who had been keeping very near me, dashed off to see.

"There's a buck, look out!"

"Bang!" sounded Jackson's gun.

"Never riz a hair!" called Mike, as the deer crashed on.

"Big buck! big buck!" called out the negroes beyond.

'Spang!"

"There goes Lou's gun," said Jackson. "What is she shooting? can you see?"

"Yes, a young buck."

"It's getting lively, Jackson."

"Wait a little, there's game here! Hear the boys sing."

The lively chant of the negroes sounded in the clear air, accompanied by the crashing of their sticks:

>Wake 'em up dare!
>Waugh and a waugh da!
>Git out possum!
>Waugh da dey!

"Da she goes," called a negro, as something bounded out of the bushes.

"What's that?"

"Big buck, sah; got horns like a dead tree."

"There's that cat again!"

Sure enough, the cat came spitting along, and dashed up a tree, sending down the bark in showers on the dogs that were close after her.

"Drap, you hussey!" said Mike, following her zig-zag course up the pine tree, with his rifle; and as she paused he sent a ball through her head, whizzing her down with a whirling motion as though she had been swung down by her tail.

"Git out, you dogs! Clare away, that's my cat!" he shouted, cuffing the dog aside, and taking possession of his prize.

"Kehunck! Kehunck!" There goes a blue heron, fanning the air with measured stroke. See him sail. He got up so slowly that one of the dogs jumped up at his long dangling legs.

"There go three deer altogether."

"Don't shoot the does, thar's no use," called out Mike.

There was only one buck, and three shots rang so close together we could not tell the report, but the buck fell over among his wives, who leaped ahead, sadly frightened. Mike cut his throat, and left his cat beside him to keep him company.

"There's that varmint again," shouted Jackson; "it's a panther!"

"Whar's a painter?" asked Mike.

"On ahead; we've seen him twice."

I heard the Doctor's voice from the other side of the island, and the quick repeated report of his double-barrel. Then a shot on our left.

"That's Lou again; push down to the beach there, will you?"

I came through the young willows that shut out the view, when I saw Lou gesticulating and pointing ahead, at the same time she was loading. I tried to see what it was, but could not, on account of the intervening bushes. She hurriedly rammed down the wad of shot with which she was provided, sowed up in muslin, and taking aim, fired again.

"A wolf! look out—he is turning in the bushes."

I ran back just in time to see the animal attempting to sneak back, when, seeing me, he turned ahead, and ran on so quickly I could not shoot, though I saw by his track he was wounded.

At the place we had now reached, the island was not more than a third of a mile in width. The trees had ceased to grow, and only a few copses of willow were found in the hollow between the ridges, and the tall grass that lined the pond. We could see the negroes away hither and thither, chasing the swamp raccoons that seemed to overrun the island, and striking at the hares that dodged hither and thither, and, escaping the men, were sure to run directly in the mouths of the dogs.

Ahead of us we could see the deer coursing over the knolls, hard pushed by the dogs, that had separated in three or four different packs, and were each hunting on their own hook.

"There's Yowler and Music. Here they come—they are after the wolf. Hi, dogs! hi, dogs!" shouted Jackson, running to a knoll where he could overlook the chase.

The negroes yelled as they caught sight of the game, and the wolf availing himself of every copse and hollow, ran on, hard pushed by the dogs, and dodging on every side to avoid his numerous foes. Whenever he entered a thicket he remained there until the dogs were about entering the other side; then he dashed away with an angry snap of his jaws that sounded like the ring of metal. As he approached the further shore, the Doctor saluted him with a double shot that stung him badly. He passed down the line of negroes, but their shouting and dancing deterred him from attempting to break their array.

"Now, Mike!"

"No no, it is your turn; I've had a cat."

"Take him, Charlie!"

I levelled my rifle, and as he ran I fired. At the report he rolled over and over like a ball.

"Well done!" shouted Lou Jackson.

I thought him quite dead, but when the dogs came up where he fell, he turned around on his haunches and snapped at his pursuers with such effect that the foremost lost a piece from his shoulder as broad as my palm, leaving a ghastly wound. The dog turned away, yelling with pain. Wag, who was always in every scrape, received another nip, not quite so bad, but sufficient to put him on the sick list for the rest of the day, and doubtless some of the other dogs would have been hurt, had not Mike fired and killed the wounded animal as the hounds came crowding up.

"Cat! cat!" "Yow! yow!" "Hit um a dip!" "Ough! ough!" were the sounds that came on the right, as a big cat broke away down the beach. The Doctor was just landing from his boat, and had a fair chance, as the animal was close by. The shot wounded the furious beast, so that it became completely confused, and being hard pressed by the dogs, it took refuge in the only *trunk* it could see, which happened to be the high curve of the Doctor's cypress canoe, just landing end on to the beach. In rushed the dogs after the animal, crowding the boat, knocking about the paddles, and forcing the Doctor up on the thwarts. The fierce animal fought with desperation against the crowd of pursuers, thrashing around the Doctor's legs, and tilting the boat from one side to the other, till it finally upset, and dogs, and oars, cat, and hunter, were all thrown into the water together. It only needed a moment of open field, and the dogs, smarting with their scratches, tore the cat almost in pieces, and left the cat-skin, as one of the boys remarked who had run down to help the Doctor, "'bout chawed up."

Jackson and I did not like to leave our places to help in the fray, though we assisted all we could by laughing, and Miss Jackson called out, after vainly trying to peer over the land, to know what the matter was.

I explained how the Doctor had presided over the fight.

"The Colossus of Rhodes!" she answered back.

"Poke! I say, Poke! Miss Jackson says you stood like the Colossus of Rhodes."

"I won't stand for a Colossus again," he replied, shoving off his boat, and resuming his paddle; "that miserable cat has scratched my legs bare!"

As our line advanced we could see the end of the island that ran out in a long narrow bar. Hundreds of gulls and black-headed terns, with snow-white bodies, disturbed from the sands, were cawing over us, and curlews and plover wheeled in circles, uttering their plaintive cries. Crowds of merganser ducks that were sitting on the shingle, basking in the sun, rushed out to sea, piling up the water in front of them, and small birds took flight to the neighboring islands, or flew high in the air to regain their accustomed haunts in the thickets. Like as some great seine that has inclosed a broad bay, at last contracts its semi-circle toward the beach, exposing to the light the flashing fishes that in vain attempt to leap its cords, while the gulls and fish-hawks wait above, so our line closed up, the prey rushed hither and thither, the black heads of the negroes above the grass, like the floats on the net, bobbed up and down, and with shout and cry, the terrified animals made their last leaps and tricks for their lives.

The first thing that broke our line was a doe, with a fawn nearly grown. The doe was let past, but one of the negroes caught the fawn as it attempted to run by, and with a blow of his knife across the back of its neck felled it to the ground, before a voice could be raised to stop him. Then a doe was pulled down by the hounds, and a dozen dogs piled up over it, very brave when its resistance was overcome.

"There go two deer to the water; see the boats pull after them—the Doctor, and Lou, and Scipio in his canoe."

"Whoop! see the turkeys—I'll have a gobbler!" I said, firing at their leader, who spread out his wings and settled down into the grass, while the hens scattered in every direction, some taking wing and flying off to the main land.

"Thar's a bear!"

"Where?"

"In those thorn bushes."

"I don't see him."

At this moment, Scipio, who had been paddling after the deer, turned his canoe landward, shouting "A bear! A bear!" and the dogs, that had been scattered about in the underbrush, made a fresh clamor, and rushed into the thorn trees, from whence they came howling back, some of them with blood running from their shoulders.

"Who saw it?"

"I saw it," said the Doctor, hurrying in from his canoe at the first intimation of a bear, as did both of the other boats, letting the deer escape; "I know it was a bear."

"Fire your gun at him."

Lem was lying down flat on his face, trying to peep under the bushes, when the Doctor, at the suggestion, fired into the thicket. At the report of his gun, out rushed the animal, stung, probably, by the shot. So quick was his charge, that Lem did not have time to get out of the way, and was run over by the brute, as dashing right through the midst of us, he hied away for the woods from which we had just come. There were too many crowded around, when he first came forth, to make it at all safe to shoot, and the moment he gained a little distance, his round stern presented a target as little vulnerable as the rump of a rhinoceros, as he ran with a lumbering gait, but with great speed, for his old haunts. But the hounds were soon after him, and as they came up they ran alongside, snapping at him without stopping him; then the smaller dogs came to their assistance, and seizing him behind, forced him to bay, which he did by standing on his hind legs, and making sweeps with his front paws at his pursuers. It was an amusing sight to see the dogs run, but still more so to see the negroes madly excited about the danger of their favorite curs, and yet cheering them on with cries, and grotesque denunciations, and warnings.

"Now for it! Whose shot is it?"

"Let the Doctor try."

"I ain't loaded; wait a minute."

"Ho! ho! that's a good one! Jackson, shoot."

Without a word of parley, Jackson fired, and struck

the mark, as we could see, for the animal flinched, and attempted to run, but there were too many dogs, and they brought him to bay again after running a dozen yards. I fired, and so did Mike, both together. The huge brute turned the way we stood, his eye gleamed a fierce glance of revenge, his jaw fell open, showing his long rows of white teeth, and then he sunk down a lifeless lump amid the ring of dogs.

"That air is rael murder!" said Mike.

As the heat of the chase subsided in my veins, I felt as if Mike's remark was true.

"Four hunters, twelve men, and forty dogs, against one bear!" called out Lou Jackson, who had been a spectator of the chase from her boat.

"I plead guilty to tyrannical oppression," said the Doctor; " deal gently with me."

"I fine you all one bear's skin, to be paid into the Court," she replied.

" Oh! that will make you a sharer of the profits."

Bruin was dragged down to the beach, under the shade of a tree, and the men were sent back for the rest of the game that lay scattered about the route of our chase wherever they had fallen. On putting them altogether in a row, it was counted, as follows : one bear, one wolf, two wildcats, four deer, one wild turkey, one sand-hill crane, seven raccoons, and hares without number.

"Not a bad day's sport!" ejaculated the Doctor, standing in his favorite attitude with his feet wide apart, and his hands in the side pockets of his shooting-jacket.

"How many did you shoot, Poke?"

"I think I shot all of them, for I fired at everything, only may be I did not kill; but I contend the sport is as good if you get the shots."

"What did you kill at your first shot, Lou?" inquired Jackson.

"That young buck. Don't you see my buckshot? they are scattered over a hand's breath of distance."

"I fired at some ducks, getting up out of the pond," said the Doctor.

"What kind of ducks?"

"There's one of them," he replied, tugging at a mallard drake he had stowed in his pocket.

"Ha! I am glad to see that; he is one of the first of the winter migration. Wait for the big flights, and we will see sport. Come, boys, off with that wolf's skin, we don't want his carcase at the camp, and so with the bear, too, I reckon."

But the negroes pleaded for the bear's meat, and it was concluded to carry him to camp. So the boats were pulled up opposite the place where the game was lying, and while a couple of the negroes were skinning the gaunt-looking brute that I had so successfully disabled, the rest carefully loaded the two canoes with the game, and when the wolf was disrobed, two negroes taking their places in the stern of each boat, gaily started on their return. We all followed the canoes, taking the line of the beach, laughing at the different accounts of the day's adventures, and the droll remarks of the men, who were in the greatest glee at the success of the hunt. The shore birds were running before us, or wheeling over our heads, and Lou Jackson was telling their names, and how their coming marked the progress of the year. The sands were hard and level, just rippled by the sea. The day was waning in that clearness of atmosphere and stillness of decay that marks the early fall, ere a leaf has dried enough to rustle. Mike's ugly face seemed to draw a reflection from the season; Poke's laugh was as musical as the waters, and, wearied with the day's exertion, I scarcely knew how pleasantly the moments were falling, until now, when looking them over through the telescope of years.

CHAPTER XIII.

THE HISTORY OF AN OLD FRIEND.

" The poor make no new friends,
But they love the better far
The few their Father sends."

THE night had drawn its curtains when we reached our bivouac, but the fire made it day between the two white tents, where our supper was spread, and where, when supper was done, we stretched ourselves in dreamy mood, watching the embers glow and listening to the tale go round. It was my turn to tell a story, but being of a philosophical frame of mind I narrated a history, and being of a modest nature was about to preface it with a few deprecatory remarks when one of my auditors rudely cut me short by saying:

"Bang away; never mind the priming."

And the following was the tale I told. It is the history of one of my old friends:

There are some persons in this world of ours that are very incorrectly estimated. They are not the talking people that boast themselves into our notice, nor the silent people that, with an air of abstract profundity, impress us with their powers, while they repress all of ours.

They are not the showy people, whose dress and equipage, house, wife, watering-place, and tight boots, dazzle us, nor the men in great places in the nation, nor the very pious men. They, perchance, are very plain men, and don't obtrude. They have not many friends. They are composed in manner, and sparse and simple in their words. If you don't know them you will not hear anything very bad of them, unless some very fashionable person says it in her manner rather than her words, when alluding to them. If you do know them, and you can't know them in a day, you will like them forever. If it is a woman, her gentle presence has filled the house for months, providing and directing so softly it was never known. She has read much, but it was in her chamber; she has opinions stronger than any partisan, but she never expresses them in conversation, only in their exercise. Her quiet eye is on you, but you don't perceive it, and she knows you before you thought enough of her to notice her, and yet, for all that forgotten presence, when the great ills come and sorrow extinguishes the light in the house, where does the household so surely turn as to her counsel and her consolation? If it is a man, his coming and going and long absences were scarcely noted, except by those who leaned on him. In his mind are stored up years of studies and observation, and in his breast there is a spring of love for simple things and honest ways, and a hidden honor that makes him a rich man, though often with scarcely a dollar to spend. Everybody says he must be rich, for he has everything he wants, though he only wants what is within his reach. Should you get to know him well, you will find in some direction or other his mind has gone out in a strong taste, and in it he so excels, that his companionship is a great instruction—a happy, hopeful story, read at the evening time, mayhap tinted with fancies, and all aglow with legends, and self-experiences of so rare a kind, you wondered you did not know him before.

Such characters are sometimes found in society, in the full sweep of restless, flattering, envious fashion, just endured, half forgotten, sometimes in literary life, sometimes toiling in some hard handicraft, where the gains they make are applied to those they love. Sometimes in the wood, or by the sea-side village.

The friend of whom I am about to speak, and who belongs to this class, is oftenest seen in rural districts, or by lakes, or the slow-moving streams of the woods. I deem it but my duty, for many a lesson taught by him and hours of quiet companionship, to speak in his behalf a kindly word, and save him and his family, as far as in me lies, from that unmerited neglect which seems to be the fate of the humble and the unobtrusive.

The friend to whom I allude is the Muskrat. Let no one smile at the name,

"Or mock the short and simple annals of the poor."

His coat may not be of as many colors as a courtier's, but it covers a kindlier heart; his house may not be of as stately proportions as a banker's, but it shelters a more tranquil soul. Writers may have slighted him, school-boys may have pelted him, poets left his name unsung, and the uncouth boor may have sought to deride him by naming him Musquash, and other opprobrious titles; but this is not the first time in the annals of the world a similar fate has overtaken modest worth. Pass by their crude opinions, and let us visit my mentor friend.

Down by many a softly-purling brook, whose sinuosities have unearthed the gnarled roots of oaks and hickories, and where the school-boy hastes from tasks to find a shady nooning, the Muskrat builds his nest. His selection of a home shows his cultivated taste, and gives a lesson to the more unobservant rustic. By the cloudy water that lies in the canals, that lead beneath the oaks, you may know his retreat. There he rests, while the day is warm, in the quiet enjoyment of his domestic pleasures, safe from pursuit in the winding galleries of his earthen fortress, but,

"When the sheep are in the fauld, and the kye at hame,
And a' the world to sleep are gane,"

when the moonshine falls on bridge and reeds, and twinkling stars are floating on the water, then this gentle friend comes forth to view. You see him, with his keen eye and grave countenance, draw himself upon a root, and with careful fingers arrange his dress and wash his face. By his side sits a little picture of his sire—a tiny counterpart, that is destined one day to take his place among the reeds and by the bridge, and rear the mimic

Down by many a softly-purling brook, whose sinuosities have unearthed the gnarled roots of oak and hickories, and where the schoolboy hastes from tasks to find a shady lounging, the muskrat builds his nest.—P age 198.

dome upon the lake. After the parent has completed his toilet he gives one or two caressing touches to that of his young heir. A moment more they sit, eyeing the bubbles or floating nuts descending the stream, or watching, their faces reflected in the moonlight waters. Who can say that they do not appreciate the beauty of the night, or the soft, murmuring music of the woods, or the fragrance of the air, laden with the odor of calamus buds and the breath of the birch and sassafras? Presently, diving down together, they disappear under the water, from whence, after a moment, they reappear, each with several muscles clasped to his breast by his fore paws, and, resuming their seats on the roots, they eat their food with the readiness of squirrels, casting the shells down at their feet, which fall on the pile of pearly bivalves that adorn the entrance to their home. Another pause follows, while they look up and down the brook.

Are they not comely in their dark-brown coat and black feet? Does not their soft hair, that sheds the water, and the strong flat tail, that steers their course, or flattens their masonry-work, befit well their pursuits? Do not their manners well become their place? Is it not true they are free from cares and inordinate greed—that they know their simple duties and enjoy them?

You say they are idle? Wait till you have seen their whole life.

Presently the father swims off on the water and across the brook. We may not see him go, for only his head is above the surface, and his tail floats like a rudder. By the wake in the water, we may tell his course, long after his round head is lost to view, and his child is following him close behind. They are bound for the low reeds on the other shore. There the calamus lifts its waving wands and spicy buds, while beyond the waterpad's broad leaf floats on the surface, and their white and yellow lilies stud the waters, and from the sandy edge of the channel the osier's round tapering wand, the bayonet flags and the sedge grass, appear above the tide and point the way the current flows. This is the playground of our friend. You may see him here when the moon is full, pulling the roots of the lilies, or the long eel-grass that is growing beneath. You can hear his quick splash and dive, and by the rattle of the cat-tails and the shaking out of their floss you know he is chasing off the wild duck's brood that intrude on his gardens. On the shore his paths are running hither and thither, wherever a better grass can be found, or the seeds of grains that have come down with the freshets have taken root, and on these grounds, which he is often compelled to cross, a deep hole is dug down to the water, and connects with the brook, in which he will take refuge if disturbed. At length, when the morning star shines dead, and the cock's loud clarion comes from the farm, the provident botanist bears away for his home, with his arms full of grass and roots to lay up for a day of need.

It often occurs that my friend has selected for his residence, being allured by the wild beauty of the scene, some lake whose shores do not present suitable accommodations for shelter. Either they are so rocky as not to be pierced, or they are so low as to be liable to be submerged with the spring rains. No more discriminating judge of the security of such shores can be found than my friend. No scenery fitness will tempt him. If there is any liability of danger on shore he **goes out to** the centre of the lake, or to a point in the lake **from** which he can readily obtain good grass, and then he **builds himself** a house. Sometimes he takes the end of a half-submerged log as a proper foundation. At other times the bottom of the pond, and yet again he will take a mass of weeds as an anchor, and construct a house that is to last for years on this slight support. His bricks are eel-grass and twigs; his mortar is mud and clay; he is his own architect, laborer, builder, contractor and upholsterer. Gradually the house progresses, without shaped like a dome, and within divided into many chambers. The door is beneath the waters, and so nothing but a diver can enter it, and being built on the open water, and at a distance from shore, nothing will attack it from above. It is formed and fashioned with a precision that no science could excel. In and out is the strong eel-grass woven, and the clay that covers the walls is patted **down** with many a sounding thwack from his broad tail until it is as smooth as a plaster wall. At length winter comes and bridges the lake, and makes an easy access to the house for the wolf and the bear. How is the Muskrat to save himself from their snuffing nose and strong claws? The careful student of nature lies all the freezing night by the side of his house, and ever and anon with his tail spatters the water over the dome, until finally the house is massed in ice so thick that none but the summer can break it. And within, in his goodly chamber, lined with the river grass, the plumage of ducks, and the soft silk of the silkweed, my friend lies with his wife, safe from enemies, from want, and from cold, and reads me a lesson of skill and providence I have not yet followed.

In some lakes I have seen as many as thirty of these little domes rising about three feet from the water, and resembling an Indian village. When the nights are still in autumn, the inhabitants of this modern Venice will be found lying about on the lake, chasing each other around the houses, or playing tag on the open water. They lie on the surface, with their tails slightly arched, which is a sign of watchfulness, and by a quick motion will disappear so suddenly that even the hunter's shot is ineffectual to stop them. One old beadle will now and then be seen mounting one of the houses, and with an august dignity survey the surrounding shores, and when well satisfied, will dive down so softly as not to leave a ripple; but if, perchance, he should see some cause of alarm, he leaps back with an angry plash, and the whole tribe disappear in an instant. Should you be tempted to fire a gun at some impudent member of the colony, before the bright flash had faded along the shore, every one will have disappeared from view. You may wait hours for another shot, and though the pond is full of them, you will never see one. Once in a while an old sentinel will float to the surface, and the point of his nose, about the size of a chesnut, will be exposed while he breathes and takes a view, and after a moment of watchfulness, it will be so quietly withdrawn that even if you see it you will not suspect it to be one of your prey.

A long time ago—I remember the woods and waters were very bright in color then, for I was a boy—there lived one bachelor Muskrat in a small pond not far from my home. After watching him some evenings, I set a trap to catch him, baited with a rosy Spitzenberg. Early in the morning I was at the pond; the trap was sprung, and peering into it through a small hole bored in the end, I saw crouched in the corner an animal with long whiskers and bright eyes, that appeared to my happy vision as big as a polar bear, but by the musky smell I knew it was my friend the Muskrat. If the woods and waters were bright the night before, they glowed with fire now, and the sun rose in the east. I carried my prize home in the trap, and tying a string to his leg, after getting somewhat bitten in the operation, secured him in the shed, and tried to tame him, but quite unsuccessfully. He refused to eat apples or cake, though always ready for a piece of my finger. When I could watch my captive no longer, I went to bed to dream of him, while he, cutting the string with his sharp incisors, gnawed a hole in the door of the shed, and made his escape. I followed his track the next day in the light snow that lay on the ground, and it led in a straight line to the pond from whence I came. I set my trap again, but though I tempted him with the rosiest of apples, he never was induced to enter. At this time the pond in which he resided froze over, and gave me an opportunity of getting out to the centre, where he had built for himself a dome as classically correct as the Pantheon. I confided my secret to a comrade, and we consulted an old work of the Northwest Fur Trade, and there learned the Indian manner of catching these animals. We accordingly provided ourselves with a small net, and going down to the pond with a pickaxe, when school was out, we commenced a regular siege. First we cut four holes in the ice, at opposite sides of, and close by the house; then with bent sticks I pushed the corners of the net through the holes, and my comrade fastened them at the four corners, thus stretching the net beneath the house in such a manner as to prevent the animal diving down in the water. By the time this advance had been effected it began to grow dark, so I hastily with my pickaxe cut a hole in the top of the house and looked in. There was nothing there but the materials for a warm bed, that had been occupied not long since. I pulled away the partition that divided the interior, but could see nothing. I put my hand in to feel, and was rewarded with a gripe from an admirable set of incisors that have left their impress on my hand to this day, and pulling out my arm, I pulled out my captive of the night before, who immediately, amid the laughter of **my** unsympathizing friend, scampered to the shore, where **the ice had left an** open margin of water, and dived beyond pursuit.

This bold burglary on our part evidently caused much alarm and uncertainty in the mind of the proprietor of the house. For the next morning, when I returned with an eel-spear, intent on warlike deeds, I found that, after putting a few armfuls of mud on the broken dome, his ratship had changed his mind, and, leaving the house altogether, had made his exodus to a safer land, under the waters of a neighboring stream, to which I followed his trail, and where I trust he still lives, undisturbed by marauding boys.

The Muskrat is no noisy roisterer. His ways are gentleness, and he only frequents the most placid scenes. He abhors the noisy rapids of the river, the clank of the wheel, or the fashionable highway, but where the stream has the softest tone, where the birch droops lowest, where the leaves in autumn lay in **yellow** and crimson wreaths upon the eddy, and the fish-hawk from his eminence can scarcely see the perch that turns his golden bars to the sunlight, so hid in foliage moves the water, there my friend finds a favorite bank, and may be seen, even in the day-time, plying his busy feet, or mounting some stone or slanting root to view the disrobing year.

To this unfrequented place, when troubled by the cares that oppress, or those greater cares that may oppress, I often come to hold counsel with my friend. I hear the waters croon, the leaves whisper, the wood-thrush warble his low chant, and I forget to listen to that inner voice complaining. I see the bold plunge of the kingfisher diving for his prey; bright eyes are peering at me from bush and hole, cautiously at first, familiarly afterward; the leafy vault above me dazzles the eye with a confused motion of waning, glimmering brightness, and catches of sunshine come and go athwart the foam and on the flowers, and I do not see the cold, hard faces that were staring at me but now. I drink the water, I smell the odor of the moss, I lean my face against the cool beech trunk; every sense is drinking in the religion of nature, and the soul, forgetting itself, goes up in the million-colored, million-formed works of creation, through their instincts, their changes, and their birth, to that pervading essence that made them all and guides them all, and placed me among them all—a very little thing in this wonderful place. And then comes forth the Muskrat; he swims out to an apple you had tossed in the stream, and, smelling it an instant, takes it in his mouth, and bears it away to yonder stone. He sees you now; a moment's pause; he is watching you; perchance he sees that softening heart that has come over you with the teachings of the hour, and therefore he does not fear you. He goes on munching his apple, while his whiskers move up and down with every movement of his grave cheek. His keen eyes wink with satisfaction. When he has finished his meal he passes his hand over his face, and dresses his robe a moment. He looks up the stream and down, but there is nothing there save a flock of wood-duck, halting for a day on their southern migration. He looks at you; do you see his contentment, his happy face, his honest ways—just enough of labor to provide him a home—just enough of leisure to learn the world his God has made? He moves into the water, and, bowing low his head to his now cheerful friend, he bids the day and you good night.

When I had finished my history, I looked around upon my auditors, and found that, with the exception of Lou Jackson, they were all asleep.

CHAPTER XIV.

THE DROWNED LANDS.

" Seekest thou the plashy brink
    Of weedy lake, or marge of river wide,
Or where rocking billows rise and sink
    On the chafed ocean's side?

*   *   *   *   *   *

" And soon thy toil shall end,
    Soon shalt thou find a summer home and rest,
And scream among thy fellows—reeds shall bend
    Soon o'er thy sheltered nest."

BRYANT.

FOR some time past, on the main land, we had been noticing the signs of the departing year, and at Bonda Key these indications became more marked and numerous. The air had not lost its balsam or the leaf its color, yet there were other shadows on nature's dial slighter in appearance, but as true in reality. The ear missed the whir in the evening air of those summer insects, whose short lives had already terminated. The eye saw a clearness in the atmosphere that brought objects several miles distant apparently near at hand, and sometimes elevated them about the horizon. Some birds that wore in summer the livery of the rainbow had apparelled themselves in plainer garments, and from day to day new arrivals among migratory tribes of the air would recall the mind to those northern hills where the jagged pine and lichened rock were already grey with the first flurry of snow. We were all standing one morning at the "creak o' day," on the island, watching the first effects of the sun before its rising, and noting the little indications of the progress nature had made during the night. Thus travellers at sea will come forth early in the morning, and for a few minutes scan the ocean and the ship, and note the bearings and the winds before they turn to the regular thoughts and occupations of the day.

"See those ducks coming?" said Jackson.

"Where?"

"Close by the main land, low down."

"Yes! they are coming this way, too."

"Teal," said Mike.

"How do you know that, Mike, have you seen that flock before?" asked the Doctor.

"By their flyin'; you couldn't throw a picayune edgewise through the flock."

The compact body of birds that seemed when first in view a fleck on the red sky, gradually extended in size until they swept high over our heads, with a sound like a strong wind in a pine wood, keeping well toward the outer side of the island.

"Jist think of them air critters bein' hatched among the icebergs!"

"But think of their all going back again next spring

to the very spot they were born on," replied Miss Jackson.

"I trust they all won't get the chance," said the Doctor, looking the way they went with covetous eyes.

"Wall, that's easy enough done with the chance they've got, stuck up higher en a meetin' house, a prospectin' over the country; they'd be booby birds to forgit their own trail. The rub was to 've done it the fust time, when it was all strange like."

"They are always piloted by some old bird that has been here before, I think," said Miss Jackson.

"How do you know that, Miss Wiseacre?"

"By seeing the flock come straight for some favorite feeding-ground, where they will always alight at nearly the same time every year. Now had there been no old bird piloting them, they would have alit in open water and found the feeding ground subsequently.

"I shot in a flock ones't in the spring-time and winged a young black duck," said Mike, pushing up his cap from his face and spreading his arms out on the muzzle of his rifle. "I tuck the thing hum and penned it up with the tame ducks, and so I kept it all summer. When fall cum the diver ducks kim fust, and then a purty considerable show of teal, but he didn't scrape his foot to them or say one word. But airly one mornin' I heerd that duck sittin' down by the bayou, quackin' away as ef he had the pip in his gizzard; (there comes a row o' black ducks now.) Wall, I couldn't see what 'twas that bothered him. I looked all around; et was comin' on mornin' like, and things out was quiet, and every minit or so he'd set up on end, and stickin' his bill up like a musket would quack three or four times. As I looked, I seen a tearin' big flock of black ducks cum from the north, high up; **they** bore around when they got over the cabin, and presently landed down by the side of the wounded duck, and sich a goin' on and duckin' of heads and gabblin' you never heered in all your born days. **It was all as** plain as a bear's track. The wounded duck was waitin' for its friends; it knowed jist when it was time fur 'em to come to the very minit, and sot out there to stop them."

"And I presume the noises they made were mutual inquiries after friends and the compliments of the season," said the Doctor.

"Asking if there had been much ice in Baffin's Bay **the** past year," suggested Lou Jackson.

"There comes another flock," said Jackson, pointing to the horizon.

"There's a grist of 'em," said Mike.

"See how they swerve one way **or another!** Look how fast they grow in size! There must be ten thousand in that flock! All night they have been travelling and yet not weary!" exclaimed Miss Jackson as the flock came pressing on in a hugh irregular shadow, soughing like the wind, and keeping straight south.

"Oh, you beauties!" ejaculated the Doctor, looking up at the passing mass of beautiful intelligent life overhead, with his mouth wide open and his body gradually leaning back to permit him to see as they passed, until his round little figure nearly lost its balance.

"Thou shall not covet, Doctor."

"Mike, can we get some of them?"

"Reckon."

"I think there are a good many on the **Drowned Lands**," said Jackson; "they have been coming on pretty thick, lately."

"Then let us try them. I don't think the Doctor will look earthward again, unless it is to shoot ducks."

A laugh followed, and the party being of one accord, it was arranged that we should spend the day in the marshes, taking a supply of food to last till night. So we walked back to camp, Miss Jackson and the Doctor chatting away about some theory of the Doctor's upon the cause of the variation of the plumage of birds, which, like most theories, was all wrong. The moment our intentions for the day were announced, the camp was in a hurry; the idlers bestirred themselves with double zeal; guns were examined; boats made ready; ammunition bags, that had not been used in a year, were overhauled and filled; and at length, when the sun arose, our breakfast was ended, and four boats were all equipped and manned with two negroes each, ready for the sportsmen. The boats were all dug-out canoes, made by the negroes from cypress logs, but their graceful shape and high sharp bow and stern made them resemble the Indian bark canoe, or the Canadian pirogue. Mike had his neatly arranged, and a beautifully tanned deer-skin was spread in the stern. The negroes, with their sinewy arms and hairy breasts bare, sat at the oars; they were the handsomest negroes on the Jackson place, but would generally run away to the woods when their master was off; so to obtain some use out of them they were always taken along on the marooning excursions. The boats lay with their sterns on the rocks, waiting for Miss Jackson. Her father took his seat and pushed off, calling out as he went—

"Come, Lou, hurry up. Who will you ride with?"

She stepped down to the water's edge and into the Doctor's boat. Push off! Away they go, moving on the water like shadows, so little ripple do they leave behind. The shore recedes, the camp-fire smoke lessens; Rose can just be seen by the beach with her hands on her hips, watching the lessening fleet; the hounds' complainings come fainter and fainter; islands are passed; new vistas open to the eye with tropical vegetation; gaudy birds on the sandy points; low swathing mist in patches on the water, and no wind to drift it away. How luxuriantly calm! The land seems all afloat!

Jackson was in the lead, and we all followed in a line after him. Presently Mike's boat shoots ahead, a feather of spray at its prow, and the sweat guttering on the foreheads of the oarsmen. Yowler's head was lying over the edge of the canoe. Mike had a paddle in his hand, steering, and I saw the deer-skin that decorated the seat had been left behind.

"Where away?" called out Jackson, resting on his

oars, as we rounded a point where numerous openings and bays presented to view, and the boats glided together.

"Any way is beautiful enough," answered the Doctor, in the highest tone of enjoyment, chanting away snatches of songs, and Lou Jackson joining the chorus.

"Hi, you Scip, you pull a baby oar."

"Git out a de way dat air clam-boat!"

> "Row brothers row,
> The stream runs fast."

"That song isn't true in fact or music, Doctor."

"There goes Mike; he will show us the way."

"The old rat, he has stolen the march! Give way, boys! All together!" and the boats filing off followed in the wake of Mike, who was making for a level shore about two miles ahead, where the bushes grew so dense you could scarcely see the land. As we approached, we could see no passage beyond, and even Mike seemed uncertain, for he steered along the beach a hundred yards distant, examining carefully, the bushes that grew close to the water, colored with red hawberries, and spiked with cactus of several varieties. After skirting the shore in this manner for several hundred yards, the prow of the hunter's canoe was turned shoreward; ours followed the leader. The boatmen bent to their work and the boats flew.

"Trail yer oars!" called out Mike.

The negroes threw their oars from the rowlocks, letting them float by the side of the boat. Mike's canoe dashed into the bushes and disappeared. Ours followed one after the other, and when we lifted our heads from the crouching position we were compelled to assume, the boats all lay floating together on a large lake completely land-locked, and cluttered up with reedy islands and bogs of coarse grass, with here and there an osier nodding among lily pads or floating scum.

With the first exclamation of delight from the negroes there was a rush in the water at one side, and twenty wood-ducks, that had been under the edge of the bushes, took wing so near us we could see their scarlet eyes and hear their piping cry; at the same instant came the pleasant and long remembered quack! quack! quack! of the black duck, as a dozen of these clergy of the marshes beat upward from the grass at our unexpected coming.

I fired at one of the wood-ducks, and so did the Doctor. Jackson banged away at the others; but as usual when in a hurry, there was not a bird killed, though a dozen or more arose from neighboring shelters at the cannonade, and after one or two circuits settled down in the grass beyond.

"Oh, Doctor, how could you miss that beautiful drake! I will shoot the next one myself," said Miss Jackson.

"You see," replied the Doctor, rather humbly, "they were too near when I first fired."

"And when you next fired, they were too far away," said Miss Jackson.

"*You* need not say anything," said the Doctor. "Why didn't you kill some of those black ducks?"

"Gun hung fire."

"Pooh! what nonsense!"

"Come, no recriminations, load up!"

"How shall we shoot?"

"Each boat is to paddle its own way through the reeds, and shoot what rises, and so we will get a good many passing shots overhead. That's so, isn't it, Mike?"

"I reckon."

"How will we come together again?"

"Thar's an island clare up to the eend of this water, and it's got one cabbage-tree on it, I reether think the biggest cabbage-tree north of Tampa Bay. We might come together thar."

"Amen!" said the Doctor. "Now let's start. I am on warlike deeds intent."

"Quack! quack! quack!" sounded close by us, and one of those wayward ducks that sometimes, against all rules, skulks behind his comrades, got up near us. The Doctor was standing up at the time, and fired, but from the rocking of the unsteady canoe he missed, as before.

"What a shame, Doctor! I shall not ride with you."

"Try him, some one."

"He's too far away!" said Jackson, with his gun half way to his shoulder.

"Shoot him, Mike!" said Miss Jackson, turning to where the hunter sat in his canoe.

Mike passed the back of his hand quickly across his

forehead, as he was wont sometimes to do when in earnest, and raised his rifle to his shoulder. A second of pause, and the crack of the piece sounded. The duck had arisen perpendicularly until it had reached a height that gave it free passage over the reeds, and then taking its direction, was bearing away in a straight line, gradually decreasing in size as its velocity increased. At the report of Mike's rifle it fell over and over, striking the water with a splash, while in the air where it was flying one or two feathers floated away on the wind.

"Well, done, that!" cried Jackson.

Lou said nothing, but her kindling eye rested on the marksman, while a smile lit her whole face, and the party separated for the hunt.

The Drowned Lands were formed by the sea banking up with a sandbar the outlet of a stream that ran through a low country. This natural dam flooded the lowlands on either side for several miles, and the soil being sandy, with a slight deposit of alluvial matter from the descending fresh waters, many varieties of grass and aquatic plants sprang up, and formed attractive food for the myriads of water-fowl that here passed the winters. Patches of cane grew on the marshy land not yet covered with water. Osiers and rushes sprung from the shallow water, and a long grass, with a tassel like the onion, opened its crown and scattered its oily seeds over the water. Now and then a floating log, or some still living bulb that had come down the stream had taken root in the shallows, and formed an island, on which rose one or two trees, and a rank vegetation of vines and grass. On the dead upper limbs of these trees the ahnega and other species of cormorants could be seen all the day patiently watching for their prey in the shallows. Fancy could not picture a more suitable home for the water-fowl, whose food was abundant in the matted grass and succulent weeds, and who hid in bending rushes for better shelter from the northerly winds.

Up this extended marsh our boats gently floated, each one following the openings that seemed best, and diverging so as to form an extended line. The negroes shipped their long oars, and used only the paddle, in order to move with greater stillness, and to pass through the narrow openings. As we advanced, I soon lost sight of the other boats, but from time to time could tell their position from the report of their guns and the rising of the ducks they disturbed. I had changed positions with the men, taking the bow of the boat, and letting them paddle in the stern.

"Dar, Maussa, black duck!" whispered Scipio, after we had paddled a short distance, changing with a wave of his paddle the direction of the canoe, and pointing it toward a mass of reeds that lay twisted and broken together, as though some wind had twisted them off half way up.

I pointed my hand inquiringly to the reeds. Scipio nodded, and the boat floated up noiselessly as a fish. We were close by them, and no sign of the game, save a feather or two on the water. The neighboring tufts of grass shut out the wind, and it was warm and still, like summer in the grassy bower, while bright little fish darted aside on either bow of the boat. Then came a flopping sound, a rattle of the reeds, and the brazen cry that so many thousand times, in a thousand hearts, has sent the blood leaping with its old memory-haunted tone, " Qua-ack! qua-ack! quack!" Some notes in this world are clearer, and some more rhyming, but there are few that when repeated, even far away, will so picture to the mind, in the twinkling of an eye, the extended reach of sedge, the downy reeds, glassy water, and young hopes, with which it is so intimately associated.

With the alarm cry two ducks broke forth, scattering the floss of the cat-tails in clouds about them, their long necks stretching out as though straining to be away. I aimed at the drake as he poised himself to bear away, and with the report of the piece he fell, head and wings pendent, with a splash on the water—a dead shot, I knew by the way he came down. The duck had gained some distance by this time, going straight away, as if terror chased her. No fear of her escape; the success of my first shot gave me confidence, and I knew the power of the little Mullen gun I held at my shoulder. Canny John Mullen, in his grim little smithy in Ann street, working away with his brogue and cunning hand—how often I have thanked him when he never knew it! "Quack! quack!" The sound was faint from the distance when I fired, but the duck rolled over and over, with its wings spinning, till it was lost to sight.

"Yah! ha! ya! Maussa; good shot. Did you ebber? Well, now, I give up—dat beats dis child!"

We paddled on, and found the first duck dead, and and the second with both wings broken, and easily secured. While loading, four ducks came flying over from the direction of the other boats. I hastily poured in some loose shot, and crouching down in the canoe, capped my gun, while I watched the birds approach, and when they were so near I could see the mottling on their breasts, arose suddenly to my feet. Scared by my sudden appearance, they breasted the air, swerving off to the right and left. Ho! what fair shots! I could have killed them with a pistol. The first barrel brought two, the second one, and the other bird departed sadly frightened.

Thus we passed on, getting fair shots every fifty yards at small bunches of ducks that arose from the little lagoons, and an occasional long shot at some passing bird that had been frightened from his proper feeding-ground by the incursion of the hunters.

At the same time that the game was abundant, the scenery through which its pursuit was leading us was strikingly peculiar. The level waste of sedge extended beyond the vision, waving in the wind. The constant opening and closing of watery passages, the little reed-locked lakes, the tortuous course we were obliged to follow, the sameness of the grouping of the reeds and little islets, repeated over and over again till the mind was all afloat as to locality and distance; the weird trees with their dead and naked arms, and the occasional mass of broken reeds and matted drift-wood that in the summer had formed the alligator's lair, all contributed to impress the mind with a feeling of strangeness and solitude. The wild birds, too, were unwontedly familiar in their demeanor. Marsh hens ran over the drifts before the boat, and gulls came screaming around us.

About three miles from where we had entered the Drowned Land, we came to the edge of open water, and found a large lake. Before entering it a glance ahead showed the further end of the pond literally covered with ducks. It was impossible, being on the same level, to tell how many there were, but from the extent of their front line they were very numerous. A hurried council of war was called to decide how they were best approached, and after two or three plans had been proposed and discarded, it was settled that we should try and paddle around on the further side of the pond so as to be near the flock, and then take our chances of their coming over us, as they probably might when alarmed by the firing in the other boats. So with much care as to the noise we might make, and some self self-control in not firing at single ducks that would rise close by us, we ultimately got around the flock, so as to place them between us and the other boats. We pulled our canoe into the thickest of the grass that completely sheltered us, and from where I sat I could see the ducks lying on the open water, moving hither and thither, and diving down for the eel-grass below the surface. I immediately recognized them as the same flock of teal that came over at the early dawn. It was a beautiful thing to see so much graceful life so bountifully supplied and protected by its own instincts in the solitude.

Away down the marsh came the frequent boom! boom! of my comrades' guns, but it did not seem to interfere with the comfort of the ducks, who still fed on, though keeping out of shot from where I sat. Soon the report of the guns coming nearer caused the ducks to crowd together with all their heads up. There was a long pause, and then a negro's voice sounded close by: "Maussa Jackson, mark!" followed by the clear ringing of a double shot, and at the sound up went my flock of ducks. Three or four arose first, and then the whole mass cleared the water; and the beating of their wings on the surface was like a long continued roll of thunder. I had no conception, before they rose, of their great multitude. It seemed as if they could be counted by tens of thousands. When they had attained a sufficient height to overlook the meadow, they wheeled like the line of an army, and apparently catching sight of the other boats, came with the bright linings of their wings turned to the sunlight, and their countless pinions hurtling through the air directly over the place where we were concealed. I had given Scipio, as a reward of merit, the musket I had brought with me, directing him to take his own time, and fire as he chose. He, however, could not wait for the best shot, but fired as one wing of the army wheeled over us. The aim was not a bad one, for a dozen ducks fell at the shot, and several more at intervals came slanting down from the flock. The effect of this unexpected attack drove the wing of the flock into the main body, clustering them together in a compact mass, when I fired both barrels. My stronger shooting gun bored a hole through the black mass, and twenty-seven ducks fell on the open water, and two or three went down aslant into the reeds. Three and a half dozen ducks was the contribution that one flock made to our booty. I still looked longingly after them as they went floating around the horizon, like banks of minute flies that wave at midsumer from prominent points on the shores of Great Lakes, undulating with the wind. But they passed away in the dim horizon, probably being unwilling to make another trial of the Drowned Lands after so unpleasant a reception.

Hardly had we secured all our ducks, after re-shooting the winged ones, before the Doctor's canoe burst through the reeds.

"Hulloah!"

"Hulloah!"

"How many birds?"

"Ah! plenty. Talk of hunting!" said the Doctor, "this is my hunter's paradise. A good boat to row you, and boys to pick up the game; no running yourself out of breath, or heavy pack on your back!" And the speaker took off his slouched hat, and rubbed his curly hair and shiny face with his handkerchief till it was all a-glow, laughing the while with his low musical voice.

"How many ducks, Miss Jackson?"

"Oh, ten for me, I believe; but they are beauties. Paddle up closer, boys, and let us see."

"Hulloah! where did you get all those? Great is Diana, but that is a pretty sight!" exclaimed the Doctor, leaning over to look at our ducks, that were neatly piled up on one of the seats, with their breasts up, and their heads hanging one way.

"These are out of the flock we saw come over to-day."

"I thought so; they just got up here, didn't they? It was a noble flock—blue wings, all of them."

"Oh! there are your ducks. Why, you only have ten altogether. Where are those you shot, Doctor?"

"Oh, I didn't care to shoot. Miss Lou, here, is a pupil of mine, and I like to let her try."

A suppressed nasal explosion from one of the boys in the Doctor's canoe informed me, if I had needed the information, that the Doctor was not a very true hand with the ducks, and that the lady was doing all the work.

"Well, there is the Palm Tree Island, I presume, not a great way ahead. Is it time for lunch?"

"Yes, I think so," said Miss Jackson, "if appetite is any test."

"Try some cold tea," said I, extending the bottle of that refreshing hunter's beverage.

"Ah!" said she, after a long drink, "that is a spring in the desert."

"Let me try a little of that spring in the desert," said the Doctor.

"Not till you tell me one thing," said I, getting possession of my bottle. "How many shots have you missed?"

"Will you give me the tea, then?"

"Yes."

"Honor bright?"

"Yes."

"Ten! Give us the tea."

"Ha! ha! you are looking at Miss Jackson when you should be at the ducks."

The boys took the direction of the palm tree, and we paddled on together, getting up two or three birds. It was a pretty thing to see Lou Jackson shoot. She had a light double-barrelled gun, the same one she had used on the deer-hunt, and when the duck beat up to the level of the tall grass and poised for his flight, she fired with such accuracy that the bird generally fell in a shower of feathers, amid the Doctor's laughter and merry jokes. He did not pretend to shoot unless there were three or four ducks rising together, and then he generally followed their flight, with his gun to his shoulder, until, when a long way off, he would finally say "Too far," and taking his gun down again, give a sigh of relief, and look around for some more game. On reaching the little island we found Mike was there before us, and the negroes had landed the provisions and prepared our simple meal. Yowler sat on the narrow beach, evidently more melancholy than usual at the unaccustomed nature of the sport, and seemed reflecting upon the worthlessness of birds as compared with deer and panthers. Wag ran around the limited extent of land several times without anything but a solitary snipe that went skapeing away, and then returned, to worry Yowler. Jackson soon came in with a couple of score of ducks, and we learned from him that the great body of the winter ducks had not yet come on. There were no geese, and no brant, and he said, what was easily credible, that late in the year a good sportsman could kill four hundred ducks a day.

"But I will tell you what it is, I have seen English snipe flying over, and as we go home we will try some of those low islands outside, and get a dozen."

"Much walking?" suggested the Doctor.

"No; you can shoot from the boat."

"I believe I am somewhat of a shot on English snipe," said the Doctor. "I remember once killing a dozen."

"You didn't have Lou Jackson in the boat with you," I replied.

"No, something a great deal worse—you were with me."

"No, never—not when you killed a dozen English snipe."

"Yes, I shot them all at one shot on the beach."

"Fudge! those were Yellow-legs."

"May be they were, but they were just as good."

"Doctor, try a piece of hot venison steak, or some cold bar?"

"No bear for me; I would be thinking all the time about his ugly teeth when he was shot."

"It is not *his* teeth, but my own, I am afraid of," said Miss Jackson, laughing; "give me some corn-bread, if you please, Mike."

"What are we to do with all these ducks?" said the Doctor; "we can never eat them."

"Yourn?" asked Mike.

A laugh.

"No, ours; those defunct, and those that are to be."

"Never fear, a camp of fourteen people requires something more than Indian corn."

"What are you toasting there before the fire, Mike?"

"Breast of crane."

"Let me try a piece!" asked Lou.

"Sartin; it's better en deer's meat," he replied, handing over a strip on the end of his toasting-stick.

"See de ducks!" exclaimed the negroes, less busy than we with their dinner, as a long train of ducks came floating over, pencilling the clear sky.

"Those are mallards," said Jackson.

"How can you tell so far off, father?"

"By the shape and color, I think; I can hardly tell how. They would be black duck, if they were not lighter in complexion. Am I not right, Mike?"

"Reckon," replied Mike, following the passing cloud with his eye till they faded away, and then continued, musingly: "Some takes kindly to that kind o' larnin'. Some kin tell what kind o' duck is comin' by the sound he makes beatin' the air. Thar was Picardo, Picardo Duck Legs he was called, because he had bow legs. Wall, that man lived in his canoe, and he could tell what a duck was a-goin' to do jist by the waggin' of his tail. He had lived on duck-meat so long he could smell a duck like a pointer dog. Thar's the natur' o' man; when God gives him a callin' he's bound to go it, or be a lazy cuss ever arterwards. Duck Legs was no a'count on shore, but it larnt a man somethin' to paddle a canoe with him."

"Come, boys," said Jackson, lighting his cigar, "it's high noon now, and there are seven miles from here to the open water, and seven more to Bonda Key, and two dozen snipe to kill on the way."

"And some more duck before we leave here," said the Doctor.

"Mind your bearings now, or we will get lost here. There is no palm tree to row back to."

"Take the range of this palm-tree, and sunset; purty good marks, both on 'em," said Mike.

"All aboard!" cries the Doctor. "Push off!" and away we went, or at least the three boats went, leaving Mike watching our departure, smoking away at his cigarette, seemingly as unconscious as his hound that sat beside him.

There were some good shots made, as we returned, at the various bunches of ducks that were hid away in the close coverts of the reeds, Lou Jackson, in particular, firing very exact, although her gun was so light that the game sometimes refused to come down. We were a good deal together, as we were paddling more to return than to get game, and only shot those birds we saw on our way. Once, while paddling fast, a wood-duck drake arose from an open pool, uttering his wheezing cry of "Oh hee!" "Oh hee!" as he stretched away. Lou fired, and at the shot he staggered and sunk for a moment, while a dozen feathers floated away, and then he rose again.

"Stop! stop!" she cried, as I raised my gun to shoot, "I hit him! I hit him!"

But the duck didn't fall, and continued his flight until lost in the distance.

"Oh, what a fool I was! I forgot all about I had another barrel! And why didn't I let you shoot? But I thought, to be sure, he would fall."

"Why didn't you shoot, Doctor?" I asked.

"Oh, I thought he would fall, too."

Sometimes we would come across a floating log surrounded by feathers, and worn smooth by the tread of the wood-ducks that would sit here half the day pluming themselves by the mirror of the water. The hazel-breasted drakes here displayed their Tyrian plumage and elegant shapes to their dove-eyed consorts, and scolded away the little bitterns that alone could compare in beauty to themselves, and who alike with them inhabited these great morasses. We sometimes would suddenly float on one of those happy families, dozing away the sunny hours, and they would arise, when we were close upon them, in the greatest disorder. The ringing of a half dozen shots, the fall of the game, the shout and laugh, would end the scene, and break upon the stillness of the solitude with a burst of fun and activity all the wilder for being so rarely heard in the marshes.

We had almost reached the confine of the open water, when Jackson fired at a black duck flying overhead, and it fell in the water, wing-broken, and immediately dove. He commenced, with the assistance of the Doctor's boat, to look for the game, probing with his paddle the bunches of floating sedge near by, while I, lying a little further off, was watching their search. While thus engaged, I happened to notice under the water a duck swimming toward the surface; it was the wounded duck trying to escape. I saw a bill protruded from the water, the duck in the mean time keeping his head and body completely hidden. I leaned over my boat and caught the nose of the cunning fellow, bringing him above water amid the shouts of the negroes who witnessed the trick.

Being joined by Mike, who had turned aside to get some roots with which to color deer-skins, we all passed through the narrow outlet of the marsh, and turned toward the low islands, where it was said we could find snipe.

"Round that grape-vine point!" called out Jackson, as the headlands we had passed in the morning again opened to our view.

The paddles had been exchanged for oars, and with long, measured strokes, keeping time to the song of the oarsmen, the lithe boats skimmed the water toward the low islands Jackson had indicated to us. On reaching the shore we found the land was marshy and wet, and about half the area overgrown with flags, now blown down by the fall winds.

"Not a bad place; is it?" said Jackson, looking around the island.

"By no means; see these little red-scummed puddles, and bare spots of mud; they'd make a snipe's bill water."

"Escape! escape!" shrieked a snipe, as he sprung into the air a few yards in front of us, tacking from side to side, and settling again on the further side of a little pond.

"There, I told you so! Hold on now till I draw my duck shot. Lou, are you ready?"

"Ready as I will be. I am going to rely on the Doctor."

"I will take a little fine shot, then. I follow your lead, Jackson."

"Mike, are you ready?"

"Yes, I reckon, 'bout, though I don't see nothin' to shoot here."

"You just keep even, and we will see plenty to shoot. Send out your dog, Doctor."

"Hi on, Wag! Hi on!" but Wag seemed to suspect some trick under such unaccustomed attention, and skulked behind his master.

The first step ahead sprung another snipe, and, being intent on the game, I shot it as it balanced.

"Hulloah! give a fellow time," said the Doctor.

"That bird flew right in the way of the shot!" said Mike, his eye kindling, and his mouth expressing a great deal of doubt and curiosity.

"Have you ever killed a snipe, Lou?" said I, the formality of the family name having been gradually dropped, on all sides, as the freedom of our hunting excursions brought us into closer intimacy.

"Yes, two; I never had much opportunity for such game, and never learned to shoot them on the wing."

"Now is your chance, then; there goes a shot."

Two barrels were discharged, one by Jackson, and one by the Doctor, but the birds went off.

"There, I know I can do better than that," remarked Miss Jackson, looking at the bird skimming over the ground.

"I'm sure you kin," said Mike.

"Escape!" "Escape!" "Escape!" croaked out three birds, as they launched away from before us. Miss Jackson fired a double shot, and one bird fell.

"Well done, that!"

"Escape!" croaked another bird, as it rose on our left among some flags. Mike, who had been watching the hunt with great interest, ejaculated, "Wall, I'll take a turn now!" and, aiming with his rifle, fired. The bird fell as if knocked by a ball-bat, and Mike on going up to it said, as he lifted it up by its wings, "Knocked into a grease-spot!"

There was a universal laugh at the quaint figure of the hunter, in his buckskin suit, and the air of derision with which he picked up his fragment of a bird, and held it at arm's length.

"Wall, ef anybody had told me that I would have ever gone a-birdin' with this ere old rifle, I would hev told that body he was a fool!"

Wag seemed to have got somewhat in the mood of hunting around, inspired by our shouts and firing, and ran about hither and yon, springing the birds up before us like a cocking spaniel.

"There!" Lou called out to the Doctor, as the dog got up another bird, "I told you that dog had a great deal of intelligence; this is the very first time, would you believe it, he has ever been hunted over snipe."

"I can certainly credit it," answered Jackson, drily, as he capped his gun.

Away went another snipe, right before the Doctor, who banged away with both barrels, and brought down the bird.

"There, I killed him! Fetch him here, Wag! Fetch, good dog."

Wag ran for the bird, but, instead of bringing him in, picked him up and ran away with might and main, pursued by the Doctor, shouting at the top of his voice, amid peals of laughter. The race was a short one, for the Doctor's figure was not adapted to running, and the island was wet, and full of little quagholes, in one of which the Doctor fell, and was unable to move a single step, and Wag, deliberately lying down on the other side, ate up the prize.

"Oh, Poke, what an invaluable dog!"

"Hold your tongue, will you, and help me out. Throw me a piece of stick to stand on. You, Scip! you lazy negro, bring me an oar. I am all out of breath;" and he polished his face with his handkerchief, as if the true remedy for his misfortune was in active friction.

"Escape! Escape!" said two more snipe, getting up right by the Doctor. Bang! bang! and they both fell at the shot.

"Hold hard there, don't shoot over me that way; just think, I can't dodge!" cried the Doctor, waving his hand energetically toward us.

"That proves your valor in the face of danger. There's Scipio with a log. Now, altogether—that's it! Why, Doctor, you look as though you had high top-boots on!"

"Never mind, it is clean mud," he replied, good-humoredly.

Wag, seeing himself unnoticed, came in to where we were standing. But, alas for his hide! Jackson caught him, and administered to him such a castigation, all the while holding him up by the tail with one hand, while he applied a stick with the other, that Wag retired from the active pursuits of the chase to the more dignified retirement of private life under the seats of one of the canoes, where he disposed of the remains of the dinner-basket before our return.

"Now we are all ready, let us form in a line, and beat down the island regularly," said Jackson, the ardor of the hunt awakening him from much of his listlessness. "Fall in, boys; one of you walk between each of the hunters."

The long, irregular line being formed, it stretched nearly across the island, and we advanced, sinking in the soft mud occasionally, but oftener finding a sandy bottom, with pools of water. The snipe were abundant; we could see them sometimes on the ground in couples, on which occasions the Doctor would always fire with pretty certain success. Most frequently they arose singly, uttering their peculiar harsh cry, and were tumbled over by one or other of the party before they had gone five yards, amid the shouts and guffaws of the negroes. Mike, occasionally, when a bird got up at a little distance, would make "a grease spot" of it with the same shame-faced look as he had when he picked up the first one, apparently doubting if he and his rifle were in respectable business.

Lou shot well, after a little practice, and she trod over the flags, with her eye fixed ahead of her, with that earnestness of look that a person attains never so greatly as when watching for upspringing game that he feels confident he can hit.

"Mark!" called Scipio, as a snipe launched in the air from our feet, the brown and hazel pointings on his back glittering like soldiers' bayonets at the charge. The first spring he makes seems to toss him twenty feet in air, and then a pause, as he collects his wings to strike out on that erratic swinging motion that is his safety and beauty. He eyes the array of pursuers behind him, and hears their strange talking; he sees before him his accustomed haunts and oozy swales, and hears the rustling of the reeds that shelter his mates. In the pride of swiftness, rings out his exulting cry, the same that had made vocal the great morasses of the Coppermine River, where he was nested, and the same by which, through the ghostly night, in the upper air, from front to rear, had kept in rank the long flight of his kindred in their semi-annual migration—" Escape!"

Pang! rings the clear shot, and over falls the wild bird among the sedge.

"Golly! Missa Lou, yah! ha! he dead!" shouted one of the negroes. "Makes dis child piccaninny agin to see his young missus wake 'em up so!" said Big Sam.

"Mark! Mark!" "Escape!" "Escape!" Two more snipe sprung up, followed by two shots, and they fell ahead of us in the grass, and then there arose three or four together. The island seemed to be full of them, and when raised, they would dodge about in long irregular circles, calling up others from the grass, until they collected in whisps above us, and bore away to some adjoining islands.

It was difficult to keep the line regular, for the negroes were full of excitement in picking up wounded birds, and seeing others spring beside them. Indeed, we wanted no dogs, for every bird on the island was raised, and there was so little heavy grass we lost no dead ones. Occasionally we would start one of those heavy grey herons that frequent such marshes, flapping up heavily from the grass, and casting his keen eye back over his shoulder at the intruders; and twice we started that tiny prince of the heron tribe, the smallest and most beautiful of all the genus *Ardea*, called the Least Bittern in the books, but which the people sometimes name the Tiger Bittern, from his brindled coat and wild eye. We shot them both, and Lou, wrapping them carefully in her handkerchief for preserving, stowed them away in one of the pockets of her hunting josey, as she styled a close-buttening canvas jacket she wore when camping out.

At last the point of the island was reached, and while the men were sent back for the boats we sat down on the beach and counted out thirty-six snipe. Taking some willow switches, we ran them through their bills, carefully smoothing down their ruffled plumage and washing off the occasion mud, and made as beautiful six bunches of game as ever delighted a fowler's eye. Even Mike consented to praise, with the reserving clause that we had wasted too much powder and shot on them. How graceful they looked beside the green-headed mallards, and the dusky ducks that were piled knee deep in the boats.

"A glorious day, well spent," said Jackson, as the island on which we had been shooting dwindled in the water, red with the reflection of the sunset, and Bonda Key opened its headland of stately verdure.

"Ay, it is!" responded one and all; and the boats flitted along the glassy waters side by side, the shadows fading and brightening with the glow of the sky, or the twilight of the shore, as one and then the other opened in the west. The hunters stretched their weary limbs in listless attitudes, and their heads swayed to the springing motion imparted by the oar. Miss Jackson sat in the bottom, trailing her hands in the water on either side of the boat, while the oarsmen sang, with deep voices and perfect time, the great old negro boat-song:

> "Gen'ral Jackson mighty man,
> Waugh my kingdom, fire away!
> Fought on sea, and fought on land,
> Waugh my kingdom, fire away!"

CHAPTER XV.

THE SKIN OF THE TIGER-CAT.

"A dragon's tail was flayed to warm
A headless maiden's heart."

A NUMBER of days flew by at our island home in the simple pleasures narrated in our last chapters. The cheering cry of the hounds, as they scoured the islands, the ringing shots in the marshes, now a long exploration in the canoes through the winding channels of the archipelago, and again some expedition to the uttermost keys, where the pelicans, dressed themselves on the sandy points in lines like soldiers, and strange sea-birds, excited our wonder and admiration, were the daily amusements of the party. Once in a while the members of the hunt would branch off, and while one party pursued the chase, another would make an excursion to the main land, or fish in the rivers. The weather had been constantly clear. One cloudless day would follow another with an exhilarating yet motionless air, that seemed as if nature had exhausted her prodigality of production, and then, breathless, had paused to dream.

Once in a while Mike would disappear, and be gone

for a day or a night, but as he never made any remark on what he saw or did, no one seemed to take any note of his incomings or outgoings. One evening, after he had returned from one of these lonely excursions, I was sitting by the willow copse on the shore, casting with my line into the channel after some large fish I had noticed were breaking the water very near the shore. The negroes were getting supper ready, and Lou Jackson came walking down to the beach, where Mike joined her, and they came toward the boats on the other side of the willows, and so near I could hear their conversation.

"Miss Lou, I've been a wantin' to see you."

A pause followed.

"That is, you don't see me every day."

"Yes, oh! yes; but then it aren't every time that a man wants to see. I mean it aren't—I mean sometimes a man wants mighty bad to see some 'un, and talk to 'em, an' sometimes I want to see you more an' others."

"Well!" said Miss Jackson, moving on slowly toward the boat-landing.

"End ef I was the Doctor, I could say anything, and talk right through a board fence; he's oncommon nice at talkin', he is," said Mike, looking earnestly at his partner's face, who looked seaward, but did not reply to this expression of opinion. "Thar's somethin' I want to say, Miss Lou," continued Mike, "end I'd a leetle reether say it to you than to any o' them folks there, for they wunt believe it, they wunt."

" Well, Mike, what is it?"

" Wall, it's this hyur; you'd better get yer father to quit that plantation of his, and move up the country a leetle, or else down to Tampa, fur things ain't all right 'bout hyur."

" What is there wrong?"

"Wall, there's somethin' wrong with them copperhead snakes, the Injins. Yer can't see it yet, but things aint right, and yer all so far away from everybody at the house that no one kin help you. Yer negroes aint worth nothin' of any 'count in case of difficulty, and yer father aint over liked in the swamp. Thar's nothin' wrong yet, and may be won't be at all, but they are jist like painters, and yer don't know where to find 'em."

"Why, what have you seen wrong?" said the young girl, stopping by her boat, and looking at Mike inquiringly.

" Nary a thing, only them fellows have been down here, and I don't like it."

" But they come to the house, why not here? You are harsh in your opinion of them."

" Because they have nothin' to call 'em here. They've been about without showin' themselves, and that's suspicious. They knew we were here, for they can see our trails all about, yet they didn't stop, and they tried to leave no trail themselves, and that's a bad sign. 'Twunt do any good to say so to your father, but you kin make him do what's safe, end so I tell you."

"Thank you, Mike. I believe you know better than

any one about such things, but I do not believe father would leave now, and I can't make him without a stronger reason than you have given."

"Wall, look out; and the time to look out is jist when everything is oncommin pleasant, for that's the blind with these sarpents. Thar's somethin' else I want to say, Miss Lou," continued Mike, after a pause.

Miss Jackson looked at the hunter as though inquiring his wishes. She leaned against the prow of the canoe that was hauled up on the beach, but did not say a word.

"Wall, I was goin' to say that—that—wall, thar haint been many Tiger-cats in Floridy, and ef thar hadn't been *any*, I reckon I would hev got that one fur you, fur you know that ef a man—ef a man likes anybody—as much as"—

Mike here made a long pause. Lou Jackson had gathered up her cloak from the boat that she had apparently come down for, and turning slowly toward the tents, seemed moving away.

"Don't go yet, Miss Lou," said the hunter, beseechingly.

"I am in a great hurry," said the girl; which, if so, was the first time she had been in a hurry since coming to the island.

"Wait one minute," besought Mike, brushing his hand across his forehead; "here's the Tiger-cat skin you once said you wanted," unfolding, as he spoke, from under his hunting-coat, the flowing robe of an animal gracefully patched with yellow and black. "It's tanned as soft as store-goods," he continued; "I shot it this day two weeks, and an Injin woman tanned it for me."

"Thank you, Mike; that is the prettiest skin I ever saw," leaning her face down until it was hidden in the glossy folds of the robe.

"Wall, it is; but I wish it was a heap purtier for you."

Miss Jackson moved on toward the camp slowly, but Mike stood with his hand leaning on the prow of the stranded boat. She had gone a few steps, when, conscious that he was not following, she said:

"Come and see how they will admire it at the camp; that is the greatest trophy of the year!"

"No, it isn't no trophy," said Mike, in an extenuating tone, not moving from his place; "it is the best I had to give you, Lou Jackson. I'd give you anything you'd ask fur." His deep voice quivered as he spoke.

"Thank you, Mike, thank you!" said Lou, turning hastily to the hunter and seizing his hand, "it is everything I want!" and then as hastily dropping it, as though frightened at her own eagerness, she walked rapidly toward the camp, bearing with her the skin, and leaving Mike standing by the boat, with his eyes fixed on her receding figure. His stalwart frame was bent, and with the breech of his rifle he ground a hole in the heavy sand. A dog, one of the wandering curs from the camp, coming to the water's edge, set up a doleful cry near him.

"Shut up, thar, or I'll send a ball after you, and let the bark all out the wrong way!" he said, and tossing his rifle in the hollow of his arm, strode away down the bay. The words that he had been pondering over, it may be for months, had remained all unspoken; the very robe that he had taken, with leagues of walking and weeks of waiting, that he had ornamented with all the taste of the woods, had only procured him a moment's gratitude, and the bold heart that for years had been unmoved by a life of peril, by ceaseless nameless dangers, by night and day, was frightened into hesitation and silence by a young girl.

The sun had gone down, the shadows lengthened on the long sandy reaches; it grew dark almost in a moment. Mike disappeared in the dusk, while from the knoll where the fires were lighted Lou Jackson was watching the way he went.

CHAPTER XVI.

SUPPER.

La découverte d'un mets nouveau fait plus pour le bonheur du genre humain que la découverte d'une étoile.—BRILLAT SAVARIN.

WHO is there, accustomed to American rural scenery, that cannot remember the summons that calls to dinner at the country farm? A stout housewife, when the sundial points to noon, walks out on the lawn, among the inverted milk-pans, where lies the house-dog stretched under the locust trees, and, turning her face toward the harvest-field gives a long, winding blast on the horn that wakes the echoes down the orchard, and over the meadow, and all along the hills, calling the farmers to their noontide meal. The watch-dog howls at the summons, and the workmen by the brook, and in the sultry grain, toss their cradles by and turn homeward, the heavy oxen saunter away in couples, and the horses are unhitched and fastened in the shade by the trough of corn. The farmer, with his stalwart sons, and "the hands," crowd into the kitchen, with their necks bare to the pleasant wind, and the sweat of their labors on their brow. The laugh is light, the words are gentle, for they are confined to the simple subjects of the crops, the weather, and the farm news. The goodwife is at the head of the table, and pours out the tea or milk; the daughters sit among the men, coming and going as occasion requires to bring water, or bread, or pie. Their attire is plain, their manners are simple and frank. Before the old man there sits a huge dish of stew; it is made of potatoes, carrots, chicken, and large squares of boiled fat pork, and he helps it out with no niggard hand, and when he has finished his own portion, he quaffs a huge cup of cider, and leans back in his chair with a great sigh of satisfaction, to wait till his youngest daughter, with brown hair and blue eyes, just opening into womanhood, brings his pie. The brass candle-sticks on the mantle-piece are filled with asparagus boughs, the oaken floor is polished with scrubbing, and the tall clock in the passage-way strikes one as the meal is ended.

There is another dinner scene that may be as often remarked in America, and equally characteristic of another class of eaters. A bell rings, or a jangling gong shocks the ear and benumbs every nerve of the back, while five and forty men rush past the waiter that is beating his brazen drum, and sit down to a large hotel table. There are spread on this table various small articles of food or ornament, such as celery, oranges, and figs, which are immediately seized, and presently every person who has evinced agility congratulates himself on having piled by the side of his plate a selection of these fruits and desserts. Waiters then hand every person a dish of soup, of that consistency that is supposed to be proper to nourish persons in the last **stage of** disease. In a moment after, the **soup dishes** are snatched away, and the guest is informed he can have his selection from any one of almost every kind of beast that walks the earth, or fowl that flies the air, or fish that swims in the water. Being a temperate man, he orders roast beef, and in a moment is supplied with a large slice of overdone, brown roast beef, flooded with a light-colored gravy, a small dish of potatoes is slammed on the table beside him, and a plate of macca-roni. He takes a spoonful of potatoes, but finds them very watery, and filled with darker colored lumps of un-mashed vegetable. He hesitates, and tries the beef; it is tasteless; he tries the maccaroni, and small streams of water run out of the pendent pipes as from a disconnected engine hose. The bread is dry and cut in small oblong pieces. He wonders what there is better cooked, and if he is a stranger, he probably looks at his neighbors to see what they are eating. The upper end of the board is occupied by ladies, that have effected their entrance to the dining-room by some side-door, and they are ar-rayed in all the colors of the rainbow, and the glitter of ornaments, and seem to **be busy** talking loudly and look-ing along **the** table. The long rows of gentlemen are busy, without the interchange **of a** word, eating rapidly of everything **that is** placed before them. While our guest is remarking these things, his plate is taken away by the waiter, **and he** notices the gentlemen are all eating dessert, or leaving the table, having finished their dinner. The waiter asks him what he will have for dessert. He demands to know what there is to have. The answer is given so rapidly, it sounds as follows:

"Ap pi—pi-p—mi pi—ca pi—rat pi!"

The guest gets confused, mildly inquires if they have any fruit.

"Yes, sah. Apple dumpling, sah."

"Very well; I will take an apple dumpling."

"Hard or soft, sah?" referring to the sauce.

"Oh, soft, of course;" referring to the dumpling.

The dumpling is dashed down in front of him, as hard as a cocoa-nut, and flooded in soft sauce, while the waiter disappears down the table, gathering up the plates with a clatter, and the room is deserted by all but the wondering observer, who has not yet acquired the local rapidity of eating.

Once more an American table looms up before me through the mist of hungry years, as I have seen it a thousand times. A low frame-house, with a porch half covered with the trailing arms of morning-glories and columbines, stands on a knoll of a western prairie. That prairie is browsed by deer in thousands, and game birds of the choicest kind feed on it in countless millions. The river winds along the valley, teeming with fish, its banks margined with water-cresses and dock, and shaded with plum-trees and fruit-bearing vines, while from his cabin-door the settler can see a hundred cattle cropping the wild grass.

Noon-time arrives, and the head of the house comes in from the ploughing to his meal, and finds the same food that was spread before him at breakfast, and that he will have for his supper, and has had at all his meals for a month past, so he should love it well. It consists of tea, Indian corn bread, and fried pork. The pork is cut in small slices, and fried until quite brown, and the bread is sopped in the gravy. There is no attempt at grace of service to make amends for the rude cookery, no white cloth to hide the table, no dainty pat of butter on a grape leaf, such as tempts the eyes as well as the palate in the Tyrolean châlet; but it is the plain simple medicine to cure a hungry stomach, administered without any sweetening.

The refinement of a family is nowhere so quickly seen as at a table, and nowhere do men's sensual selfish instincts become more prominent. There is the centre of the family after the day's wandering, there its first meeting after a night of forgetfulness; there we give hospitality to the stranger, there the tongue is loosened, the wandering thoughts called back, and the heart is warmed into expression by generous wine. The feasts of Lucullus were celebrated for their wit, according to the fashion of the day, and the simple suppers at the Mermaid were the signals for the intellectual tournament of England's greatest minds. "He has eaten with me," is the Arab's talisman to protection, and the Christian has made a supper the emblem of his religion. Then what constitutes a supper, even the simple half of a meal, being the food and its preparation, apart from its physiological bearings, is worthy of thoughtful study.

"As to that other half of a dinner, the people that are to sit around it, they being chosen only on festive occasions, to them I do not allude. Equally important to a man's physical being, as to his moral health, is the character of his food. It may be insufficiently cooked, crude, and indigestible; it may be overdone, sodden and heavy; it may be dried to a chip, until the nutritive juices are evaporated, or it may be fried to an oily mass that requires the strongest stomach to analyze. Then, again, the food that was originally ample and rich may be so wasted by the culinary process, that what was once abundant is prodigally reduced. One or the other of these faults universally affects nearly every dish that is placed on the American tables. To avoid such evils, and cook sufficiently without wasting, and in the most economical quantities, is a high art of life, and one of the simplest and most overlooked. It is slighted by the intelligent, and left in the hands of the ignorant, and those whose duty it was to govern are punished in health and property for their own neglect. Almost every one can remember having eaten of simple meals that were as good as any king's; sometimes they were found at a private table, where white hands, that were dear to him, have spread the cloth; sometimes they have been served in some out of-the-way Gallic auberge, when the hungry traveller was even doubting if in a place so destitute he could find anything to eat; and again it may be, they have been spread in that chief of all hostelries, that reckless home of self-reliance, the camp beneath the greenwood tree. Oh, dear beyond all *cafés*, and green when Verey's shall be forgotten, is that spreading **blanket-cloth, those bark platters, and flashing fires,** by which so many meals have been cooked and heartily eaten. Don't **laugh, Epicurean, who reads these lines in** a big city, **where for years** fancy cooks have manufactured spiced dinners at Midas prices, and **do not** say **it was only** the **appetite,** and not the dinner, that was marvellously good. Though it is easy to cook when **you** have skillet and spider, bake oven and basting spoon, griddle, pan, sauce-**dish, pot, skewers, rotary jacks,** earthen dishes, and a **double acting patent** kitchen range, yet still there are **more good meals cooked in this** world without them **than with them, and** this reminds me of the last dinner we had at our camp on Bonda Key.

There had been **a long** hunt that had lasted from daybreak till almost sunset, and we were tired and hungry, and a certain feeling of approaching separation had come over us that made exertion necessary, and so we **went to work** with a will to cook a good **meal. It is true, our** utensils for cooking were few and simple; **they** consisted **of one iron** kettle, **one tin coffee pot, and** a dozen tin **cups—a small** *batterie de cuisine* for a legitimate cook, **but they were** ample for us. The fire had been burning for a week, and thus there were plenty of hard coals. The material consisted of some Indian meal, bear's meat, venison, wild ducks, wild turkey, red-fish, turtle eggs, and **snipe.** The cooks were Mike, the Doctor, Lou Jackson, and myself; the scullions were all the negroes of the island.

"Poke, you attend to the birds, will you?" I said, handing over a bunch of snipe that Rose had just picked as clean as apples, and that were all nicely drawn, and had their bills stuck in their breasts as though trying to plume their lost feathers.

"No *sir*," replied the Doctor, emphatically; "*any* body can cook snipe, *I* am going to attend to the side dishes—*les entremets, vol-au-vents*, and the *pâtés.*"

"Nonsense! there are no side dishes, and plenty of substantial food that can be roasted," interposed Jackson.

"Yes, yes, Doctor, give us an *entremet*.

> 'Of candied apple, quince, and plum, and gourd,
> With jellies smoother than the creamy curd,
> And lucid syrups tinct with cinnamon.'"

"Wait awhile," said the Doctor; "I will show you a dish that will make you forget poetry."

As he selected a couple of flat stones, and commenced pounding up some biscuit that were so hard they had been declined by all the party since the commencement of the hunt.

"You, Sam, bring me a fork," said Jackson, as he approached the fire with a square of the loin of bear's meat, nicely cut for roasting. The fork was produced, which was a stout branch of green wood, and carefully pushed into the sand at such an inclination that the meat would be between the fire and the wood; the roasting piece was carefully impaled thereon, and in a little while was hissing away before the heat as musically as if **in a Dutch oven.**

Mike had, in the meanwhile, plucked a pair of young black ducks, fastening their wings to their bodies with **little sassafras skewers so they should not** get burned, and tying them by their legs to long strings, hung them near the fire on high sticks. **They looked like bales of** cotton, or like horses when they are suspended **by tackles** to be hoisted on shipboard. **The** strings being then tightly twisted, gave a rotary motion to the birds that **presented every** side equally to the **fire, and** prevented **them from burning.** A few fragrant leaves, and a dozen **oysters being** stuffed in each **one,** answered **in** the place of dressing.

Lou Jackson prepared the corn-bread as only a South-woman can, and it was laid on a flat stone that had been carefully selected, and had served for this purpose for several previous dinners, and it would have been a pleasant amusement to see the white dough gradually becoming mahogany brown before the fire, had we not each been busy with the more delicate **duties** of the **kitchen.**

I made the boys cut some long wooden skewers, and Rose, **having** cut a deer's liver in small square pieces, an inch in diameter, we impaled a half dozen of these little cubes on each skewer, and stuck them up before the fire at a safe distance from the coals. A piece of bear's fat of the same size as the piece of liver was stuck on the top of each skewer, so that as the heat of the fire gradually melted it, the liver was basted by the dropping fat, without any further attention being needed. Next a redfish, with its scales left on, but carefully drawn, and wiped dry, was rolled in green leaves, and buried deep in the hot ashes.

Poke, by this time, had completed his ship-biscuit powder, and been to the beach with Pompey Duffield Sah, from whence he returned with two large bivalve shells, resembling gigantic clam-shells, which had been left by the waves on the beach, which he carefully washed, and greased with bear's fat, and then sprinkled with his ship-biscuit powder.

"That a poultice you are going to have there, Doctor?" said Jackson.

"No, gruel," I suggested. Poke maintained a scornful silence, continuing his labor and making another trip to the beach with Pompey, from which they came with the tin pan full of oysters, which he proceeded to divide equally among his four half shells. When the shells were full, he sifted the balance of his ship-biscuit over them, and placed them in front of the fire.

"Scolloped oysters, by the moustache of Soyer! Doctor, you're a genius," said Jackson.

Lou Jackson made the coffee by boiling the water in the tin coffee-pot, and then tying up a sufficient quantity of ground coffee in a canvas bag, placed the bag in the pot which was kept simmering over the coals. Mike had cut several slices of venison, and laying them across two iron ramrods as a substitute for a gridiron, was carefully watching them cook, from time to time giving the ducks a twist, that made them revolve on their gallows like martyrs suffering two of the extreme penalties of the law at one time. Jackson set up the snipe as sentinels around one side of the fire, and the iron pot was hung over the coals, and in it was placed bits of bears' meat and venison, the breast of cranes, pieces of ship-biscuit, and all the little odds and ends of game, which, being fit for nothing else, seem especially intended for making a stew. To this was added a wild pepper or two, and some green leaves and roots that the negroes had gathered, and every time the water bubbled a savory smell issued forth that made one entertain a more lenient opinion of Esau, in spite of the thousands of years of misjudgment that have been visited upon him. And lastly, as a crowning honor to the meal, a pumpkin was produced; a real golden pumpkin, with its honest ochre face wrinkled into lines of swelling rotundity, and suggesting the rows of rustling corn, among which it had obtained its plethoric shape. The boys had brought it from the plantation in the boat, and though some might say "there is an article that will bother these improvising cooks," it was hailed with exclamations of delight and welcome. A plug was cut in its upper side, where the stalk joined the fruit, and when the piece was taken out it formed a cover to the interior cavity, to which the short stalk answered for a handle. The seeds were carefully removed from the interior, and in their place was poured as much heavy brown sugar as would fill the cavity, when the cover was restored to its place, and the emblem of plenty was seated in front of the coals, where his jocund face reflected the bright flames, and the simmering viands that were cooking beside him with a pleasant glow, like that which shines on the countenance of an old patriarch, when down the Christmas table peer the bright eyes of long lines of merry grand-children. The turkey-hen had been in the meanwhile transfixed on a stake, with its maw crammed with chestnuts, and was clucking out its despite against its warm roost, vaporing out its savory humors, while Rose was squatted behind it, screening her face from the fire with one hand and basting the bird with the other as the fire blistered its tender skin.

"Now for the omelette!" exclaimed the Doctor, turning away from a long survey of the various articles of food that girdled the fire; "bring me the eggs, Sam."

Sam approached with a grin on his face, and his hat full of soft shell turtle eggs that had been procured from the sand.

"You'd better roast them in the hot sand instead of trying to make omelette," I suggested.

"Or boil them in the stew," said Jackson.

"No, gentlemen, an omelette soufflée I have decided upon. If you want some in the stew I can spare you six; they will be as hard as bullets by the time the stew is done; but I must have an omelette; I am really suffering for an omelette; and he began breaking open the little round eggs in **one of the tin** cups, singing all the while, with a merry tone—

"Who can help loving the land that has taught **us**
Six hundred and eighty-five ways to cook eggs."

When they were all broken he set one of the men at work to beat them up with a bundle of switches, and turned his attention to tasting the stew, that was being seasoned from **the contents of the mess-box,** and tasted by all the persons who expected to eat therefrom. Each one gave his opinion, **and each one** was finally satisfied; the Doctor **threw in six turtle eggs** for my satisfaction, and allowed **an additional pod of red** pepper for Jackson's decided taste for spices, while a fox squirrel, that is a dry kind of **gymnast for cooking** alone, was quartered, and thrown in to complete the mess.

"Round about the caldron go,
In the poison'd entrails throw;
Double, double, toil and trouble,"

began the Doctor in a declaiming voice.

"Hold your tongue, destroyer **of** appetites!" called out **Lou** Jackson; "don't mix bad ideas with the stew; **that is worse** than putting in tough meat."

"Poetry, ma'am, is never out of place," answered the Doctor, gesticulating with the forked stick with which he was stirring the stew. "Poetry is salt to life's omelette; poetry is the poor man's gold—the coffee to a dinner. —You Sam, twist the ducks; don't you **see** they've stopped?—Poetry ma'm, is suggestive of dinner and dinner of poetry, for

> "When the oldest cask is opened,
>   And the brightest lamp is lit,
> When the chestnuts glow in the embers,
>   And the kid turns on the spit;
> Then then the story is told,
>   And the rhyme so bold"——

"Doctor, your pâtés are burning."

"Dear me, what a miserable operation! You Sam, why didn't you see that coal snap?"

"Didn't like fur to stop maussa's speech."

"Ha! ha!" laughed Jackson, "you had better get the plates ready, Scip; where are the plates?"

"All here, sah," said Scipio, bringing in a dozen or more pieces of white birch bark neatly rounded and smoothed with the knife; and behind him came Cæsar with the tin cups all brightly scoured. Some of the men had reared a wooden table when we first came to the island; this unusual luxury for a camp was elevated about two feet from the ground, and formed a convenient centre for the family that sat around on the sand where fancy dictated. The plates were arranged on the table, one to each guest, and a pile in store for other courses, for it was a thing unknown in this camp of plenty to use a plate the second time.

"Turn the pumpkin, some one; don't you see it browning."

The Doctor paused while measuring a handful of sugar for his omelette to see the cooking progress. Rose basted the turkey, ejaculating from time to time, "Gi, he hot." Mike sat like a Turk on his crossed legs, gradually withdrawing the venison steak from the heat, and Jackson, who never gave himself much concern about the dinners, stood overlooking the coffee-pot. It was a pleasant dinner in cooking, and when it was announced by universal acclaim that it was done, we all felt that we had earned our appetites.

First came out the fish from his hot bed, a black steaming mass, that bore more resemblance to a sacred crocodile embalmed in the pyramids than to an article of food; but as one by one the wrappings of wet rags and leaves were removed, bringing with them the skin and scales, and his fishiness was gently rolled over on a piece of clean hollow birch bark and placed on the table, white, flaky, and steaming hot, a universal ha! from the convives heralded the success of our first course. To **talk of boiled fish,** where half of the peculiar **flavor of a trout is left in** the water, or *sole au gratin* that is smothered in sauce and mushrooms, is a mark of gratitude for past enjoyments and the dinners we have eaten at Mackinaw or at Magny's, but if the nostril has ever inhaled the pure steam, the condensed just liberated essence of a cold water fish, baked in the ashes, or the tongue ever moistened under the first pure morsel that entered the mouth, he will forget those artificial combinations that have hitherto deceived him, and believe only in the simplest cooking as the best. The fish was soon disposed of, and Mike handed over his venison steak, hot and rare, just cooked enough to make it tender.

"Ah! Mike, you rascal, it's not the cooking that makes that venison so tender; you have had the selection of the whole deer," said Jackson.

"Would you have me take the heels?" asked Mike, sarcastically.

And thereupon there arose a great discussion between them as to the safest cut from a deer, as Jackson had some of the old yeoman's ideas of venery, and Mike was in no wise a stranger to this, one of the most considered arts of woodcraft.

"Hi, dogs!" called Lou, as the hounds crowded around her for the scraps of venison that we had not eaten, and licked the hand that fed them. "Down, Jip! back, Boz! back Lady! Bring the turkey, Rose."

"And the bar," said Mike, tossing his wooden platter into the fire and taking another.

"And the oysters," said the Doctor.

"And some corn bread," said another.

"Ho! for a boar's head and a flagon of wine, and we would make a royal carouse!" cried Jackson.

"Were we kings, we would not have hunter's appetites," said I.

"And might have the gout," intimated the Doctor.

The turkey was placed on the table, flanked by the piece of bear's meat, and between them the oysters, and my brochets of liver. The corn-bread, brown and smoking, was broken up and piled on the board. And, finally, the tin pan, the only tin pan in the company, was half filled with the savory stew, and put under the Doctor's nose, to his evident satisfaction, and his face broadened in spite of himself, as the delicate fragrance of venison, eggs, bird, and bear's fat, mingled with chestnuts and savory herbs, ascended to his nostrils.

Hunting-knives were applied with vigor, and, after a short interval of busy silence, there was nothing left on the board but a portion of Bruin's carcass, the stew, and one half of the turkey-hen, and these would have stood but little chance, had not there been the remembrance of the ducks and snipe that were still by the fire, not cooking, but just smiling, as the Doctor expressed it. The stew had been pronounced good, but not as good as it will be to-morrow morning, for a stew is like wine, and improves by keeping, and a gentle cooking, oft repeated, makes it more grateful still.

"Now, Doctor, I think the time has come for the game," said I; "don't you?"

"I do. Let the game be served," said he, with a wave of his hand.

"You will have to serve it yourself, then," replied Lou. "Rose is eating among the men; just hear them laugh!"

The loud, clear notes of the other party sounded from the farther side of the fire, where they were discoursing huge pieces of venison and bear's meat with a series of cachinnations that resembled the morning rejoicings of a gang of turkeys.

"You Rose! the coffee!" shouted Lou; but the girl did not hear, and Lou had to bring the coffee herself, with the Doctor and Mike bearing the ducks and the snipe. The birds were laid out in state on bark platters, and the coffee, after first removing the bag of grounds, was carefully poured out in equal portions, in the five tin cups that ornamented the table.

Now, there are various kinds of wild ducks, and without referring one to the natural histories, under the head of *Aves*, the reader to count the varieties need only to recall to his recollection the various sensations received from eating them. Sometimes they have been tough— leathery tough, these were the Old-wives; it is generally only the young wives that buy them; others there are that taste like mackerel, these are the fishy ducks; others that are dry, like corned beef, these are Pharoah's lean kine; others again that are just duck, and nothing more, you would hardly suspect them, under their stuffing of acrid sage and rancid onion, to be duck—if you saw their feet, you might be positive; these were the common wild duck, peppered with shot, jammed in crates, putrefied by time, and bought by hotel-keepers and noodles; when cooked, they are anything you choose to name them.

Another kind of duck, like those the Doctor was putting on the table, is a young, fat wild duck, either a Wood-duck, Teal, or Black-duck, and, as such, is peer to any game that ever feasted a hunter. It was nested in a tussock of grass, on some of the sedgy shores of the great northern rivers, and there it lived on seed and succulent grasses, and when it made its first migration southward, it stopped at the wild rice fields that fringe the shores of the big lakes, at Sodus, on Sandusky Bay, the Thousand Islands, or the morasses of the Calumet River, in Indiana, and then for a day or so at the celery beds of the Chesapeake and Delaware, and then on the rice-fields of the Carolina or Georgia planter. It is so conditioned that its breast is flat, and its back is white with underlying fat, and by the color of its feet you can say it is its first winter out. Treat such a duck gently, cook him as you would roast an apple, and with no more sauce, and when he is done, not crisped like a roast pig, but gently done, bear him away from the fire tenderly as you would a baby, carry him lovingly as the Doctor carried the two that we had cooked, and flank him with nothing discordant and gross, but with some game bird, and nothing better than an English snipe, and then thank the Lord who giveth us our meat in due season, for never since man had dominion over the fowls of the air has there been cooked a daintier dish.

Two ducks and five snipe would probably be to five persons the same inconvenient animal that a goose is said to be to one—too much for that one, and not enough for two; but then when the day has been spent in hunting in the open air, it is another matter—so we pronounced the ducks the best ever killed in Florida, and ate them all.

"But what of the omelette?" I hear you ask.

Oh! ah! yes. The omelette was not what was properly expected of a dish prepared with such flaming announcement; either from receiving too much sugar, or from some want of lightness on the part of the parent turtle, or from some dissipating effect of just a few drops of brandy, to give it an essence, that the head cook confessed to have put in it, or from some other unexplained reason, the omelette never soufléd, but remained perversely dense; it might better have been called an *omelette au plomb*. Lou Jackson suggested that the heat had so far generated the young turtles that their shells made it tough. Others insinuated that the brandy appropriated for the omelette had been perverted from its use by the Doctor, and therefore the omelette grew downhearted. But it was no great loss, after all. We concluded we had eaten enough without it, and gave it up with a sly laugh at the Doctor.

As the dinner progressed it had become dark, and now only the blazing fire lighted the foliage and the rippling beach, and only the faint call of the raccoon in the woods answered the heron and the duck in the marsh, and gradually we sank down to our usual places, talking in a low tone, and casting remarks back into memory, and away into the future, now telling a tale, now half singing a song, until we dropped asleep.

"But what of the pumpkin?" I hear you ask.

Oh! that we kept for the next day.

CHAPTER XVII

HOME AGAIN.

> "Be thy intent wicked or charitable,
> Thou comest in such a questionable shape
> That I will speak to thee."
> HAMLET.

If the reader will leave for a short time his hunting acquaintances of the Key, and visit another contemporary camp, he can see, in fancy's eye, one of the chief men that, at the date of our story, controlled the destiny of the Floridas.

Halleck Tustenuggee was a Mickasukie chief of much repute, as well for his bravery and endurance as for his complete knowledge of the resources of his native land, his eloquence and his cunning in all the wiles of Indian diplomacy. Being born of the Mickasukies, the original owners of the soil, and being related by marriage to the principal men of the tribe, he possessed a wide influence that was sustained by his strength and manliness of person. Gaily colored quills were plaited in the long black hair that fell from the crown of the head, and his costume was more uniform than that of the savages of the northern tribes, and resembled the hunting-shirt of the frontier hunter. He was six feet two inches in height, and slightly made, with a sullen, stolid face, that seemed in repose to be without intelligence, but which brightened into intensity when animated. Halleck Tustenuggee's favorite camp was located on the upper waters of the Ouithlacouchee River, on a live-oak island that reared itself the only stable land amid leagues of morass. Here were erected neatly thatched cabins, and store-houses of food and ammunition, and here, guarded by the solitude, the quicksand, the tortuous lagoons, and the scaly reptiles of the swamp, were always to be found a merry company of little swarthy imps that played in the grass, and sober women that sat all the while with their blankets wrapped around them, as still as the dead monks in the Piazza Borgonona.

No white man, it might be said without a word of exaggeration, had ever seen this island; therefore, a perfect description cannot reasonably be required, and any criticism on the description, as given, will lack proof to make it effective. The buzzard alone, from his slow circles in the zenith, had marked the camp smoke, under the long-hanging moss. Only the panther, from the labyrinth of the magnolias, or the alligator under the fallen trees, heard the children's laugh, or the squaw's song to her swart pappoose. So the stores of maize and powder were never burned by the enemy, and the dried and wrinkled scalps that hung to the tent-poles, some by their silken tresses and some by their short grey curls, continued to smoke and dry in the fire-light and the sunshine, unreclaimed and unavenged.

To explain the unconquerable aversion that has always existed between the white man and the Indian on the North American continent, needs the description of many aggressions and revenges that each has inflicted on the most susceptible feelings of the other. The white man has colonized the land of the savage by suffrance, and then by reason of the necessity of his position, kept them by force. By superior foresight he has bought their peltry at trivial prices. He has imported infectious diseases, has corrupted with alcoholic drinks, has cut down preserves of game, has amassed wealth, and power, and space, while his simpler-minded neighbor has been stunted under his shadow. All this happens even when the relations of the two races are amicable, and treaties are observed with fidelity, and the aborigine knows that, as the white man prospers he must decrease—that the white man's life is the red man's death. But the outward peace in a little while disappears. Some settlers' cattle have disappeared from the woods, and the Indian is charged with the theft; the charge is probably true. Some brave, in visiting the settlement, has been intoxicated, and killed or maimed a white man, who has insulted him. The law claims a compensation. The law is made by the white man, who regards the Indian with contempt and dislike, and the compensation is graded by his judgment, and not by the meagre wealth of the Indian. Retaliation follows the distraining; a foray avenges the retaliation; then a burning village and the scalping-knife brightens the night, and brings on a campaign that for years converts the border into a debatable ground, like the Valley of the Shadow of Death. The white settler, at a distance from relief, and guarding his cabin only by force of arms, regards the sullen, wary, crouching foe with a bitter hatred that he bestows on no other enemy, and his hatred is handed from father to child, and perpetuated by tradition and song, and many a vacant place by the fireside. The chieftain looks back over a life of battles that were always disastrous to him, and that has left his tribe a handful of broken men, and recalls the peace that was more injurious than war, the worthless bargains, hollow promises, poisonous gifts, discordant counsels, mock ceremonies, and cloaked hatred.

Little wonder is it, then, that when some chiefs of shrewder foresight than others come to power among the Indian tribes, they form combinations, recount their wrongs, and, urged on by the national enthusiasm, make one bitter burst for revenge and immortality! Such a chief was Halleck Tustenuggee, and such was the history of his people; and the settlers on the Gulf and the verdant bottoms of the Suwanee remember his last charge, so unexpected and so bloody, as the fishermen of the Mexican Gulf remember the tornadoes that come out from the south in the middle of the summer afternoon, and go wailing and wrecking all that was basking in the tropical stillness.

Tustenuggee had consulted with all the divisions of the Seminoles. Runners had come and gone, some in canoes and some on foot, to all the different outlying parties.

The women had been removed to the recesses of the swamps, extra quantities of lead and powder had been purchased, a census had been made of all the white inhabitants residing on the debatable land, and the forces had been appointed so many braves to each department; at the same time, no change in the demeanor of the red men marked their determination; they came and went the same as before, and bartered and hunted without a word of mistrust or dislike. The very day had been fixed, and the hour; and that night, while the laugh was so loud by the camp-fire at Bonda Key, and while soothed by the murmurs of the sea, we passed away to the land of dreams, the red eye of Indian warfare was on us all the while, and we knew it not. While we were cooking and eating our meal, and when we laid down to sleep, a tawny figure was turning its basilisk face toward us from a clump of thickly clustered trees that grew some fifty yards from our tents. It could not be seen in the shadows, and the land breeze that blew from us to it prevented the dogs smelling it, and giving indications of its presence. No motion attested weariness, no sound betokened its cat-like arrival. It was the skeleton at the feast.

As the morning warmed the east, the figure melted away with the wan colors of the sky, and when Mike left the camp to loiter around, for his usual morning walk, he found the dew disturbed on the grass, and following the slight trail, he carried it to the edge of a bayou, where he noticed the rushes were divided as though they had been bent by some body passing through. As he watched them carefully they still arose, closing more and more of the opening, and regaining their erect position, showing that whatever had disturbed them, had but just departed. The hunter surveyed the whole bay and the opening bayous with a careful eye, and then followed back the trail to the clump of trees where the scout had spent the night, and examined the place carefully. He then made several casts around the camp, each one of greater circuit, examining as he went every indication of the presence, during the night, of any other person, and finally returned with his measured tread, and took his accustomed place by the fire.

From the survey he had made, he knew there was but one Indian on the island; he knew by the track, the new footmarks overlapping old ones, that the Indian had come and gone in the same direction. He knew that he was there to watch the hunting party, and for no other reason; and by the matted grass in the thorn bushes he knew that he had passed the most of the night in the same place. It was no straggler, for he had an object; no hunter, for he was without dog or comrade. Whatever Mike's reflections were, he kept them secret, and smiled at Lou's jests and chatted as quietly with the Doctor, while he superintended the loading of the boats for the return trip, as though he had not left the camp.

The tents were struck and packed, our few skins and trophies were stowed away in the canoes, and when we had finished a hearty breakfast, and Rose had cooked sufficient venison and corn-bread to answer for our dinner, we embarked and started once again for Far Away.

Mike had given directions at starting as to the course we were to take, and himself led the way. This was not the same route we had taken in coming, but deflected very much to the southward. Soon the island on which we had passed so many pleasant days, was blue in the distance, and I envied the pelicans that were sitting on its sandy point, careless denizens of a happy land, to whom time brought no necessity for change, and who only migrated at their pleasure; until a headland of water-oaks shut out my isola-bella, and the boats wound in among a group of islands that hid us from any view but those of the shores that immediately surrounded us. Mike's canoe, that led the way, paused for a moment, and as we rode abreast he spoke to Jackson, who was with his daughter and the Doctor, and asked them to row on slowly with the other boats through the channel that opened ahead, and await his coming in the first broad piece of water they came to. The boats all passed on, but Mike, who was paddling alone with Scipio, immediately turned back and ran ashore on the low island that had shut out our view of Bonda Key. Landing on the beach, he bade Scipio wait, while he crossed over the narrow point of the island, and standing among the heavy moss that reached down from the trees, narrowly scanned the open water beyond. Bonda Key exposed its full length of blue; beyond were other lesser sandy keys blinking in the sunshine; nearer, the low tangled islands upreared their winter verdure, save when the magnolias or pines interpersed their green domes, or the gaudy creepers blotched them with scarlet. Long flocks of ducks crept along the horizon, or swam in nearer clumps; but it was for none of these the hunter was watching. At length from behind an island, that had momentarily hid the view, a canoe, impelled by a single paddler, glided over the water, apparently making for the place where the hunter stood. Mike returned to his canoe, and paddled to the point of the island where an old tree, undermined by the water, had fallen over with its load of vines and moss, and then pulled his boat under its shelter until it was completely invisible from any spot but the water in front. The canoe that was approaching from beyond soon reached the end of the island, on the side opposite to the one where Mike was concealed, and a young Seminole stepped to the shore, and crouching on one knee, cautiously peered around the point. A moment's survey satisfied him, and returning to his canoe he paddled on as rapidly as before, and turning the point of the island continued his course down the channel where our boats had passed, and where Mike lay concealed. He was dressed in buckskin breeches and moccasins; a belt supported a heavy hunting knife, while the upper part of his body was completely naked. His head was bare, and a daub of scarlet paint ornamented each cheek and either breast. His blanket lay beside him, and with his eye fixed on the winding channel ahead, he was paddling rapidly past, when Mike, with a muscular push against the overhanging tree, shot out into the lagoon so far that the two canoes floated almost side by side. In spite of his training and his stoic blood, the Indian was startled, evincing his surprise by a quick motion and an aspirated ejaculation, as his hand involuntarily laid hold of his gun. Scipio was paddling the canoe, and Mike's rifle was lying across his knee, while with an appearance of most simple assurance, the hunter said:

"Good morning, brother, were you looking for me?"

"No—yes"—replied the Indian, too much taken by surprise to collect his thoughts immediately; "I saw canoes ahead, and I like company."

"My brother been to the Keys hunting?" continued Mike.

The Indian answered by a nod of assent, a gesture that he hoped the hunter would believe.

"And is now going up the river again?"

"Yes," replied the Indian, willing to favor the first supposition.

"Then we go together," said Mike, propelling his canoe a little forward in the direction the Indian was going.

"Yes, but I am tired with much rowing, I will not keep you back," answered the savage, evasively.

The boats now lay side by side, and Mike, with his rifle in his hand, deliberately stepped from his own canoe to that of the savage, saying, as he did so, " Ingin Mike will help his brother paddle his boat if he is tired."

A keen glance and an impatient look proclaimed how much the Seminole was averse to this polite offer. His eye roved around the bayou as though expecting some treachery, and then rested on Scipio's face and his musket that lay beside him. There seemed to be no help for him, and if he had any suspicion as to Mike's intentions, he could not confirm them from anything he saw in the sun-browned face that confronted him. His hand left his gun, and the ill-assorted couple commenced paddling down the lagoon, while Scipio followed behind, his white teeth glistening as he laughed at intervals a low laugh, with a chorus of words and pectoral chuckles.

The surprise of our party was most unqualified as the strange boat paddled out from the winding lagoon to the open water, and took its place in the rear of the little squadron. The negroes eyes opened with a language of ejaculation that was louder than words, and Jackson eyed it as a mallard drake would stare at a cormorant who should dare to sail in among his brood. Nothing, however, was said of our visitor, though from front to rear were passed many covert jokes at his expense. We kept on our course industriously, and by noon were all in the mouth of the river, and stopped for our lunch and a little rest on an island, the smallest of a group of three, that lay side by side. Jackson wanted to stop at a larger island that we had just passed, but

Mike said that a little island, with good company, was better than a large one with bad company, and so we complied with his wishes, though not knowing what he meant.

The important feature in our lunch was the pumpkin that had been cooking all the previous night, and that had been carefully carried in Jackson's canoe. As Rose brought it up from the boat on her head, the Doctor smiled, I laughed, and Lou looked eagerly forward, as a child looks at an unopened Christmas box.

"Take off the cover of Pandora's Box, Lou," said the Doctor.

"It won't come off, it's glued fast," said Lou, tugging at the stem.

"Give me a chance," said Jackson, aiming a blow at it with his hunting-knife, which did not produce any impression on the shining surface.

At length by the aid of a hatchet, it was split open, and the interior revealed itself to our admiring eyes. The pumpkin had baked soft, and imbibed the sugar melted by the heat, and candied in irregular shapes, like the interior of a crystallized rock hung with brilliants. The steam was pendent from the sides in drops, and a breath of sweets exhaled when opened that carried one's mind back to the dinner-basket of childhood, and as each one of the party possessed himself of a piece, and sat munching away, we must have looked like so many monkeys regaling themselves in a melon patch. I became poetical and repeated Whittier's lines.

"Oh fruit of loved boyhood! the old days recalling
  When wood grapes were purpling, and brown nuts were falling,
 When wild ugly faces we carved in its skin
  Glaring out through the dark, with a candle within."

Jackson became disgusted with the rhyming.

An hour's rest and we were again on our course, Mike all the while in the Indian's canoe, and leading the van. The wild fowl were numerous along the river, though we did not stop to shoot, partly because we were loaded with game and partly because Mike had requested us not, though he would give no reason, briefly saying, in reply to our questions, "It's a leetle better to travel fast and hunt slow than it is to travel slow and hunt fast." Large flocks of ducks were all the while being driven ahead of the boats, flying short distances each time they got up. Flamingoes and cormorants were winding from point to point, and knee-deep in the tide great blue herons waded, and snow-white cranes dressed their plumage. As vista after vista opened around the bends of the river, or up the lateral lagoons, new forms and colors opened to the eye. There the stately cypress trees stood in the water, like the pillars of a rustic Venice, and the mound-like cones their roots threw up extended all across the basin; while above, the swinging vine had caught its tendrils in the opposite tree, and thus back and forth festooned a royal *porte-cochère* to nature's mansion. On the other side, a fallen tree shut in an open passage and formed foothold for brier and creeper, and vines that aspired to the highest pinnacles of the forest and bowed the trees with their passionate embrace. The lunge of the alligator, the cry of the bittern as he rose from the reeds, the scream of the fish-hawk, circling in the air, and chasing the tern, seemed fitting music for so strange a scene, and soothed and interested the mind, while the low song the oarsmen sung did not disturb the wild inhabitants of the air, or mar the unity of the scene.

The river grew familiar, and Lou Jackson recognized remembered trees and openings, and soon we saw ahead of us the bluff that marked the landing at Far Away, and then the logs that formed the rustic wharf, and then the seat under the oaks, and then we landed once again on familiar ground; and leaving the boys to "tote the plunder," wound our way up the hill toward the house, Jackson taking the lead. The young Indian seemed to have made up his mind to accompany us, if not pleasantly, at least without any manifest reluctance, though I noticed Mike was always by his side.

As we mounted the hill I looked for the flock of sheep that usually fed on the bluff, but they were not there, though in a moment we passed one of the wethers dead by the side of the path. Before I could remark upon this, I heard a cry ahead from Jackson, and hastening forward we saw the cabin was not there, but a pile of of ashes that was drifting hither and yon by the wind, and a column of smoke, that ascended from the ruins, marked the place where it stood. The sheds were burned, and the sheep pen. The little kitchen, where so many pleasant dinners had been cooked, was gone.

There was no voice or sound, no neigh of horses or bark of dogs, or bleat of sheep. The only living thing there, was a group of buzzards that, heavily gorged, flitted up on the stones that formed the chimney. Looking to where they arose we saw a naked body, half-eaten and scalped. It was Aunty Blase, the old cook. Her eyes were protruding, her bare teeth were grinning at the spectator, and by her peeled skull, we knew who had been the visitors at Far Away.

After the first cry of horror that escaped Jackson's lips he turned around to Mike, and his eyes fell on the Indian prisoner, who had taken advantage of the surprise of the party to glide away among the trees.

"Hound of hell!" shouted Jackson, "I know your work," and he levelled his rifle at the Indian, who was bounding away down the glade. A mocking cry answered the shot, and the spy disappeared in the woods.

"After him!" called Jackson, starting in pursuit.

"Hold thar, hard!" exclaimed Mike, springing after the planter and taking him by the shoulder. "You'll lose your own har in thar and won't git his'n. Besides, I'm of the 'pinion that the sooner we get in fightin' trim, the better for us. Them sarpents has made a clean sweep and thar is nothin' more for 'em to do here; and so I reckon they've gone arter us to the Keys."

Mike spoke earnestly, and Jackson stopped and returned to the rest of the party that by this time had collected together by the ruins. The negroes were moaning and making a noisy lamentation over the remains of Aunty Blase, rocking themselves to and fro, and throwing their hands up and down. The Doctor was examining the wound on the poor old negress with a professional eye. It was the first time he had ever had the opportunity to see this style of dissection, and Lou Jackson sat down on a log and wept as if her heart would break. Aunty Blase had been a friend of many years to her, and had baked the cakes at the feasts that yearly honored her birth, and many a time had slyly cooked favorite dishes for her young mistress. It was no wonder then that Lou felt as though she had lost an aunt in reality, and not merely a dependent.

A short consultation was had. Mike detailed the fact that the young Indian that had accompanied them back had been watching their camp last night, and stated his belief that he was there for the purpose of informing his tribe of our movements and of our return, in order that they might be prepared to surprise us, either at the camp or on our way back; that his unexpected capture had frustrated the plan, or delayed it, and that there was no time to be lost in getting into a more open country, if it should appear, as he suspected, that there was a general rising of the savages along the coast. The reasoning was so correct that it was immediately adopted. A shallow grave, hastily dug, preserved the remains of the old cook from the buzzards, and a short survey and a "hulloo" satisfied us that the few other people that had been left behind had been carried off by the savages, and then with the goods we brought home, we hurried back to the boats, and in a few minutes were speeding down the river. No song of oarsmen now ; no laugh or jest ; it was the hurried exodus from impending fate, "and the boldest held his breath for a time."

Tustenuggee the Mickasukie chief, now commanding a band of the Seminoles, at the time of the return of Jackson's family, was lying with his men in one of the little elevations that raise themselves from the swamps, on the upper shore of the Ouithlacouchee, where he had retired after the sack of the plantation house, to wait for the return of those whose unexpected absence had deprived him of half his revenge. Among the spoils he had carried away from the last night's sacking was a case of spirits that had created a debauch in the savage band, and from the chief to the youngest warrior, they had all succumbed to its influence, and passed the day in alternate riot and stupor. But when the scout who had been sent down the river to watch the hunters, and whose fleetness of foot had saved him from Jackson's vengeance, arrived and told of the return of the party, the chief was immediately aroused, and shaking off his sluggishness, hastened to take such steps as were necessary to secure his prey. Runners were sent out, some to the site of the despoiled house, some to the river, and some to the country lying north of the river, and through which the settler's family would necessarily have to travel, if it sought to escape by land to the upper settlements, that at this time were but sparsely settled, in the direction of Pensacola.

Hardly had the different scouts been sent on their errand before one came hurrying back with the word that the boats were descending the river again, and, like a pack of dogs on a fresh scent, the whole band hurried down to where a point ran out into the river. They leaped from root to root, and crossed the marsh where a hare would have floundered in the mud; they swung themselves, by hanging vines, over deep pools of black water, and their tawny bodies as lithe as the copper-head snakes that slid from the logs they trod on, appeared and disappeared through the tangled woods until they at length reached the point of land around which the boats were sweeping, impelled by four oars each, and keeping well out in the river. Tustenuggee watched the flotilla coming with an eye that would have transfixed a lonely traveller, so much had it grown and brightened by excitement. He knew his prey was escaping, for it would be a long shot to those canoes, and no matter how strong his own force, he would be unwilling to hazard an open attack on sixteen men as accustomed to the rifle as those before him, and one of those Ingin Mike, whose prowess all knew and feared. The Indians were careful not to be seen from the boats, and crouched down behind any cover they could find, hoping that some of the canoes might approach near enough to afford them a shot. But Mike, who led the fugitive fleet, was too wary for that, but inclined the boats away from a point that he was conscious might afford a cover to a foe, and nearer the low timber that, growing in the water, would form but a poor footing for an ambuscade. The negroes bent to their oars, and the boats skimmed fast, making the curve in beautiful order, and had entirely passed the point, when the shrill report of a dozen guns sounded on the stillness of the forest, and the water near the boats was spattered by the bullets. Then followed the tremulous, fierce, prolonged war whoop, and as it died away, Mike's taunting answer, with a gesture of derision, came back. Two or three of the savages had not fired with the rest of the band, but had reserved their shots for a better opportunity. The opportunity came as the last boat, steered by Jackson himself, swept down with the tide. He had seen the futility of the preceding discharge, and regarding the boats as entirely out of range of the guns, had rather cut the segment of the semicircle than followed its outer curve. As he came opposite the point two guns were discharged almost simultaneously, and at the report Jackson dropped his steering-oar, and raised his hand to his side.

A taunting cry was echoed from the shore, and a number of the Indians ran out as far as they might come, mocking the fugitives, and delighted at the apparent effect of their shot. Jackson raised himself up, staggering, and attempted to bring his rifle to his shoulder, but could not; he spoke to Lem, his favorite servant, who put his arm around him, obedient to his master's command.

"Way enough, boys," he called out in a low voice.

The men paused on their oars, Jackson's lips com-

pressed as the rifle came to his cheek, and at the sharp report, one of the two Indians from whom the last shots came, tossed his arms in the air and fell from the bank where he was standing with a splash into the stream and swirled off with the black water.

"Ha! ha! ye black devils," **laughed Jackson,** sinking down in the bottom of the canoe **from the arms of the boy that was holding him.**

"Oh, maussa! you hurt; dear maussa, speak, maussa!" cried **Lem,** kneeling over the planter, and unbuttoning his vest.

The wounded man looked fixedly, and a guttural noise came from his chest at every breath and a perspiration dampened his **iron** grey locks. The boat, unheeded, turned and drifted with the tide, and Mike's canoe, in which Lou Jackson **was** riding, seeing something wrong, **waited till we came up to them.**

"Father," said Lou, as the canoes swung together, speaking in a **low, hurried voice,** "I am here, your daughter, Lou."

Jackson did not speak, **though he** looked shoreward with a wandering eye.

"Dear Father! God is **good; he will not** do this! **speak to me, say it is not so!**"

Jackson's **lips moved, we** listened, and low **and** faint, we heard a nursery prayer:

"Now I lay me down to sleep,
I pray the Lord my soul to keep,"

and then some words indicating that he was thinking of

home and the garden walks. The stern heart was retracing life's steps again; it saw its childhood's home on the Altamaha, it heard its mother's lullaby, the evening prayer, it felt the good-night kiss, and smiled. The dangers around were forgotten, the war whoop that was sounding mockingly along the shore was unheard, Jackson had retraced live's voyage to its source, and was home again.

We all saw the relaxation of muscle that followed the last hesitating word, and knew its meaning. Lou sunk back into her boat vacantly—listlessly staring, without a word or a tear. The negroes wailed a low cadence of sorrow gazing on their master with streaming eyes.

"Wall, he's only got the start of us by a piece, it's a few days airlier or later; but them dogs don't get his hair—that's a comfort; and may be it'll do him good to hear my rifle crack, if he hain't gone far yet—it used to make him smile." And saying this, Mike levelled his piece at one of the savages on the shore, who were watching, in groups, our movements.

At the crack of the heavy piece, that carried a ball further than any gun on the coast, an Indian in one of the groups shivered, but by holding on to a branch above him he saved himself from falling, though we all saw he was wounded. Mike put his hands to his mouth and gave the war whoop, but neither the ring of the rifle nor the wild cry of battle awoke the dead, and obeying the dictates of prudence we resumed our oars and hurried out of the river for the more open channels of the islands.

CHAPTER XVIII.

THE BURIAL.

"They truly **mourn who**
Mourn without a witness."
BARON.

DEATH is a great truth-teller. He throws us back on our littleness, and makes us turn about, feeling for protection, or staring for explanation of his mysteries. We see ourselves divested of reputation, of wealth, and the million little circumstances and forms that clothe us, and in his presence we stand naked to our own eyes. There is nothing in **us** different from **the dead** clod beside us, that a moment before was one of us, and that a moment hence we may be. **We speak** short, and only what we mean; we act fairly, and not for any appearance; **we** feel the stirring warnings that are of our spirit, and that are taunting our million **cares for the flesh,** mocking its littleness and its flickering termination.

In social life, the love of self and dread of others is not shaken off even at the **grave.** We bury our dead **man** with pomp and proper etiquette. There are invitations, and crape dresses, hearse, bells, monuments, criticism, and seclusion from society; even in our death **we are** worldly, draping the dead truth and its morals with liv ing fictions and fashions. In the woods death is more direct in approach, and you less able to shun his company. There is no art to help the stricken, no luxury for the languid, no shrive for the dying. When the destroyer has left his mark on your comrade and gone again, the open eyes gaze at you, the stiff body is in your arms; no one speaks of it, or over it; it preaches in mute language for itself; there is no hearse, no mourners, no newspaper article, no sexton, no rites; you and your friend are alone together—he is dead, and you are living. Prithee, hunter! pray for yourself, for you know the flies will crawl in and out your nostril to-morrow as they do in his to-day.

The night had well set in as we again caught sight of the low outline of our camping-ground, after the hurried flight from the river with our sorrowful burden. We lay off in the open water until Mike had made an examination of the land to see that there had been no one there after our departure, and when we saw his fire-light signal we rowed to the beach and disembarked. The negroes spoke in whispers, the boats were half unloaded, the guns carefully examined, and lay ready for use; the very hounds felt the blow that had fallen, and crept listlessly to the fire, and laid down wondering, all save poor old Duke. Duke was a sterling dog, though somewhat aged; his bed for years had been his master's couch, his platter his master's hand; and now he kept by the blanket that was spread over the stern of one of the canoes, and licked a white hand that fell from beneath, and at intervals half whimpered, as does a hound when dreaming of the chase.

Before establishing ourselves for the night, we made a thorough examination of the island, and posted one of the men on the upper end, to act as sentinel in case any canoes were seen, as they would necessarily have to approach from that way. Then one tent was raised for Lou, the smoldering fire was rekindled, being first sheltered from observation by the tent, and by a screen of bushes, and we addressed ourselves to sleep, though this was done more to encourage the men to take some rest than from any desire on the part of the others for forgetfulness. Some lay down, and soon were oblivious of all earthly troubles; others dozed, and started, and mused by turns; only Lem, of all the negroes, seemed to keep fully awake, and his low moanings were pitiable to hear. The night was perfectly still, and the same familiar cries came from the marsh that we had so often listened to; but now they had a mocking sound. The "stars dreamed their path through the sky," and with the waning moon made a thin light that seemed cold and ghostly, and a mist arose from the sea—the sure precursor of a storm.

Mike presently left the camp, and walked down by the beach, and the Doctor and I followed him, for the purpose of talking, and arranging some plan for the morrow.

"Well, Mike, what are we to do with Jackson?" said the Doctor, after we had taken a long look at each other.

"Thar aren't but one home for him now; but what's to be done with his darter?"

"Take her with us," said the Doctor.

"Where shall we take ourselves to?" I asked.

No one answered, and each looked at Mike as the surest adviser. The hunter sat himself down on the sand cross-legged, in the Indian fashion, and, after a pause, said:

"It's clair we aren't wanted hereabout, and it's mighty onsafe for the young woman. Thar has been a risin' of the Injins everywhere, and the only safe place for a crowd as big as our own is in the boats. The Injins wun't fight us by day; it's only when they ketch us on the sly, fur they know they aren't a match for honest folks, no how. Ef it warn't fur this ere young woman, and Rose, and the boys, we might lay around and rub out some of those varmints, and like enough get back some of the people they stole from the house. But it's a mighty onsafe game to play, with a handful of niggers to bother one, and I reckon we'd best make tracks."

"But where shall we turn to?" asked the Doctor, looking around him.

"Well, ef we go north, it aren't a great way to Lorenzo's clearing, but I kind o' think Lorenzo has lost his hayar night 'fore last, with the rest on 'em. The surest place would be Tampa Bay; thar we'd have the Fort, and from thar Lou Jackson could pass up to where she would."

"Poor girl! poor girl!" said the Doctor. "What is

to become of her? She seems very calm; I was afraid she would feel it more. She has not shed a tear or made a sob since it happened."

"A hound don't yowl much when he's hard hurt," replied Mike.

"What of the body, Mike?" I asked. "We must bury it some time, and where."

"Them sarpents won't let it stay buried long; they want his hayar."

"You don't mean to say they would despoil his grave for his scalp?"

"I mean they are 'bout among the islands, nosing us out this minute like wolves."

"Oh, Mike!" said the Doctor, looking around anxiously.

"'Taint likely they'll find us to-night, though they know pretty much where we be; but their spies'll be in all the passes at light to see where we go, and what we take with us, and they'll dog us to Tampa, and ef they can't get our hayar, they'll try to get his'n. We can't carry him four days' journey to the fort."

"We could bury him in the sea," said the Doctor, "and there he would remain undisturbed."

"His darter wouldn't give in to that," said Mike.

"How do you know?"

"Wall, I reckon."

"Then how can we bury him, and when?"

"The sooner the better," I replied. "Bring him here to-night—'twould be least suspected."

"And how hide the grave?"

"Build the fire over it," said Mike.

And so it was agreed that the burial should be made in the night, and that the party should leave before light should expose their motions to the enemy. I was deputed to acquaint Lou Jackson with the plan, and to obtain her approval. I found her in her tent, that opened to the fire, half lying and half sitting against a roll of blankets. Her eyes were shut, and she seemed asleep, but when spoken to she answered without moving. I told her of our plans for the morrow. She answered in a low distinct tone, that it was all very well. I spoke of her father, and that it was necessary to have a burial so secretly as to preserve the grave from the knowledge of the enemy. She consented by a single word of assent in the same composed manner. I then spoke of its being done immediately, and asked her if she was willing. She turned in her habitual manner, as though deferring the question to some one beside her; it was her manner of asking her father, that had always in the family been regarded as a question, and answered by Jackson without a word. Then as if recalling to her mind that there was no one to respond, she looked around vacantly with a troubled look, pronouncing the name of Mike.

"Yes, child," said the hunter, bending his frame to the entrance of the low tent, and replying to the unasked question, "that's best."

"Very well," she said; and seeing her indisposed to talk, I left the tent.

In a few minutes the fire was removed from the spot where it had been burning for so many days, and the pile of ashes pushed aside. Then with sharp sticks for mattocks, and paddles for shovels, in a little while we dug a grave in the sandy soil. Four men took the canoe, covered with the blanket, and guarded by Duke, and carried it up by the grave. The fire waned and flickered and the moon was nearly set. The heavy gaily-colored Indian blanket was wrapped around **the** dead man, and his hands were folded, " as though praying, dumbly, over his breast." Nothing was said, but the plaintive moans of the negroes and Lem's wailing cry were the only sounds of sorrow. Lou looked on with eyes wide staring and followed every motion of the attendants, but no word or gesture escaped her. The body was then laid in the grave, and then followed a pause; so silently we stood, the very air in the trees seemed noisy, and the negroes ceased their lamentations and crowded round Duke, who stood at the head of the grave, looking sadly in, while his long ears touched **the ground.** We looked one at the other for a sign, and the dead man looked up at us from the grave. Where now is the prayer of the living, and the hope for the hereafter?

The Doctor spoke with a voice so low, that but for the silence we **could** not have heard it : " Dust to dust, ashes to ashes." Then, as if seeking words to continue the **service he could** not remember, he broke forth in that great confession : "I believe in one God, the Father Almighty, maker of heaven and earth, in JESUS CHRIST, his only Son, our Lord." His voice, that was faltering, grew strong, the tears that were raining o'er his cheeks grew dry, and the triumph of his voice, as he proclaimed the resurrection of the body and the life everlasting, was like the march of a triumphal chorus, to which all responded, Amen!

Mike stepped into the grave and turned down the blanket over the face of his friend, our host and our comrade, and laid beside him his hunting-knife and rifle—a kindly care he had learned from his Indian habits—and then the grave was filled up, all the dirt was carefully placed back, or thrown in the sea, the ashes drawn to their place, and the fire re-kindled. The boats were reloaded, a piece of canvas was stretched on poles to imitate a tent, and one canoe that we did not need was left in plain sight on the beach, with a log or two half in the water to represent the others. This ruse was done to attract and occupy the attention of the Indians, who would be searching for us the next day, and who would thus be drawn away, for a time, from our real course. There lacked about two hours to daylight when we took to the boats and called away the dogs. They all came but Duke, who still sat by the fire, until one of the negroes carried him to the boat and placed him in; but as we started he jumped out and ran back to the spot where he had seen his master buried. The negro went back again, but the dog resisted and set up one of those long plaintive howls for which the true deer-hound is so remarkable, and which echoed from shore to shore like the call of a bugle. Lou was sitting in the boat, but at the sound of the dog's voice she sprang out, and running back to the hound, threw herself down on the sand with her arms around his neck, and broke out convulsively sobbing. It was the first tear she had shed since her father's death, and the torrent restrained was the more powerful.

"Oh! Missus! Jesus help us!" moaned Rose, swaying her head from side to side.

Mike rose up in his boat and looking seaward, brushed his hand across his cheek, saying: "Thar aint no show of light yit awhile."

In a little while Lou came back to the boat, leading Duke by the ear, and having taken her place with the Doctor, the boats glided off into the darkness and the mist, and using only the paddles, passed like phantoms out of sight.

All that night we rowed, and the next day, and availing ourselves of the smallest of the open islands for resting places, avoided surprise.

Whether the Indians ever followed us I know not, or whether they ever found the grave of the recluse planter by the sea. I never again visited the island, and the craft and ceaseless vigilance of our guide carried us safely amid the dangers by storm and warfare that constantly surrounded us during the four days that were occupied in getting to Tampa Bay. The scenery we sailed along was beautiful, and from time to time we would stop to beat up an island for necessary game, but the memory of the grave under our camp-fire, and the ever-present sorrow of Lou and her attached slaves, so abode with us that it did not seem a pleasure trip. Mike was the same regular, patient, watchful man. His eye saw everything, and a motion or a word directed attention to all that was curious. His boat was constantly by the side of the one in which Lou Jackson was riding, and his voice and manner were singularly low and gentle, when conversing with her, for so rude and wild a figure. Lou was very quiet, and at night her eyes would be constantly wet with tears, but it was an uncomplaining sorrow to which man can add no solace, and which is only bettered by that forgetfulness that the Creator in his kindness has permitted to come over the heart of man to heal even his "deep stabbed woe." In the destruction of Far Away, Lou Jackson had lost nearly all the property of every kind that she owned. Of the twelve negro men that had accompanied us on the hunt, six only were the property of her father and six had been hired, and would now have to be returned to their owner at Pensacola. Lem and Rose, together with five men, would accompany their young mistress and return from Tampa Bay to St. Augustine, where her father's relatives resided, by the first vessel that could be found. This was the meagre plan that she had laid out for herself, as we sailed down the coast. At length we made the point of Egmont Island, and entering the broad bay saw once more the American flag, and stepped ashore in security under the guns of the Fort.

CHAPTER XIX.

INDIAN HISTORY.

" True they have vices—such are nature's growth
But only the barbarian's—we have both."

BYRON.

When Florida was ceded by Spain to the United States, in the year 1821, it was inhabited by several powerful tribes of the natives. The Seminoles, residing in the Alachua country, in the centre of the peninsula, were a branch of the Creek Indians, whose villages margined the Chattahoochee River, near Columbus, in Georgia, and the name of Seminole, or *Runaway*, originated with a secession of this branch, which occurred at a remote period. Micanopy was their principal chief. The Tallahassees inhabited the northern and western portion of the peninsula, their chief town being at Tallahassee, the present capital of the State. Thlock-lo-Tustenuggee, or Tiger Tail, was their head chief.

The Mickasukie tribe, under Ar-pe-ik, or Sam Jones, and subsequently under an eminent warrior, Halleck Tustenuggee, had their hunting-grounds on the waters of the Ouithlacouchee, and the heavy swamps that border it.

South of Lake Okechobee another tribe found a secure

home in the fastnesses of the everglades. They were called Spanish Indians, and their chief was named Chekika.

The Creeks of Georgia came down to assist their kinsmen in the wars that ensued, and were led by Octiarche, and subsequently by that chief whose name has added so much to the romance and dignity of the Indian character, Osceola. The whole number of Indians in Florida at this time was estimated at from fifteen hundred to as many thousands. To this was to be added an equal number of negro fugitives from the slave States or the children of free Spanish negroes, all of whom were living with and adopting the habits of the Indians. So wide the extent of country over which they roamed, and so inaccessible their villages, that even the existence of some tribes was unknown until after many years of warfare. The tribes were different from each other in government and location, and some of them were hostile to the others.

After the cession of the province by the Spanish, the United States immediately sought to control the haughty nations that peopled the newly acquired territory, many of which had never been subject to Spain, and to induce them to cede their lands and delegate their government to the Government of the United States, upon the condition of protection and alliance. To this end three Commissioners were appointed by the United States, at Fort Moultrie, near St. Augustine, in Sept., 1823, who caused thirty-five of the principal men of the northern tribes to sign with their marks a treaty, denominated the treaty of Fort Moultrie. The first article of this treaty stated that themselves and their tribes have appealed to the humanity, and thrown themselves on the protection of the United States, "and do cede all claim to the whole territory of Florida." The United States Government, in its turn, agreed to pay six thousand dollars in goods, and an annual payment of five thousand dollars.

Immediately upon the execution of this agreement, settlers poured in and commenced cultivating the lands relinquished by the Indians, and many quarrels as to the intrusion and the rights of person and property arose between these two classes, so antagonistical in every element of character.

This difference of feeling led the United States Government to propose, and carry into effect, in May, 1832, a conditional treaty known as the Payne's Landing Treaty, signed by seventeen chiefs, whereby the Seminole Indians agreed to emigrate to the territory of Arkansas, west of the Mississippi River, providing they should be satisfied with the country, after first sending some of their chiefs to examine the land, and to give up to the claimants the negroes said to have escaped. Seven chiefs accordingly went, and in March of the following year, at Fort Gibson in Arkansas, the seven chiefs ratified the Payne's Landing Treaty, and without first making a report to their tribes, made the original treaty irrevocable.

No sooner, however, had the delegation returned and

it was told to the different tribes of Florida that they had entered into an agreement to remove, than they, without dissent, repudiated the treaty, refused to relinquish their native land, or surrender their negro allies. They haughtily answered the different runners and Indian agents, commissioned by the whites, and withdrawing to their villages in the Cypress Swamps and hummocks, prepared to defend their homes as best they might, according to the ancient hereditary rules and regulations of Indian warfare. At a council summoned by General Thompson, when Micanopy, Cooacoochee, Alligator, and other chiefs of high renown were present, Osceola, who was then a young chief, being called upon to answer if he would sign the treaties, strode up to the table in front of the officers, saying, " The only way I will sign such a treaty is this," and drove his scalping-knife through the parchment deep into the table, while the conference broke up in confusion. The call to arms sounded through the land, the Indians pillaged the settler to obtain military weapons, and burned his cabins, drove off the cattle, and waylaid the soldiers, and the United States Government threw her best armies into the country, to have them destroyed by the miasma and the Indian arrow, patiently renewing the losses in the regiments, and supplying millions of money for a period of over fifteen years. The amplest supplies were afforded for the prosecution of the war, and the first soldiers in the country such as Generals Jackson, Clinch, Scott, Worth, and Taylor, led the armies.

This was the condition of Florida when in the latter part of the winter of 1840 and 1841 we found ourselves involuntary prisoners at Fort Brooke.

A low octagon fortress, with a palisade inclosure of sharpened timbers, situated at the end of Tampa Bay, and that formed the headquarters of the American army through the many discouraging years of the Seminole war. The temperate climate of the coast, and the commanding and safe position of the fortress, made it a pleasant and safe residence amid the miasma and disorders of the interior country. It was also the depot for military stores, the arsenal for ammunition, and the harbor for the gun-boats. Civilized and savage warfare here displayed their pomp and coloring in close relief. The painted savage, with his wives, camped daily by the walls, or traded with the sutler; the Indian runners, who alone could thread the inner wilderness, came and went to distant outposts; and the little brown canoe of the savage, so thin in texture that a pin could pierce it, and so light in mold it left no wake in the water, floated side by side in the ripples with the heavy gunboat of the soldier, that some day was destined to rake and crush to pieces its slighter opponent—fit emblems both of the power and feebleness, of the people of which they were respectively the types.

Fort Brooke often contained within its casemented walls other and greater contrasts, and more stirring emotions than the material landscape and pageantry of war and race. Here came the young recruit, emulous of fame, with armor newly dight, and hither returned from the cypress swamp or pathless everglade the soldier whose brief campaign sent him home wounded, wasted, broken, with his weapons untarnished, save by the rust, and his glory unmade, except by his sufferings. Here fled for shelter the settler's family from their burning home, the shipwrecked sailor from pursuing storms, and here the haughty chieftain came with his armed band, wrapped in his wrought mantle and his stoic dignity, to treat for peace or vindicate his race; or the captured warriors in their damp prison shivered on the prison ships in sight of the warm life of their native forests. Here "talks" were had with the tribes, treaties signed, expeditions fitted out, forays revenged, and the barbaric life of the woods mingled and flowed side by side with the chaster forms of civilization, as the Oswegatchie pushes its black current into the blue waters of the St. Lawrence, and mottles the flood with its curious contrast.

The war that had been waging for over ten years through the length and breadth of the peninsula was apparently no nearer its termination than at any previous period. Small bands of Indians had been captured at different times, always by some *ruse*, and not by open warfare, and exported by ships to the far West. Several noted chiefs had been slain in defending their homes, and many villages and corn-fields been laid waste, but braver warriors seemed to take the place of the old ones, and new retreats had been found in the most inaccessible swamps, wherein the Indian woman might nurse her babe and till her corn-fields, while the braves revenged their losses by some foray so distant, unexpected, and bloody, as to countervail all rules of warfare, and render useless all prevention, and impossible all redress. This was not one perpetual war, but a succession of wars, separated by treaties and truces more or less long, and more or less faithfully kept. During these truces, sutlers, relying on the promises of the United States Government, made settlements in the territory, and with the fearlessness and temerity of the American borderer, pushed their outermost farms within the lines of the Indian territory. Sometimes, under favor of a particular Indian chief or band, they were protected for years, and remained safe while others were massacred. But at length some wrong done to their people would so excite the Indians that no individual favor could be a protection, and the outposts of the settlers were whelmed in flame and blood.

Far Away had been an instance of this kind of reliance upon this most uncertain estate, and its existence had been prolonged by the hospitality of the planter; but courtesy could not avail in the hour of general retribution, and the revenge bred by years of accumulating wrongs swept over the homestead like a spring freshet.

In a few days after our arrival, a government vessel, sailing by way of Key West for St. Augustine, offered Lou Jackson a passage, with her people, which she accepted, and departed, carrying Duke with her, and leaving Mike, Poke, and myself, again to our own resources, awaiting some opportunity for the indulgence of our roving propensities. But roving propensities were now only to be indulged under military escort, or else at the risk of our *hayr*, as the hunters pronounced it; so for the first few weeks we contented ourselves with the curious scenes that were daily transpiring in the inclosure of the fort, or the most limited walks directly around the pickets. Occasionally some scout would come in with the report of a soldier, or a runner, lying dead on some of the routes, and a guard of soldiers would be sent out to bring in the body, and give it a burial in the little burying-ground that was located just beyond the picket. The sight of the revolting exhibition of Indian warfare, however, soon passed by, and we forgot the terror that environed us in our desire for activity, and the enjoyment of the sports of the chase and the observations of the varied beauties of animal and vegetable life so prolifically developed.

Is it strange that, when the morning *réveillé* of bugle and drum awoke the loud gobble of the wild turkeys not yet flown from their roosts on the cottonwood trees on Hillsboro' River, we could not resist the call, but would occasionally steal out with our rifles, "jist to clair out our shootin' irons," as Mike said. Day by day these little excursions extended themselves, and we became so accustomed to the danger, that, like the villagers that build on the slopes of Vesuvius, we had forgotten the fires beneath.

CHAPTER XX.

A BEAR IN DIFFICULTY.

"*Snout.* O Bottom! thou art changed: what do I see on thee?
Bot. What do you see? you see an ass's head of your own, do you?"
MIDSUMMER-NIGHT'S DREAM.

ONE morning Mike and I left the fort in our canoes, with Scipio and Cæsar, to look for some game on the islands that were scattered along the beach in the many indentures of the bay to the southward of the fort. An hour or two of paddling brought us where a low island was fringed with the tangled roots of the black mangrove. This peculiar tree frequents the salt-water shores, and springs up from a multitude of roots that raise the trunk of the tree from the ground. The pendent branches then droop until they touch the water beneath, where, clasped by oysters and other parasite shell-fish, they are anchored to the earth, and, taking root, send up many shoots that thus ramify and interlace like miniature banyan trees. A large portion of the peninsula of Florida is fringed by this hardy hedge of vegetation. Behind a border of this kind we saw the towering forms of some gumbo-limbo trees, and the oval leaves of the sea-grape, and, finding an open place wherein to conceal our boat, landed and commenced to hunt down the island.

It was early morning, and the dew was still on the grass, and the mocking-bird had not yet finished his matinal song.

"There's a dog's track," I said to Mike, directing his attention to some footprints fairly marked on the sand; "there may be some Indians camping here."

"No" said Mike, following the tracks with his eye for a moment; "a wolf."

"How do you tell?"

"A wolf's got two long fore toes on each foot, d'ye see?" pointing to the mark on a piece of clay soil, where the animal had leaped over a pool of water, leaving a deep scratch on each side that showed plainly the formation of his foot; he's gone sometime in the night; they are great travellers, they be, and like enough he's now on Topolika River."

A little creek ran into the island, containing about an inch of water at low tide, but into which, with the flood tide, fish were accustomed to feed, and the shores of this inlet, at its narrowest part, were strewed with the heads and tails of small fish, such as the young of bass and redfish, while the whole shore was tracked with the prints of some animal. We stopped before the signs, and Scipio, his natural instincts fully alive, exclaimed:

"Gi! dere be shocks ob coons here o' nights fishin'."

A closer examination satisfied me that such was the case, and that some raccoons were in the habit of repairing here when the tide was ebbing, and heading off the fish that had ascended the stream, to seize them on their return to the sea. Scipio and Cæsar consulted long over the marks, with an air of much importance, and then informed us that such was "de fac'." Moreover, Scipio assured me that he had seen, on moonlight nights, raccoons engaged in these industrious pursuits, and standing knee-deep in the retiring tide, using their broad fore paws for hands, scoop out the fish, and throw them far up on the beach, while a fellow-fisher of the same family, wading down the creek from above, with splash and squeal, would drive the frightened denizens of the brook into the very paws of their cunning foe. Cæsar indorsed the same story, which I would readily believe from the nature of the animal, but which I cannot think that Scip and Cæsar ever had the forbearance to watch, while they had the means of pouncing on the raccoons.

Not far from the creek lay a hollow log that Scipio judged might be the resort of his friends, the raccoons, and, trimming a willow stick for a probe, after one or two careful examinations into the different knot-holes, he began a vigorous series of punches, while Cæsar stood at the end with a club elevated to knock over the prize. Instead of a raccoon, to our great amusement, out slid a huge rattlesnake, disturbed in his morning nap, and shaking his tail with a whirring sound, like the wing of a quail when rising. Over went Cæsar in his haste to get away from his dangerous prize, exclaiming, as he ran:

"Gorry mighty bress us! what for you call ee coon? you purty nigger, dun know snake fur coon!"

There were no signs of deer on the island, though quantities of birds of every description, that roosted in the mangrove bushes, and resorted to the pools and the beeches of the island for food, and made the bushes laugh with their various notes. The Key West pigeon was here, with its burnished colors, and the ground dove, with its plaintive note; the oriole gleamed in the willows like sunrise, and the mocking-bird so peopled the bowers with his many-tuned throat that the stranger would believe a hundred voices were singing at once. When, through vistas of the mangroves, we caught sight of the sea, the porpoise was rolling in pursuit of the fish on the bar, while the pelican and cormorant were following his motions in revolving circles high in the air. All created things, in their multitude of ways, were fulfilling their destiny, and each grade of life, by the other fed, ran its appointed round to make its part in the measured whole of that great cycle of animal life, of which man knows but a few members, and whose rules of revolution seem to his dull vision to be the mere instinct of appetite.

"Bar!" said Mike, interrupting my reflections.

"Where?" said I.

"Smell him."

"Nonsense!"

"Yah! ha! ha! ha!" said Cæsar, tugging at the leathern leash by which he held Mike's hound; "Yowler smell him, too!"

Mike took the strap in his hands, and we silently followed the lead of the dog. In a moment we passed a tree that had been stripped of its bark for a distance of five feet from the ground, and the bark scattered all about, while the hard inner wood of the tree was all furrowed by the nails of the animal.

"An old He," said Mike.

"How do you know that?"

"The she ones are 'bout havin' young, and are hid in the big swamps," replied Mike; "and he's a fat one; see, his hind toe marks don't touch his front ones. If he'd been a rael lean one, they'd a well-nigh overlapped."

The marks we saw soon led us to the edge of the bushes, and then out on the open sands. We followed carefully until a roll of sand affording a cover for us, we crawled up behind it, and carefully concealing our heads behind bunches of grass that grew scattered about the summit, beheld our game in the undisturbed pursuit of his morning avocations. The surf was rolling in, and there were many things lying about on the sands that had been stranded by a recent storm: here a tortoise-shell, and there a cocoanut, and further on a board, and some fragments of a vessel. Bruin was busy inspecting these flotsam that had drifted into his domain, and his manner of doing so was as follows: He would first look at the article, then smell it, then touch it with his fore paw, and then he would deliberately seat himself in the sand on his broad posteriors, with his hind legs projecting in front, and his toes turned up, and, lifting the article under consideration to his mouth, turn his head on one side, and try to crack it with his teeth. The indescribable air of burlesque gravity with which this was done made me laugh. Added to the individual awkwardness of the animal was the fact of our unsuspected observation, and the scene appeared doubly ridiculous; and when the negroes chuckled aloud, the bear would only discontinue his investigations for a moment to take a survey, and then renew them again. The cocoanut he found too hard to bite, and so, after rolling it over two or three times, threw it into the sea again. Then he examined a large tortoise-shell, and putting his claws in the side, with his arms a-kimbo, pryed it open, to find it empty. Next he picked up an orange, and sitting down, as before, ate it with evident satisfaction, his fore paws resting during the time of his mastication on the toes of his hind paws. Occasionally he would reach around and scratch himself in the same manner as a negro, whom he laughably resembled in very many of his manners.

Presently he discovered a small cask, and after applying his nose to the bunghole to scent the character of its contents set to work to arrive at the interior. But the half-barrel was strongly coopered, and in spite of bites, and boxes, and hugs without number, it remained intact, though an oily juice ran from the bunghole and smeared Bruin's paws, who eagerly licked them dry. At length, by a good deal of biting, he enlarged the bunghole so that he could get a paw in, and by this means fished out the sweets, holding the cask up with one arm, **and dropping** the other into it, and then into his mouth, like a little negro on a molasses barrel. **But this mode** of getting at the contents did not seem sufficiently expeditious to Little Tommy Horner, who, pre**sently** getting up on his feet, inserted his nose in the bar**rel,** and then his head. Now a bear's nose is **very** sharp, and goes through a small place very easily, but does not have the same facility for coming out, owing to the hair and ears being set backward, and the heavy folds of skin that hang around the neck. In this instance Bruin made the discovery of this difference, and, like the weasel in the flour barrel, soon gave symptoms that he was fast. He began to pull back, but as he pulled the barrel came **with** him, until he rolled over on his back, pawing ineffectually with his hands at the convex sides of the barrel, which revolved around his head **as on** a pivot, but would **not come off.** Mike smiled out aloud, and the negro **yelled with laughter. The** bear, hearing the sound **of our voices, probably increased by the reverberations in** the hollow barrel, took fright and **ran for the woods,** making directly to where **we were lying,** and carrying the cask on his head like a helmet. **We** could not have shot at that half-barrel, even had we been able to fire our guns, which we were not, from laughter, and therefore scattered right and left as the animal rushed up **the hill; as he** crossed the conical peak he lost his foothold, and rolled head over heels in our midst. Then picking himself up, he started in the direction he happened to be when he regained his feet, and ran directly into the sea.

This turned him about again, when Yowler, who had escaped from the negroes, seized him by a leg and forced him to halt. At this he reared himself on end, and commenced growling and waving his paws all the time, resembling more a picture of Bacchus than a wild animal. We ran down to where he was standing, when Scipio, with a blow of a club over the head, broke the barrel, scattering the mackerel with which it was filled, and released the animal from his confinement, who rewarded the negro with a blow from his paw that knocked him on the sands, when Mike and I, with a simultaneous discharge of our rifles, laid him lifeless. This was a very large bear, and from the abundant mast still hanging in the woods, and from the quantity of shell-fish on the island, was very fat. We brought our canoe round to the beach, and in a few hours were again with our trophy safely back to the fort.

CHAPTER XXI.

HOW WE CONQUERED HALLECK TUSTENUGGEE.

>———" but quoth he,
>'It was a famous victory.'"

THE winter had passed away and spring had come, opening the pyramid of silver tulip-flowers of the palmetto royal (the *yucca gloriosa* of the naturalist), while we were watching a chance to leave Tampa Bay. One day the commanding officer detailed a company of men to cross over the peninsula to the forts on the other side for the purpose of keeping open the communication, and learning the situation of the enemy, as well as of the troops operating in the interior.

We accepted the chance, and the next day found us with our packs slung on a mule, two canoes for ferrying across rivers, and a company of about forty men winding through the pine lands that lie east of the bay. There had been an old trail cut through here, marked by blazes on the trees in the open woods and here and there a log felled bridge-like across the creeks that intersected the swamps; but the trail was only useful as a guide, although it is marked on the charts of that day as a military road.

The dear-bought experience of the American troops had not been profitless, and the company we were with was as well organized as it was possible to be. The men were frontiersmen, quick in the use of the rifle, unterrified by the appalling sights and sounds of Indian warfare and—what was of vital importance—accustomed to the country, and skilled in woodcraft. They could support themselves, if need be, in a swamp, or build a town there without foreign assistance. The rules adopted for crossing the country were as follows: No more baggage to each man than was absolutely necessary, and this baggage to consist only of food and ammunition; each man to carry his own share. One guide was placed ahead of the detachment about three hundred yards; within sight of him and of the column, another. These men were the most experienced of the hunters, and generally one a friendly Indian. To their knowledge of the geography of the country the party was indebted for the directness of its route, to their quick eye for its security from ambush, and to their observation of every passing footstep on the land, marks of paddles on the shallow bottom of rivers, or the slimy projecting logs, its acquaintance with the movements of outlying parties of Indians, or the recent passage of friend or foe. How small these signs might be, and yet be detected, how blind and yet be read, is one of those mysteries of the woods that are disclosed only to the observant and the practised. Their very description excites incredulity. The passage of one of these scouting parties through the Indian country was a curious scene, and impressed one with a feeling of awe. The old tokens by the way, here a ford named after some bloody massacre, and there a little log pen whitened by the bones of those who fell there at bay together, hemmed in by the pursuing savage, were so frequent and well-remembered, that the soldier crossed the woods with a ceaseless watchfulness. He travelled all day with his utmost speed, lest his pursuers might come up on his trail, and at night lay down in the darkness without his fire, that his covert might not be disclosed. The celerity of the passage was the safety of the party.

Thus we crossed over to Fort Fraser, on the Hitchipucksasi, and two days more brought us to Fort Gardiner, on the ford of the river that connects two of the largest of the lakes of central Florida, Lake Kississimee and Lake Tohopekaliga. These forts were nothing more than heavy cabins built of logs, and defended by palisades, sometimes garrisoned by a company of men, and sometimes only houses of refuge. The one last named was in the margin of the cypress swamps, and was one of those huge shallow tarns, whose black waters, encumbered by logs and cypress knees, and encroaching into the dense forest by interminable arms, were more intricate than the labyrinth of Crete. The Indians excelled in the navigation of these lakes. Their canoes left no trail, and they could be hovering about for weeks, without the scouts discovering their presence. If they wanted to leave, they knew of water connections through to a score of other lakes, or they could flee away to the South down the Kississimee

River, to the great Okechobee Lake in the everglades.

Some portion of the land around the fort was of the same nature as that commonly known as everglade. Properly, the everglades are confined to that portion of the peninsula lying between the uttermost southerly point, Cape Sable and Okechobee Lake, a space of about two degrees of latitude, though some are found further northward.

No language save that of the painter's brush can depict the desolate immensity of one of these treeless swamps. There league after league of rank grass waves on every side, unrelieved by hope, to the explorer, of termination or prospect of change. Here and there a thick leafed cactus, or cabbage-palmetto, or a clump of leafless cypress, grows upward, draped in the moss the stagnant water has bred. Fallen trunks of old trees are tangled with palmetto roots beneath the grass, having drifted in the summer rains from the place where they grew, or gaunt dead water-oaks hold out their arms, from which the flesh of leaves has dropped away, or still clings pendent from the fingers. Strange birds fly over, screeching in foreign tongues, and trees and stumps and grass show by green deposit on their sides the different heights to which the water that floods the waste had arisen on different months.

In the dry season this broad extent of country is nearly dry. During the rainy season of spring and summer the water lies over it in varying depths from two to twenty inches. Through the grass are seen winding channels made by the prevailing currents and lagoons, from whose black muddy bottom grows the pond-lily and other floating grasses which intersect the prairie and turn back the pedestrian. It would seem as if the rolling of the sea had built an embankment of sand around all the coast, shutting in this low-lying tract as does the cushion on a billiard-table, so that it could be only drained by evaporation, or settling in the shallow lakes and lagoons.

Through this Stygian pool the hunted Indian doubled and wound, or turned to strike pursuing soldier whose toilsome march he had been watching for days, or he disappeared into its mirage with his family, like ghosts, without a trail and beyond all successful pursuit.

The story of this war has yet to be written. On the one side were Generals Scott, Clinch, and Worth, names that were dear to us, and millions of money, and loving chroniclers of our gallant deeds. We hunted the Indians with troops, boats and dogs, and renegade spies crueller than the hounds, and we entrapped their chiefs at the council board, and broke up the organization of their bands. On the other side was a people deriving their weapons only from their foes, insufficiently provided and suffering every want. They resisted our attack with patriotism and battled in swamp, and water, and reedy fastness, for thrice as many years as we were fighting the War of Independence, and no historian to record their protests, their prayers, their councils, their sufferings, or heroic deeds. We know that Molly Starks were there at every battle, for their bodies lay on the field when the fight was done. Bunker Hill was represented in every cypress gall. The cruel winter at Valley Forge they underwent, though their torture was the miasma and the heat. Their capitol was burned at Palacklickaha, and its fruitful fields were destroyed. The old prison-ship lay moored for them in Tampa Bay, and their highest chiefs were captives in its hold. They had their Sumpters and Marions, in Chekika and Hospetarke their Pulaski in Holartoochee, and their Washington in Osceola; and had their Arnolds been discovered, as ours, they would be living still, an independent people.

If men are to be esteemed for high virtues in proportion to the obstacles they had to overcome in attaining them, and if the praise of comparative great deeds is due mostly to those who have from lower life made them eminent, the brave resistance of the savage in his swamp is a higher deed of chivalry than the war of a civilized people, with its wealth of reason and example, and if it does not stand on historic page in brighter light, it is because the page is written by the civilized race as defence and not as a veritable history.

One morning, as the sentinels around the fort were relieved, a stranger came up to the relief, was recognized, and then sauntered into the camp. A huge, rough, talkative fellow, a hunter by trade, and now following the camp, like many others, half for the fun and half for the gain; one of that peculiar southwestern race, a sort of cousin to Mike, not in blood, but in position. Mike was a little more gentle and observant, Potter a little rougher and jollier, more rollicksome, hailing everybody, singing wherever there was eating and drinking, and running every danger to be present at a fight. His leathern suit, rifle, and knife, were the prominent features of his dress, and a keen eye and huge mouth and limb, the first points noticed in his person.

Mike knew him, and recognized him with a smile and a question:

" Up ?"

" No, down."

" S'Gustine ?"

" Wall, you'd better b'lieve it."

" Seen Injins ?"

" Stacks of 'em—slinkin' about like coots on the St. Johns. Squaws, too; somethin's up—reckon they're a-goin' to purr a little; sent a letter to the old man. Who's your old man here now?" continued the hunter, pulling out, as he talked, from his bullet-pouch at his belt a little roll of birch-bark; " took 'em an all-fired time to write it, and had a big pow-wow to read it when wrote. Scissors! I saw some good looking Injin gals at that camp. Came as near being tuck that time as ever I did; felt my hayar jist fallin' off; thought I was wolf's meat that run. Yer see I'd been dodgin' tracks all day, so's to git to this clearin', and night cum on. I sez to myself, Go it, boots! and made a bee line. Fust thing I knowed I had walked right into an Injin camp. No fire—fire'd gone out—cuss the fire! Pitched slam-bang over a red-skin asleep, and in a minnit there was forty atop me. 'Hold up!' sez I; 'I'm Injin, don't you know me? I'm come with a letter from the great white chief,' and I held up an old bit of paper that Jake had given me at S'Gustine, with the writin' on about bringing some stores. They swallered the bait, and I sot there half an hour readin' off in Injun the cussedest lot of nonsense you ever heard tell on. Then they wrote this answer, and I started fur here? Didn't I make dirt fly for the first ten miles betwixt me and them!"

Having rattled off his account of the adventure, that left no more mark on his danger-loving mind than an every day encounter would have done, he tossed his rifle in the hollow of his arm, and lounged over to the cabin occupied by Colonel Worth.

The missive he delivered was on clear white birchbark, and pictured a broken hatchet, and a half-circle of Indians sitting around a council fire. Being translated, it read: "We have broken our weapons of war, and are now consulting about peace; only half our chiefs are here—we are waiting for them at the council."

This message was on a par with many others that were constantly passing between the Indians and white leaders, always on the part of the Indian procrastinating and guarded.

From Potter we learned many items of news from the east coast, but none that served to interest us so much as the information of Lou Jackson. It seemed that a month before Lou Jackson had been in St. Augustine, and had embarked in a revenue cutter to go down the coast with a relative who had been appointed light-keeper somewhere in the neighborhood of Key Biscayne.

It seemed strange that after the danger experienced at the plantation she would so soon go off to an equally exposed and lonely life. Could she not find a better position than that of a light-keeper's assistant? Or did the lonely life it promised agree with her disposition and her feelings of sadness?

Mike expressed his feelings, looking southward as if he could see the lighthouse, by the words "Waall, waall!"

However there was no explanation to be had, and after talking it over, we turned to the frolic of the camp and the Indian negotiations, which seemed rapidly approaching a definite result.

A few days more at the lakes, and we found ourselves at Fort King, having accompanied Col. Worth with a detachment of troops by the way of Warm Springs, where there was a collection of Indian chiefs who had come in for a conference.

This was one of the occasions of periodical truce, so common in this war. Each party was glad of cessation—the soldier to be relieved from marching and incessant watchfulness, and the Indian to gain time to recruit and purchase a stock of ammunition. At such times the precincts of a fort was the scene of a pageant. The chiefs came in under the white flag, without their arms, bringing their wives and children, and pitching their camps right under the guns of the fort, and the sutlers traded with them as with the soldiers. These chiefs retained all their stoic dignity of manner and gaudiness of dress. Regarding themselves as in a measure in council, they dressed with care, and studied to impose on the respect of the whites or each other. Some of them were men of much influence and honor among their own people, nearly all of them were objects of great curiosity to the troops who had been so many months in their pursuit, and who connected their names with some bloody massacre, or hard-fought battle.

The leader of the present band was our old friend Halleck Tustenuggee, who had left the marks of his black fingers at Far Away, on our last visit there. He was standing at the gateway as we came in, the war paint washed from his face, and his heavy black hair drawn back from his head, and plaited down behind with the feathers of the roseate spoonbill; a heavy blue blanket hung from one shoulder, in which was wrapped one arm, and the other hung freely at his side. His bearing was noble as words could describe, and if there had not been in his eye the glittering cruelty of his race, something akin to the fascination in the tiger's eye that stops you as you pass his cage, he would have stood with credit for a Roman general. His wife and children were with him, and two subordinate chiefs with their wives. The main body of his band, twenty-five in number, were a few miles distant, near the camp at Warm Springs, participating with all the abandon of the native character in games of ball and quoits, wrestling and dancing. Nothing was omitted on the part of the officers to make the truce pleasant. Provisions and whisky were distributed and presents made, and, to crown all, a great feast was prepared, to which all the warriors were invited. When at the table, the commanding officer announced to them that they were prisoners; the soldiers, already instructed, sprung to their arms, and the band that no force could conquer were bound prisoners for life.

A messenger was sent to convey the tidings of the capture to Colonel Worth, who was entertaining Tustenuggee at Fort King. The rider came fast through swamp and woods, for his life would be little worth should the day's proceeding be known to Tustenuggee, or any outlying Indian, before he reached a secure shelter. He approached the fort at a moment when the commander was sounding his Indian guest upon the ever-recurring subject of their emigration. The officers were seated in front of their quarters, the Indian chiefs stood before, and the idlers of the camp were gathered around listening to "the talk."

"A horseman is coming from the south," called out the Doctor, relieving his pockets of one hand to shade his eyes.

"Come as ef he was sent," remarked Mike.

The sentry challenged, and the rider came in with his answer through the open gateway in the palisades and up to the doorway where Colonel Worth was sitting, and delivered his missive. Tustenuggee stood before him in his Roman attitude until the dispatch was read, and watched the while the countenance of the colonel, but the hard-bearded face gave no sign.

The rider dismounted and stripped his saddle. A brief order was given by the colonel to the orderly who stood behind him, and the Indian chief resumed his talk.

"My heart and the hearts of my chiefs are white, not from fear, but in love. You sent me the flag of the five fingers (white flag, with white and red hands clasped). I know you want friendship. I trust you. Tustenuggee is here. Listen, white man; what he says is true—listen, Great Spirit; what he says is true. His answers are the answers of his people. He is chief of the chiefs."

The Colonel—"The chief has spoken like a brave man, and his words in council are like his deeds in battle. We all honor him, for he will listen to reason. He has lost many men in the wars, and the rest are weary. But the white soldiers still come, and will come on forever. The white man has many soldiers, and many weapons, and much ammunition. It is not good for the red man to fight against him, for he will waste away, no matter how brave. The white man has offered his red brothers lands in Arkansas many times. Some have gone there—Tustenuggee has refused. The white man now offers for the last time, and he wants to know if Tustenuggee will move at once with all his people."

Said the chief: "Hundreds of winters ago the Great Spirit gave to his red children this land, its woods and its waters."

He enunciated emphatically and pointed slowly to the sky above him, and waved his draped arm around with a majesty peculiar to the oratory of his race.

Old Primus, a snowy-haired Indian, translated into English as he spoke, and a secretary at the table wrote down the conversation.

"Where was our white brother then? Where then was that shadow?" pointing to the shadow of the flag on the officer's quarters, as it fluttered back and forth on the greensward. "Forty years ago, God made Tustenuggee. Then our white brothers lived to the north. Did the Mickasukies war against our white brother, and ask him to emigrate to Arkansas? The Mickasukies were big then, and the white man very little. The white man was so little that he could not do his own work, but had black man to help him.

"Tustenuggee has always lived here. Tustenuggee's people have always lived here. They have loved the soil; they have dropped their seed here, and their seed has taken root. The roots have gone down far into the earth. The white man is a great wind. He comes from where we can't see. He blows against the red tree. If he blows hard enough the red tree will break down, and his seed be scattered, but the red tree has grown too long to take root elsewhere. My people are like deer— they have been hunted, and are shy. They start when they hear a twig break. They hide when it is day. The white man has hunted them for many winters. He has burned their cabins, he has rooted up their cornfields.

They are sick at heart. The women can find no covert to bring forth their young. The men dare not light a council-fire, or come together to talk. The chiefs cannot know the minds of the people, for they are scattered. Let there be peace. The red man will keep it. He who breaks peace will be punished. The red man will hide his hatchet, and take his hoe. The white soldier may go home. Then, when the tribe comes in from the hummocks, we will talk of moving. Runners will go to Sam Jones, to Octiarche, and to Tiger Tail. Our hearts will be open—the sun will shine on them—the smoke of powder shuts out the sun now. When that is gone we can see clear. Tustenuggee will not promise what he cannot pérform; Tustenuggee is too great a chief to lie. His tongue is straight. When peace comes he will see clear. Then he will read the white chief what is written in the hearts of his people about moving. Tustenuggee has spoken."

The Indian stepped back, and wrapped his blanket around him.

The colonel arose, and said: "Halleck Tustenuggee, I read your thoughts. You have wanted a truce to buy ammunition and provisions. You would then do as you have done before—take to the swamps and renew the war. This stratagem is now to be ended. At Warm Springs, to-day, all your warriors have been taken prisoners, with their wives and children, and will be sent forthwith to Arkansas. You and your chief are also prisoners, and will accompany them."

Tustenuggee looked around him with a quick gesture. The gate in the palisade fence was drawn, and the soldiers were under arms. His eye flashed, his breast heaved, and, as his young chiefs made a desperate, but unavailing attempt to escape by scaling the palisades, he quietly drew his blanket over his head and sat on the ground.

No word was said by the bystanders. The intense interest of the scene chained every tongue. The sentinel stopped on his round. The soldiers gathered from their avocations. The orders given by the colonel for the security of his prisoners was delivered in a low tone, and as they moved away to the guard-house our hearts seemed to beat again as if after the spectacle of some great tragedy.

Thus ended the career of this great chief. The woods knew him no more. His race lost his fiery valor, his vindictive vengeance, his far-sighted policy, and the influence of his name. He was one of the haughtiest and most uncompromising foes the white man ever had, and was only taken by the same means that Osceola had been before him.

That night, while most of the camp had retired, or were quietly sitting by the fires that lighted the inclosure, a savage scene was enacted in the guard-room where the prisoners were confined under a guard of soldiers. A large fire was lighted and the captives sat around it, among them several of the Indians taken at the other camp, that had been forwarded for security.

It appears they had been canvassing the means by which they had been made captive, and one of them had intimated that it could only have been effected by the treachery of their chief.

The words were no sooner out of his mouth than Tustenuggee was on his feet. Bounding over the fire, he struck the bold speaker in the breast with both feet, then seized him by the throat, and as those in the yard, attracted by the tumult, reached the window of the building, they saw him almost strangled in the tiger-like clutch of the raving chief. Before help could be rendered him, Tustenuggee had seized the ear of his antagonist between his teeth and bitten it off, then throwing aside his prey, he ground the ear between his teeth, and spat the clotted flesh in the faces of the guard, then, raising his sinewy form to its grandest height, and waving his arm, he gave the Indian whoop, and called out with a wild voice twice, "Halleck Tustenuggee! Halleck Tustenuggee!" and fell back to his seat, trembling with excitement and the rush of his passions.

The strange accessories of form and color, the armed guard, and red fire-light, the savage act of the barbarian, impressed the scene on our minds as the act of a demon. It held us enchained, and we looked on the actor as a caged lion.

On the morrow he and his chiefs were on their way to Tampa Bay, to be sent by ship to New Orleans.

CHAPTER XXII.

THE "PAINTER" IN THE PIG PEN.

"I was with Hercules and Cadmus, once,
When in a wood of Crete, they bay'd the bear
With hounds of Sparta; never did I hear
Such gallant chiding."
                                    MIDSUMMER-NIGHT'S DREAM.

The days were getting rapidly warmer in the interior, cut off as we were a large portion of the time by the close woods from the free winds. The ducks had gone to the northward long since, and with them the snipe and many song birds. To take their place, the flowers were opening to the spring on every side.

Hunters are rarely botanists. None of their wants are aided by its knowledge, with the exception of the knowledge of the points of the compass, told by the moss, or an acquaintance with the texture of different woods, or the medicinal properties of a few plants. They are equally unused to the description of flowering plants. The pointed cutting of a deer's hoof on a cactus leaf to them is a greater study than the most radiant flower that ever fringed its pulpous leaf. They cannot give technical descriptions, and but few natural ones. They may not call the stars by their names, or classify the active life that peoples every muddy pool, or makes a decayed tree a miniature world.

Yet, for all this, there is no race on whom the sweet influences of the Pleiades fall who are more open to their soothing—none to whose eyes the radiations of the flower afford a keener pleasure—none to whom the fragrance of the woods opens a more vivid association, or who are more observantly drinking in, night and day, those Æsop lessons that man puts into a fable, but that God talks with in letters of life. The constant silent observation of what is around him makes his recognition quicker; his natural active life makes his senses keener, and the soft, damp, fragrant wind that touches his cheek in passing, may tell him of a change of weather, of the wet swamp that he is skirting, and may even whisper the kinds of trees and plants there growing, and whether in bloom or no; the plants will tell the soil, and he may know the very animal life that lives in the woods before him, by what on another cheek would be a passing wind, and nothing more.

Even the roughest hunters at the Fort could show this observant taste. Mike had it to a great extent. Potter had it, though burlesqued by the wild, random manner of an impulsive boy. We would often get them talking in order to lead them out. Evening was the ordinary occasion of many tales and practical jokes. The men would gather around the huge fires, sitting and lying in every attitude. Negro interpreters, Indians and soldiers, the volunteer hunters, that gained their living by supplying the garrison with game, and the officers, in uniforms that the swamps had left no longer uniform or neat. Names well known in the Florida wars were called and answered to. There were Primus and Gopher John, the Indian scouts, and Holatter Mico, the royal chief, and Vose and Wilcoxson, officers, and Mike, Potter, and a score of others whose local fame then ran as high as Maréchals of France, though in a narrower sphere and for a shorter term.

There were drinks of government whisky, and smokes from pipes shorter and blacker than a Killarney man could fix in his hat-band, and Irish jokes, and yarns of monstrous length, that were roughly criticised or excelled by some other more incredulous still.

Potter gave us one. Seated astride of an empty barrel, with his rifle across his knees, his buckskin cap pushed back on his head, his blue flannel shirt-collar rolled back, exposing a breast as broad and shaggy as a bear's, he told us the following story with gesticulations and amid peals of laughter:

"Wall, you see how it was, Squire, is this."

The speaker took a long pull at his pipe, gave a hitch to his suspenders, and then, ejecting the dense smoke in volumes through his nostrils, commenced his narration.

"I was living that year on the coast, purty nigh St. Augustine. It was late in the year and the night was oncommon dark—wall, it was—and the wind roared ugly. Yer could hear the trees smashin' up in the woods every five minits when it buckled to a little extry, and when yer put yer head out o' the door, as I did once in a bit to see, you couldn't have seen Talyhasse Capitol House ef you had rubbed your nose agin it. The big breakers were poundin' on the bar, and yer could see 'em one by one whare they struck, for the phosper lit 'em up like blue paint. We had a screechin' fire in the chimney, and it was right good to look at. The old woman was a-mending clothes in the corner, and I thought it war a cussed sight better bein' a home body and turnin' in by the side of one's own wife than a-roosting all night in the open range, as I had bein' a-doin' for a month back.

"Parson Smith war thar, too; he had dropped in goin' up to Pelatky on a revival trip, and seein' the blow comin' on staid all night, and he was talkin' religion to Marthy by the fire, drying himself and convartin' a soul both ter once. Parson Smith was a likely man and a racl talker. They called him Doctor, and he wrote his name Rev. Eliakim Smith, M.D. M.D. stood for Medicine Doctor, though that war somethin' of a lie, for he war a horse-doctor before he took to religion, and he had a kind of oily way of rubbin' his hands down his legs as he sat by the fire and talked away that would take the spavin right out of a woman, and convart her in two-forty.

"Wall, there he sat a-rubbin away and watchin' the taters roastin' in the ashes and the bacon frying in the pan, and talkin' of Election and Delilah, and them other holy women folks in the Bible, till I begun to feel holy myself, and thought I was in the land o' Canaan, when I fancied I heerd a painter screech. I was wide awake in a minnit. 'Holy Moses!' sez I. The Doctor hadn't heerd the painter, so he thought I was getting grace, and he right away buckled into me with all sorts of Bible sayin's, and my wife jined in, but I jist riz up and went to the cabin wall, where there was a little winder that I had cut to look out toward the woods. I pulled out the shutter and put my head through, but yer might as well have looked into the Kentucky cave, it was so dark. The wind come in, too, so strong and chill-like, that it made the Doctor and my old woman draw up a little closer together. I listened a while to see if I could make out any signs of the critter, but it war no use. What between the surf a hammerin' on the bar, and the branches crackin' in the woods, and the squalling of the gulls that had blowed in from the sea, you couldn't a heerd a neighbor asking you to take a drink, and I reckon that is what a man hears quickest. Once in a while one of the big water-oaks would topple over in the woods. I knowed it had *blowed over*, for it made such a smashin' of little branches when a hull tree come over, and then a short tug or two as the roots broke. Then agin yer could hear one of them tall pines on the ridge break. There was no give there; it would break short off with a crack like four or five rifles. I would have bet I could have told the very trees that snapped, I knew 'em all so well. Then agin the wind would die away, and you didn't hear nothin' but the rain.

"'Jist the night fur them varmints,' says I, drawin'

my head in again; 'they allers come down in a storm, kind of unsuspectin' like; that's their natur.'

"'Yes, nothin' so deceaitful as the 'Piscopalians,' says the Doctor.

"I knowed what he was after; the Doctor went tooth and nail aginst the 'Piscopalians, and so did the 'Piscopalians 'ginst him. That's the natur' of religious people.

"'No,' sez I, 'it was the painters.'

"'Painters! where?—have you seen a painter?'

"'No, but I heerd one just now.'

"'You don't mean it,' sez he, and he went right over to his saddle-bags that was lyin' on the bed, and tuck out two of the longest kind of Spanish pistols, and primed 'em up, sayin' all the while somethin' about how with the jawbone of an ass he had slain a thousand men.

"I didn't believe the critter, for he was given to blowin'; but Marthy she jist swallowed it all like batter cakes.

"I seen old Boz, who was asleep by the fire a whimperin' away—you know how dogs take on when they're dreamin'—raise his head quick like and make a straight pint for the t'other eend of the cabin, whare the logs was a little open like. He stood there for about a minnit and then came back and laid down agin. I knew somethin' was up, and that screech I heerd war true music. The old woman seed the dog, and she broke in with—

"'Yes, that's so; when I, my old man, and the dog, both smell painter, I knows there is painter. Two dogs don't both make a false pint to once.'

"At this Doctor Smith he walks to the door and

unlatches it; the wind blew it wide open. I saw a pair of long white horns outside, and that minnit the Doctor gave jist one of the biggest yells yer ever heerd a wild Injin make; one of his pistols went off; I don't know ef he fired it off, or it went off of itself, and the preacher went over backwards as my yoke of young steers came a rushin' right in the cabin. Lord! yer could a heerd me larf a mile.

"The critters was a frightened in the storm, and maybe had smelt the painter, and were mighty glad to get in the house where the light was; but they weren't half as frightened as the Doctor was. He hadn't any more pluck in him than an old hen on a rainy day; he was right wilted down, though he tried to show how the bullock had hit his arm and that had fired the pistol.

"We got the critters out agin presently, though they didn't want to go and I sot a thinkin' about it, and wonderin' how it was they were so onusual skeery, and the old woman had fixed the Doctor somethin' warm, and I hadn't heern any more of the painter for an hour or more, when all of a sudden, queek, quee-ee-ee-ak, we heerd the old sow go, and a thumpin' noise, and the cattle bellowed and run around the house.

"Thar, I knowed it," says I as I grabbed my rifle, upsettin' the teapot, 'cuss the painter, he's got the old sow.'

"Lord, you should ha seen that cabin empty itself. Boz and the other dogs first, and then the Doctor and his pistols, and then the old woman, though she was the smartest man of the lot, fur she brought out a big pitch pine knot all afire, to see what we were goin' after.

"I put right for the pig pen; that was about eight rods off from the house, and where the pigs were a squeelin' bloody murder all the time. That's what bothered me. I knew if the painter had got a pig he must have killed it right off, and then he would up and away with the carcass. That's the natur' of the varmint. Could it be an old she painter a havin' one of her cubs out exercising him, and the cub couldn't lug off his share of the game?

"We got up to the pen. It was a log cabin about twelve feet square, built of heavy logs, jist to stop such doin's as this. 'The dogs had their noses to the cracks baying away like all fired, and the pigs were a snortin' and squealing inside; but the strangest thing was, that the door was tight fast, the chain across it, and the big oak pin drove in as tight as ever.

"'Whar is the painter?' says the Doctor, as he came sidelin' up, lookin' behind every stump.

"'That's jist what I want to know,' says I, as I cum around the buildin' to look for his hole, but without findin' it. The pigs were a squealin' away as if they would split their throats, and the dogs were a dancin' and a howlin. The old woman was a sayin' somethin', but you couldn't hear what it was, for the wind blew as bad as ever; it only wanted that cussed painter's screech to make it all complete; and jist then, as I am a livin' sinner, the varmint gave his screech, and it was inside the pen.

"I say, Squire, it would ha done yer good to have heard that screech, and ha seen that scrimmage. I've hearn the varmints screech many a time when they and I have been in the woods all alone, but then it was kind a soft like, as if he was a doin' it for his amusement when he was lonely; he puts it then in the best metre, of course, and it isn't disagreeable, unless he might be too close to you. But here he didn't smooth it down, his dander was evidently riz, and he yelled out as if he was filing a ninety horse power saw with the Rocky Mountains, and wound up with a spit that jist took the hair off a steam whistle. The young pups drew back a little and howled, and the old dogs went nearly mad because they couldn't get through the cracks between the logs.

"The Doctor was for settin' fire to the cabin and burning him up. The old woman was fur cuttin' a hole in the door and shootin' him. That was kind of onfair to the varmint, I thought. Sez I, 'I'll show you a prettier trick than that; I'll jist open the door, and then, Marthy, if you hold the light steady, I'll take him with a poke in the ribs that will stop his stealin' my pigs. There is no miss fire to my gun, and that won't be imposin' on a varmint that's down.' I put my hand to the peg that held the chain, when the Doctor, taking the ends of the logs that stuck out at the corner of the cabin for a stairs, jist put himself on the top of the pen in a shake of a deer's tail. I smiled softly to myself, but I didn't say nothin', for thinks I to myself, if the varmint does come out here, and I do miss him, or only wound him, the dogs will be on him like a shot and then he'll go to tree right on top of the cabin, that's sure.

"So I tugged at the peg, and every time the chain rattled, the Doctor edged back on the top of the cabin, gettin' up to the ridge, I s'pose, for a sure seat, when all of a sudden he disappeared. Heavens and yearth! he had come backwards onto the hole the painter had dug in the roof, and had tumbled in.

"Yer should have heerd that man scream! The painter wasn't nothin' to it. Painter might have been some louder, but then it wasn't so skeery. It fairly made me shaky to hear him. As he come down to the ground inside, there was such a bustling around in that little building! pigs and painter and man, all seemed to be stirring about pretty lively, and to all the other noises the old woman set up a screechin' that made me more shaky than anything else.

"'Quick!' she hollered, 'pull open the door—quick! Oh, Eliakim! oh dear!'

"I pulled as hard as I could, but the cussed peg had swelled with the rain, and yer couldn't budge it, and the chain was the ox-chain, as went all across the door.

"'Tear it down, you old pirate!' says the old woman to me, and she took hold of it with both hands, but she might as well have tried to pull down the cabin. And all the time, between the howlings of the dogs and the squeelings of the pigs I could hear the Doctor a praying away one minit as loud as he could bawl, and at another minit callin' to me to come and help him.

"'Run,' sez I to the old woman, 'run to the house for the axe.'

"Away she started, leaving the torch with me, and she run like a wild Injun. I kneeled down so as to get on a level with them, and puttin' the pine knot so it would shine through, I peeped in at the varmint. Lord! he was a beauty. Crouched up in the fur corner of the cabin, he stood with one foot on the wall, ready for a jump. His glossy bay coat shone like a horse. His eyes looked like two blue lights out on Florida Keys, and his open mouth all the time dropped water down on his whitish chest and on his feet. Once in a while he'd take a look up at the hole in the roof and lay down his ears, as if to jump at it, but it was a leetle too high for him, and he couldn't get room enough to make the leap. Oh, he was a purty critter. His feelers were as long as a ramrod, and when he looked up at the roof they lay so far back that they reached the wrinkle that crossed his shoulders, the only wrinkle on his body. I wanted to take a shy at him, but it warn't no use, the cracks were so narrow I couldn't begin to sight over my rifle, and knowed if I wounded the beast it would be all day with the Doctor. 'Oh,' thinks I to myself, 'ef I could get my pigs and the Doctor out, I'd manage some way so as to take him alive, and make a spec out of a real live painter. 'Twould be the first ever seed in Ameriky, I reckon.'

"Just then the Doctor broke out afresh, half a screech

15

in', half a prayin'; he seemed to be kind o' confessin' to the painter, for he was goin' over what a sinner he had been, and talking about Daniel in the lion's den, and the sword of the Lord, and somethin' about Gideon, and Samson and the young lion, and yer never did hear a critter get out so much that was pious in so short a time. I think if I wanted to convart a sinner I'd shut him up with a painter, I would.

"Just as he was sayin' somethin' about reposin' on the protectin' arm, the painter gave a jump for the hole in the roof.

"Jehoshaphat! what a jump! he got his fore claws on to the shingles, but the shingles give way and down he cum with a spiteful screech. With that the pigs rushed around in double quick time, and Eliakim, forgetting his praying, hollered for me and Marthy to come and help him. He was like the old woman who said she trusted in Providence, when her horse run away with her, till the britchen broke, and then she guv up.

"Poor fellow, I felt for him; every time the painter moved, he and the pigs moved too, and they were hazed around that pig-pen in double quick time, for the painter is a restless brute, and can't abide standin' still.

"Soon the old woman came back with the axe, and I commenced cuttin' the peg that held the chain. This riled the painter, and he commenced runnin' round livelier than ever, and away went the pigs, gruntin' and squeakin', and away went the Doctor, runnin' and

THE "PAINTER" IN THE PIG PEN. 339

jumpin' over the dead sow the painter had killed, prayin' away and callin' to me by turns. "Oh, Potter! quick—be merciful to me—a—a—painter's comin'—as you hope—to—be—saved—blasted sow—oh, ough—salvation!"

"A stroke or two of the axe cut off the plug. 'Stand aside Marthy,' sez I, as I pulled down the chain and threw open the door. I had my rifle to my shoulder. The first thing that cum out was the Doctor; it nearly cost him his life, for I was just a pullin' on him when he said somethin' and saved himself; then came the painter quicker than greased lightning; as he struck the ground outside after his first jump, I pulled on him. The ball struck him just in the shoulder, breaking one leg; he fell, but was on his feet again quicker than thought, and every one of the sixteen dogs, pups and all, on top of him.

"Phew! what a tussel! 'Go it, pups!' sez Marthy, holdin' up her light. 'Go it yaller backs.' That old woman was clare grit—well, she was. Gone now, poor soul!" and the frontiersman wiped his eye with the sleeve of his hunting-shirt—" killed herself learnin' to read.

"The painter fetched himself up on his hind legs, like a bar, hissin' all the while. One leg hung down—that was the broken one—the t'other one he fetched around among the dogs, and knocked 'em over like nine-pins. Old Boz took some of it, and it keeled him up straight, and then Tinker, and Sumter. I seen 'em getting cut awful, and so I walked into the muss with the axe. One cut did the business. It took him just over the ear and druv into the brain, and thar's his skin, now aint it a beauty?

"Wall, the Doctor was in the house when we cum in with the painter, and he was still holden on to his pistol. He was just used up, and all my larfin at him, and all Marthy's Schiedam Schnapps didn't cure him. He took the fever and ague, and couldn't leave the house for a week, and when he went he war so weak in the back that he could hardly sit on his horse.

"He stopped there purty often again that winter, goin' and a comin', but cf we ever heard anything out doors nights he would always coax me to go off and see what it was, but he never left the house, and was purty sure to lock the door when I was gone, to keep the varmints from comin' in. That's the natur' of a doctor."

CHAPTER XXIII.

POKE RECEIVES A CUR'OSITY AND TELLS A YARN.

" Oblivion here thy **wisdom is,**
Thy thrift the sleep **of cares;**
For a proud idleness like this
Crowns all life's mean affairs."

EMERSON.

THE Indian prisoners had gone with most of the garrison to Tampa Bay; the fort looked desolate in contrast with its previous crowd and excitement, and we were anxious to start for the east coast.

Our party **had made** preparations **to** descend the Ochlawaha **to Lake** George, and **thence down** the St. Johns, and Mike had employed his leisure, and our negro boys, Scip and Cæsar, in building **two** dug-out canoes. In these our "plunder" was carefully stowed, and with a **store of salt** provisions from **the fort, one pleasant** day **we embarked and swept away down the current.**

There is something of unusual novelty in descending a Florida river. **An aspect of** dreariness that only long habit overcomes, quiets the tongue and awes the heart. The black turbid river boils in circular eddies, or spreads **in** motionless lagoons, far into the neighboring woods. The stiff cypress trees stand naked with their feet in the water as though relying for foliage upon the grey Spanish moss that hangs from everything in tresses and curtains of wondrous length, sometimes reaching from the upper limbs into the water, and marking the direction of the current. Where the lagoons opened into the river there was constant doubt as to the course of the channel, for the lagoon might be broader than the true course, or the latter totally shrouded from sight by the draping moss or jammed trees. Sometimes the leading boat would wait for its fellow, calling to it a few feet off to come through some curtain of vegetation, where it had just found a passage. There was no animal life here save reptiles, and little vegetable beauty. It was a stagnant waste, overhung by the dead growth of ancient times.

Then, too, there was a watchfulness against Indian contact that made our passage seem more like a flight than a hunt, and when some alligator rushed from the bank to the water, the noise would startle us and bring back the scene when Jackson died on just such a passage down the Ouithlacouchee. Two, or three days brought us into pleasanter life, and our eyes were greeted with the open water of Lake George and the varied vegetation of its low-lying shores.

It was curious to watch Mike make his entry on the lake. As we approached, our boats came nearer and paddled slower. We hugged the shore closely, and when the first faint roll of the waves of the lake came into the river, he motioned us to stay, and glided down among the rushes in his own canoe, watching the broad

open water with a keen, careful eye. We slowly came
up and followed him as, parting the reeds, he wound
along the shore some quarter of a mile, till where the
grass began to grow thin. Then beaching the canoes
where they could not be seen from the lake, we unpacked
our provisions, and, seated where we could overlook all
the water, and yet not be seen. ate our dinner and took
our noonday nap.

The propriety of Mike's caution in a little while
became apparent. A canoe came out from one of the
outlets of the lake a mile down, and crossed over to the
side where we were sitting. In it was a single Indian.
This was followed at a short distance by another with
three women, and both boats disappeared in a cove.
Had we been on the lake we should have been seen, or
had we continued our course we must have met them.

"What's that mean, Mike?"

"Injins."

"Yes; but what are they doing? Is there a tribe of
them here, and are they on a war party, or what?"

"No; it's a band; they've got their squaws with 'em.
They're travellin', fur they paddle, leastwise the squaws
do, as ef they were tired. And there's more on 'em
somewhars, for there's too many squaws there fur that
one red-skin. Keep quiet and they'll show their hand."

Before night three other canoes passed the lake in the
same direction, and turned round the projecting point
where the first appeared.

The evening came on apace. The sun set—a globe of

fire. The pencillings of red on the lakes shortened; and then disappeared. The birds that had fished all day in the shallows settled in the trees to roost. The earth wrapped itself in darkness as a mantle, and left to dews the freshened air.

"Wall," said Mike, after a big yawn, "let's do somethin'."

"Yes, and that something must be to get out of this place as soon as possible," quoth the Doctor.

"No!" replied Mike, with a comical accent.

"It's very well for you, Mike, who have *a gift* for Indians, to hang about them, but I don't think I care to have my ears bitten off, like Tustenuggee's aid-de-camp."

"We're all right so long as we squat here, and make no fire, or any trails, but when we come to go away we may meet more Injins in the river."

"But the faster we go, the less likelihood of meeting."

"Wall, we will go. Shut up, Yowler, you dod-rotted dog!" to the hound, who was attempting one of his houndish yelps. "But first I must see who them creeters is, and ef you'll keep quiet here awhile, I'll go look."

So, in spite of the general dissent, Mike took one of the canoes and disappeared in the darkness, while the negroes crept up close like monkeys, shivering with fear of the darkness and danger, and we chatted in low tones of the scene around us. There was a steam on the water that looked like a gathering fog, and made it dark close to its surface. The night was hushed, and the heavy booming of the alligator bull came down the lake like the muffled roar of a lion.

In an hour Mike returned, with his quiet salutation, stepping ashore and tossing something in the Doctor's lap, saying, "Thar's a cur'osity for your collection."

The Doctor picked it up, but it was too dark to tell what it was. It looked like the boy's toy called a sucker, made of a circular piece of leather, about three inches in diameter, with a string fastened to it.

"What is it, Mike?"

"Somebody's heyar."

"A scalp?"

"Reckon."

"Where did that come from? It is not a fresh one."

"Stole it from those beggars; too lazy to watch their own boats!"

"How many of them are there?"

"Nine, and five squaws. I stole the only scalp they had, and jist marked my cross on their canoe with my knife, so they'll know 'twas me. It's that cussed old Tiger Tail. Drat his red skin! won't he swear some to-morrow! I reckon we'd better go. Marbee it wouldn't be safe to be loafin' 'beout here when he finds his canoe punched and his scalp stole."

No one obeyed this suggestion to depart with more alacrity than the Doctor, who already felt Tiger Tail's fingers clutching his own scalp-lock in revenge for the lost one, and a few minutes found us on the lake pushing fast and silently for the St. Johns.

The next morning we learned the cause of the movement of Tiger Tail's band. The flight of several flocks of water birds, and the chattering of the blue jays, gave us warning of the approach of some stranger, and, taking to the bushes that fringed the banks, we watched for what would appear. Soon we heard the measured stroke of oars, and then several Indian and negro scouts in canoes passed without observing us, and then swept along six barge-loads of soldiers—a part of the Second Regiment moving up the river on one of their forays, by which they sought to disturb the security and products of their foes. The American flag was flying at the bow of the leading boat, and the merry laugh of the men, and the loud joke and call passed from front to rear, showed how inadequate they were to catching their fleeter foes.

"Hulloa!" said Mike, pushing out his canoe from the reeds, "goin' a fishin'?"

This sudden satirical salutation brought the boats to a halt, and sent half the soldiers searching about for their muskets.

"Where are you from, and where to?" was the answer of the officer.

"Oh, cross country, goin' a pleasurin'," responded Mike.

"Seen any Indian signs?"

"No signs in partickalar; stopped at Tiger Tail's camp a piece back," replied Mike, gradually moving down the river, and away from the boats.

"That's the band we are after. How soon do you think we will come up to them?" The boats getting further off all the time.

"Never!" responded Mike, paddling down stream at full speed. "Ketch a fish-hawk jist as soon," he continued in an undertone.

The boats had resumed their course, when the officer, who seemed to know our hunter, hailed us once more.

"Hulloa!"

"Hulloa!" said Mike.

"Come and guide us, and you will be well paid."

"No; you're too many of you, 'taint no use;" and a turn of the river carried us out of sight.

That night we camped early, perfectly secure from annoyance, for the passage of the troops up the river had, we judged, driven away any lurking Indians. Indeed, the only band in the St. Johns which we were approaching had been Tiger Tail's, the rest being occupied with the treaties and negotiations that had been in progress on the west coast. So we kindled our fires and cooked our meal, and laid down to talk and dream of old adventures, or half-forgotten hopes.

Mike assured us that he had no tales to tell, mumbled about Tiger Tail, and wondered where he was leading his band, then ventured some remark about Lou Jackson, half to himself and half to his hound, and then fell asleep. The Doctor being called on for a story, gave us an account of a fire-hunt in the woods of the Adirondac.

As nearly as I can remember, it was as follows. I can't repeat the words, only the ideas. They were pleasant; he was a poetical fellow, that Doctor, when it grew late in the evening.

Beyond Little Tupper's Lake, some three or four miles further on in the wilderness, toward the Racquette, lies Little Rock Pond, a mere dot of glass set in the emerald woods that stretch for miles away in every direction, unbroken by human thrift and unmarked by the fruits of that primal curse that caused the thorns and the thistles to be brought forth. Connecting these two sheets of water is a narrow stream so insignificant that it joyfully runs its way nameless and unknown. The hills stand back on firmer bottom, and the little valley bordering the river is filled with succulent grass, reeds, swamp alders, and rose-trees that blossom and bud for the wild game alone. Here Stalknecht and I had a camp and were spending a month together, keeping house in the only decent manner there is of living in this free country, where the servants are all a little better than their masters. (Poke was violently opposed to Irish servants.)

Hank, my guide, and I one night paddled our boat up this stream to its source in Rock Pond, and when darkness had come we lighted our jack-light, and, setting it in the bow of the boat, he took his seat in the stern with the paddle, and I mine in the bow with my double-barrelled rifle, and we commenced to descend the stream. A jack-light is so arranged that it throws a bright light in front of the canoe, while it leaves the boat in utter darkness, and the hunter, thus sitting in obscurity, is enabled to see anything in range of his light with perfect distinctness. So we began to descend the stream. Our voices, subdued to a whisper, were presently hushed altogether. Not a sound disturbed the perfect stillness; no splash of the paddle in the dexterous hand of the guide; no noise of motion; we floated on the water as the moon floats when "with white fire ladened" she sails out into the still night. The weird trees, naked of leaves and shirted in moss, flashed out in light, and then fell back in darkness, save when their tops marked the sky beyond. Bush and flower, reeds pendent with their heavy seed, and lancifoliate lilies, with their deep blue plumes, lateral lagoons, gemmed with water-plants and bordered with their larches, came out into the light, dropped into the darkness, and were succeeded by others in clumps and clusters, and festooned by blackberry vines. Ghostly-looking sights, stumps that had supernatural shapes, and tombstone trunks, blanched white by rain, marked the banks.

Kee-honk! kee-honk! screams a blue heron in harsh, aspirated accents, as he springs into the air, fanning the night with his great wings in measured beats that can be heard long after he is beyond sight. The muskrats come out in the circle of light before the boat, in wonderment at the pale fire that awakens them, and dive beneath the waters when the boat is on them. The boat swings around in the turning of the stream, and I see the erect head and large ears of a deer. It is a doe, for there are no horns. A moment of pause to be sure that I am right, and the ringing shot awakens a hundred echoes, and clouds the air with smoke.

"Why, ye'nt seen no deer, did yer?" asked Hank.

"Yes, a doe."

A dip of the paddle sends the boat to the shore, and then discloses to my mortified gaze, the charred limb of a tree, standing up in the grass, the veriest spectre of a deer.

"Well, your doe is dished now—ha! ha!" laughs Hank.

I load my rifle rather humbly. "Ready—push on!"

"Don't you want to see if you hit it?"

"No; push on, will you."

The boat glided forward again, mile after mile, in the same spectral journey, as fast and as still as the dead do ride in the ballad of Leonora. My mind floats along with the water-bugs that run ahead of me and the shadows. I see the stars floating in the water, and those overhead likewise, and many more stars than ever shone in these latitudes. In fact, I got asleep. I don't think I had slept long when I was awakened by a shrill noise, resembling the letting off of steam from a small steam-engine when the valve is suddenly opened and as suddenly closed again. I have heard such noises in a country church before the commencement of exercises, when some plethoric deacon blowed his brazen nose, only, if anything, the night-bugle was a little more emphatic, and several times repeated in quick succession. "What's that?" I whispered.

"Deer," responded Hank, in a whisper, swinging around the canoe so that, as the light moved, against the woods, the motion of the boat brought forth two or three more sneezes, and then we heard a heavy crashing through the bushes as the deer dashed up the hill, awakening the echoes with his nose, more terrifying than Bardolph's fiery beak to all the bottom land; for immediately, from the other side of the brook, another great buck took up the cry, and rushed up the hill to the summit, where he stood some minutes, stamping the ground and startling the darkness with that most singular of alarums.

"Two big bucks," said Hank. "There be'ent much good huntin' here any longer; we've got back to the lakes agin, and them bucks has called off all the others."

"But it won't do to give it up so, Hank; we must have a deer, or we won't go home till morning. Think of the hungry mouths in camp."

"Wall, I suppose we can try them sand-beaches round on the south shore. I kinder think the bucks fodder on the sand beaches more'n on lily pads this time o' year."

So around we went, glaring our Cyclopean eye over the open lake, and causing the loons to laugh like monkeys. One or two islands stand out in the open water where the brook makes in, and we passed around their jutting rocks to the southern shore. The water began to shoal, and I could see the white sand on the bottom, from which here and there the osiers reared their taper wands, and, as the air came wafting from the land, it brought the odor of the white water lilies, the queen of all the water flora. Skirting the osiers we could see the sword-grass growing rank beyond, and presently our ears heard a splash in the water. A moment more of slow drifting motion and we heard the tramp, tramp, of some animal wading in the water. A little nearer we floated, the rifle in hand and the senses concentrating on the grassy marsh. A little nearer, and the eye caught a motion. Brighter grew the light as the canoe floated up and reddened the grass and reeds, and we caught in the darkness ahead a bright, blue light, and then another, the reflection from the deer's eyes. Then we heard a suppressed snort. Another stroke of the paddle, and a deer stood out in the grass, his head thrown up, and his eyes shedding pale light. The boat is directed straight toward him, and the paddler is as still as a statue. I aimed and fired. From beyond the smoke I heard the splashing and dashing of water, and a big buck dashed past me, and then two others, all rushing off together for a belt of timber that arose close by us on our right. As they ascended the bank, I aimed at the hindermost with my remaining barrel and fired, and at the sharp ring of the rifle he fell back convulsively dead.

We hastened to the shore, and, carrying with us the light from the boat, we found the deer I had first fired at, lying with a broken shoulder, just dead, in the high grass. The second was lying among the lily pads where he had fallen, the ball having passed through the centre

Another stroke of the paddle, and a deer stood out in the grass, his head thrown up, and his eyes shedding pale light.—Page 352

of his neck, breaking the spine and killing him instantly. They were both large bucks of six tines, with their horns fully grown. It seemed a marvel—something that was as supernatural as the weird scene around us—to see those two noble beasts that, a moment before, were the wildest forest things that range the earth, so still and heavy in among the lilies and the sword-grass.

"Wall, wall, that was purty well done," said Hank.

But Hank's praise could not lighten the dull leaden weight of the stags, nor relieve my mind from the lurking impression that the coming by night into these solitudes, to shoot down two of the lords of the soil while at their food, was not the part of a brave man. But what is the use of moralizing? Some men sin without thought, others with much; but I opine that the much thought don't deter from a repetition of the sin.

With a good deal of labor we hoisted our two deer into the canoe, and paddled home to the sleeping camp, and then—

"Tuck a drink," said Mike, whom we all thought fast asleep, from under his arm.

A drink! no sir, I was more intoxicated with my hunt than a gallon of whisky would have made me.

"All who believe Poke's story, signify it by saying I."

"I," said Poke.

"I'se sure maussa tell far true 'bout firin' in de stump part," suggested Scip.

The Doctor was displeased, and went off to lift the night lines, and the rest of the party to dreams.

CHAPTER XXIV.

WOODLAND CHORUSES.

"In the long nights of winter when the cold north wind doth blow
And the howling of the wolves is heard amid the snow."
MACAULAY.

As we descended the St. Johns River, the water scenery gradually enlarged and became more characteristic. The wider volume of water set back the forest to a farther distance, and not only removed all question of Indian bullets, but the change from the heavy woods to the open vista made us freer in feelings and more rapid in our motions. The boats moved faster, and wind and current in our favor, with trolling lines astern for seatrout, and the negroes singing their Methodist air—

> "In a few days, and a few days
> We're gwine to glory,
> In a few days,"

we rapidly sped northward to our final destination and the scenes of civilized life.

One day we passed an Indian canoe. Mike said the paddler was an Indian, though he looked more like a negro, and had a long talk with him. They used the Indian language and we could not understand them, though from some names we heard spoken we judged their conversation went back to Tiger Tail. The Indian once, we thought, mentioned Jackson, and once gave the native motion for taking scalps.

After he was gone Mike seemed moody for a day, and then the meeting with the Indian was forgotten.

The jumping mullet were frequently seen in the waters here, and at night we could catch them in abundance in our canoes by carrying a torch. They sprung from the water toward the light, frequently two or three at a time, and fell in the boat, their pearl-colored scales glancing and flashing in the torchlight. In some places they are called moth-fish from this peculiar instinct. In later years the raftsmen on the river availed themselves of this habit, and placing lights on the sides of their rafts collected quantities of fish that readily leaped the low edges of the raft.

The nights were very dark, and during a portion of the time we were descending the river, yet as we were in haste to be home, we kept on our way sometimes till late in the evening, marking our course by the black line of forest that margined the shore. Some of those nights were exceedingly solemn. The mystery of the darkness, the splash of the leaping fish, the murmur of frogs and moths, the rushing wings of the night birds, and now and then the heavy bassoon of the alligator, in whose bosom the spring of the year had awakened tender recollections of his mate, all added to the awe and novelty of our voyage.

Sometimes, too, we could hear the plaintive whine of the panther or the howlings of wolves, that, scenting us from shore, challenged our distant passage that left them no bones for their supper.

These wolves are funny fellows. You would hear one howl away down the river just audibly above the insect hum. Then an instant's pause, and another answers from the opposite shore, and then one close at hand gives a yelpish whine as though he had been intending to howl, but a bone that he had in his mouth stopped him, until he laid the bone down and hurriedly had his howl out.

We pitched a camp one night at dark in a grove of orange trees a little up from the shore with everything to make us comfortable. Opossum, venison, fish, and doves were hanging before the fire; the night was dry and pleasant, our camp was well located, and we had every anticipation of a cheerful night, until the Doctor, who never could resist the chance of throwing a line, must needs hook a small alligator in the river on his night line. It was all very easy as long as the animal was in deep water—he was a caught fish—but the moment the Doctor dragged him up to shoal water where he could obtain a good footing, then the Doctor was caught, and had either to be pulled in the river or let the line pay out and the brute get back to four fathom water.

Soon we heard a call for help, and, after a number of facetious suggestions offered and refused, one of the negroes paddled out a few yards, and, when the animal came up to the surface, put a rifle to his head and killed him.

The hook was cut out of his mouth, and the body floated down the river a few yards, and, as we learned in the morning, lodged against the bank.

The discomfort of the Doctor's fishery now became apparent. Supper being dispatched, every one rolled over, pulling off his boots for a pillow, or laying his head on his arm. The first sleeper had just begun to emit the first hoarse breathing which a listener would call a snore and the sleeper would swear was not, when we heard, "Ah-ha—whoo-a-whoo-oo-oo!" from a little way down shore. "Bow-ow-ow-owe-owe!" said every dog in the camp, in different tones of shrillness, depending upon the acidity of their tempers. Up on end came every sleeper.

"What's that?" quoth I.

"Cuss the wolves!" quoth Mike.

"Dar's a prime psalm singer, settin' the tune," quoth Scip.

"Cause he settin' tune, yer mussent kick around like all afire," quoth Cæsar, holding on to his shin, that some one had kicked.

"Wag, here Wag, don't go there!" called the Doctor to his cur, that had not the least intention of venturing beyond the circle of the fire-light.

Everybody turned over; wolves are never dangerous, unless to your provisions, and in a moment more there was silence and a sound of strangulation from the Doctor that foreboded his profoundest sleep, when " Ooh-oohooough," came the old note, followed by the rush of the dogs and the same series of questionings and yawnings and objurgations.

There seemed to be a concert near us; for the moment one wolf would get tired, another would take up the refrain until it was soon apparent that there was no more sleep for that night.

We only took cat naps, eating a little now and then and sometimes taking a drink, talking, conjuring up all the old stories of wolves that we had ever heard or read of, good bad and indifferent, they were all repeated, —wolf had no mercy shown him that night. If he could have understood our language I am sure he would have howled louder in anger at the character we gave him than ever he did in hunger or melancholy.

Mike's opinion of him was that he was a "dratted mean cuss, feered to hunt deer alone and fodderin' on his own young ones when he can't ketch nothin' else."

The negro boys entertained the belief that the luminous appearance from their eyes at night arose from their feasting on the slain in battle, and a suspicion that they sometimes visited grave-yards for other purposes than pensive meditations.

The Doctor told how that the power of a wolf's jaw was greater than that of any animal—that it had a power of, I have forgotten how many hundred pounds, and something about his facial muscles that no one understood.

I told the following story of an adventure. It don't

seem now half as natural as when the wolves were howling an accompaniment, but it is true, nevertheless.

THE WOLF CHASE.

During the winter of 1834, being engaged in running a line in the Aroostook country in the northern part of Maine, I had much leisure to devote to wild sports. To none of these was I more passionately addicted than to skating. The deep and sequestered lakes of this State, frozen by the intense cold of the northern winter, present a wide field to the lovers of this pastime. Often would I bind on my skates, and glide away up the glittering river, and wind each mazy streamlet that flowed beneath its fetters on toward the parent ocean, forgetting all the while, time and distance in the luxurious sense of the gliding motion, thinking of nothing in the easy flight, but rather dreaming as I looked through the transparent ice at the long weeds and cresses that nodded in the current beneath and seemed wrestling with the waves to let them go; or I would follow on the track of some fox or otter, and run my skate along the mark he had left with his dragging tail until the trail would enter the woods. Sometimes these excursions were made by moonlight, and it was on one of these occasions that I had a rencontre, which even now in a warm climate and with kind faces and bright fires around me, I cannot recall without a nervous looking-over-my-shoulder feeling.

"I had left my friend's house one evening just before

dusk, with the intention of skating a short distance up the Kennebec, which glided directly before the door. The night was beautifully clear. A peerless moon rode through an occasional fleecy cloud, and stars twinkled from the sky and from every frost-covered tree in millions, and the great zone of the milky way and the lucid planets were all copied in the mirror-like ice, till your foot seemed treading the jewelled vault of heaven. Your mind would wonder at the light that came glinting from ice, and snow wreath, and incrusted branches, as the eye followed for miles the broad gleam of the Kennebec, and like a satin ribbon wound between the dark forests that bound it. And yet all was still. The cold seemed to have frozen tree and air, and water, and every living thing that moved. Even the ringing of my skates on the ice echoed back from the Moccasin Hill with a startling clearness, and the crackle of the ice as I passed over it in my course, seemed to follow the tide of the river with lightning speed.

"I had gone up the river nearly two miles, when, coming to a little stream which empties into the larger, I turned in to explore its course. Fir and hemlock of a century's growth met overhead, and formed an archway radiant with frost-work. All was dark within, but I was young and fearless, and as I peered into an unbroken forest that mirrored itself on the borders of the stream, I laughed with joyousness, my wild hurrah rang through the silent woods, and I stood listening to the echo that reverberated again and again, until all was hushed. I

WOODLAND CHORUSES.

thought how often the Indian hunter had concealed himself behind these very trees, how often his arrow had **pierced the deer by this** very stream, and his wild halloo **had here rung for** his victory. And then, turning from fancy to reality, I watched a couple of white owls, that sat in their hooded state, with ruffled pantalettes and long **eartabs, debating in silent conclave the affairs of their** frozen **realm, and** was wondering if **they, "for all their** feathers, were a-cold," **when suddenly a sound arose; it seemed to me to come** from beneath the ice. **It** sounded low and tremulous **at first, until it** ended in a prolonged yell. I was appalled. **Never before** had such a noise met my ears. It seemed more than mortal, so fierce, and amid such an unbroken solitude, as if a fiend had blown **a** blast from an infernal trumpet. Presently I heard the twigs on shore snap, as if from the tread of some animal, and the blood rushed back to my forehead with a bound that made my skin burn, and I felt relieved that I had to contend with things earthly, and not of spiritual nature; my energies returned, and I looked around me for some means of escape. The moon shone through the opening at the mouth of the creek by which I had entered the forest, and considering this the best course, I darted **toward it** like an arrow. 'Twas hardly a hundred yards distant, and the swallow could scarcely excel my desperate flight; yet as I turned my head to the shore, I could see two dark objects dashing through the underbush at a pace nearly double in speed **to** my own. By this great speed, and the short yells which they occasionally gave, I knew at once that these were the much dreaded white wolf.

"I had never met with these animals, but from the description given of them, I had but little pleasure in making their acquaintance. Their untamable fierceness and the untiring strength which seems part of their nature, render them objects of dread to every benighted traveller.

> "With their long gallop, which can tire
> The Deer-hound's hate, the hunter's fire,"

they pursue their prey—never straying from the track of their victim—and as the wearied hunter thinks he has at last outstripped them, he finds that they but waited for the evening to seize their prey, and falls a prize to their tireless cunning.

"The bushes that skirted the shore flew past with the velocity of lightning, as I dashed on in my flight to pass the narrow opening. The outlet was nearly gained; one second more, and I would be comparatively safe, when my pursuers appeared on the bank directly above me, which here rose to the height of ten feet. There was no time for thought, so I bent my head and dashed madly forward. The wolves sprang, but miscalculating my speed, sprang behind, while their intended prey glided out upon the river.

"Nature turned me toward home. The light flakes of snow spun from the iron of my skates, and I was some distance from my pursuers, when their fierce howl told me

I was still their fugitive. I did not look back, I did not feel afraid, or sorry, or glad; one thought of home, of the bright faces awaiting my return, of their tears, if they should never see me, and then every energy of body and mind was exerted for escape. I was perfectly at home on the ice. Many were the days that I spent on my good skates, never thinking that at one time they would be my only means of safety. Every half minute an alternate yelp from my fierce attendants made me but too certain that they were in close pursuit. Nearer and nearer they came; I heard their feet pattering on the ice—nearer still, until I could feel their breath and hear their snuffing scent. Every nerve and muscle in my frame was stretched to the utmost tension.

"The trees along the shore seemed to dance in the uncertain light, and my brain turned with my own breathless speed, yet still they seemed to aspirate their breath close in my ears, when an involuntary motion on my part turned me out of my course. The wolves close behind, unable to stop, and as unable to turn on the smooth ice, slipped and fell, still going on far ahead; their tongues were lolling out, their white tusks glaring from their bloody mouths, their dark, shaggy breasts were fleeced with foam, and as they passed me they glared, and they howled with fury. The thought flashed on my mind, that by this means I could avoid them, viz., by turning aside whenever they came too near; for they, by the formation of their feet, are unable to run on ice except on a straight line.

"I immediately acted upon this plan. The wolves having regained their feet, sprang directly toward me. The race was renewed for twenty yards up the stream: they were already close at my back, when I glided round and dashed directly past my pursuers. A fierce yell greeted my evolution, and the wolves, slipping upon their haunches, sailed onward, presenting a perfect picture of helplessness and baffled rage. Thus I gained nearly a hundred yards at each turning. This was repeated two or three times, every moment the animals getting more excited and baffled.

"At one time, by delaying my turning too long, my antagonists came so near that they threw the white foam over my dress as they sprang to seize me, and their teeth clashed together like the spring of a fox-trap. Had my skates failed for one instant, had I tripped on a stick, or caught my foot in a fissure in the ice, the story I am now telling would never have been told. I thought all the chances over; I knew where they would first take hold of me if I fell; I thought how long it would be before I died, and when there would be a search for the body that would already have its tomb; for oh! how fast man's mind traces out all the dead colors of death's picture, only those who have been near the grim original can tell.

"But soon I came opposite the house, and my hounds —I knew their deep voices—roused by the noise, bayed furiously from the kennels. I heard their chains rattle; how I wished they would break them, and then I would have tried 'turn about is fair play.' The wolves, taking the hint conveyed by the dogs, stopped, and after a moment's consideration, turned and fled. I watched them until their dusky forms disappeared over a neighboring hill. Then, taking off my skates, limped up to the house, half cured of romance in the woods and tired of the name of wolf.

"But even yet, I never see a broad sheet of ice in the moonshine without thinking of that fetid, **snuffling** breath, and those fearful things that followed me so closely down the frozen Kennebec."

As the tale ended, an unseen auditor, who from his covert in the bushes was indignant at my account of his people, yelped out, Oo, who-oo, who—oo—o—ah, aigh.

"Hear the vowels," said the Doctor, "a, e, i, o, u, and sometimes w and y.

"Drat the cuss!" quoth Mike, throwing a blazing knot into the bushes, "has he got no decency?"

CHAPTER XXV.

LIFE IN THE LIGHT-HOUSE.

"The rocky ledge runs far into the sea,
 And on its outer point, some miles away
The Light-house lifts its massive masonry,
 A pillar of fire by night, a cloud by day

"The startled waves leap over it; the storm
 Smites it with all the scourges of the rain;
And steadily against its solid form
 Press the great shoulders of the hurricane."

Far to the southward of what has been the scene of our story, forming one of the barriers between the sandy coast of Florida and the surging Atlantic, lies Key Biscayne. Southward still, innumerable little islands of white sand show their backs above the tide, and then Key Largo, Indian Key, and Key West, sweep in a curve around the point of the continent, warding off with their coral arms the blows of the angry Atlantic, and the soft allurements of the Gulf Stream. To the westward on the main land stretches from ocean to ocean the labyrinth of the Everglades.

There were no permanent settlers in this country a few years ago, though at Key West was congregated a reckless company of men whose boats found shelter from the storms among the islands, and who gained a livelihood from the shipwrecked vessels that monthly dashed to pieces on the coast. Most of them were desperate men, without families, only cultivating the soil to plant cocoa and plantain trees, and relying upon the sea for the supply of their wants. Their low craft could be seen among the innumerable reefs at the beginning of every storm, like sea-gulls foreboding the tempest, and hovering for its waifs.

In the interior of the peninsula the Indian still remained secure in his morass, and from Key Biscayne at times his camp-fires could be seen bright against the midnight sky.

The only thing that was human on the coast, contrasting with the cruel shore and the more cruel wreckers, was the light-house on the Key. The great charity reared itself between the howling wilderness and the beating surges, an oriflamme over the strife. It stood on a jut of beach at the lower end of the island, where the palmetto trees dried out in the sand, and only the long sword-grass grew around in scattered spears. A boat with a mast lay on the shingle, and a log canoe, and close by the light stood a little low white house, with two square windows and a door toward the sea, and two square windows and a door toward the bay. A tiny porch covered each doorway, and the little windows were opened and closed by heavy wooden shutters. The only vegetation near the light was one tall, twisted cocoa-tree, whose tuft of heavy leaves were so high in air they formed no shelter from the sun, but crackled with a shardy sound, and when the wind blew fresh from sea, from time to time the tree loosened one of its large cocoa-nuts from its stem, letting it fall to the ground with the thud of a cannon-ball.

The prospect to the eye from the lantern on the tower was a weary stretch of sand islands between the sea and the bay, and beyond the bay the desolation of limitless swamps. Heavy surges beat on the shore, long hot days made the land glimmer in the mirage, and the tower and the little house cowered before the breaker, or danced in the white heat.

Here Lou Jackson had come, and with her father's brother was living in the house and keeping the light.

It is difficult to explain the motives that in some persons lead to their course of life. The human heart is not alike in all, and words that are meaningless to one fall on another like blows, and acts that are ordinary to one's standard are monstrous to another's. Analyze most of our acts, those that are disconnected from sudden, transient impulses, and we will find at the bottom of the retort a deposit of pride that would color the whole solution. It may be unsuspected—it certainly is to the extent discovered, but our words are couched in its language and many of our acts—all of those in public—are under its stern will. "Shall *I* yield?" says Pride, emphasizing the personal pronoun, and refuses what the heart would have granted. "Shall *I* accept a favor from these people who ought to be no more capable of giving favors than I?" and avoids and declines just what the judgment says is needed. "Shall I let him know I love him, and overtly respond to advances he has been making?" and the pride acts a lie, leaving the soul longing, sighing, hoping for that other soul that was abashed, and has departed.

Lou had a little foot, and it was laced over its high arch with an Indian moccasin. The wrought buckskin became the foot, as the foot was tapping the uppermost step in the lantern, while its owner, with her arm on the window-sill, sat looking seaward. Here was her accustomed seat as the sun fired the everglades at his sitting, and left the ocean still as a child tired with his romping, and every evening, for the month that she had lived at the Key, found her in the same spot dreaming away the twilight, and when it was dark brightening the eyes of the passing mariners with the expectant flash of the great lantern.

The spits of sand that ran up and down along the coast were margined with little rollers that broke in foam along their seaward side, and then fell back to renew the attempt, while dowitches and sand-pipers with nimble tread pursued them back and forth. The blue line of the horizon, where it cut the roseate sky, was marked by the sail of a ship. It was not the ways of the shore birds that Lou was watching; her mind was not following the path of the ship. She was conning over her past few years of life. Figures came up to her misty eyes, dead friends, and other homes, strong men, and patches of wood, and camp-fires, and old longings. There were tears in her eyes, and her foot ceased to tap the iron step, and she leaned more over her arm and looked harder out to sea. Then appeared her lonely life, and the wild imaginings and romances it had created, and her form straightened again. Her short lip curled, and the tears dried up.

She thought of her wealthy kinsfolk in the States, and how with haughtiness she had thrown back their proffers of assistance and sympathy. She thought of her own active life, her self-educated tastes, her superiority to her sex of the same age, not boastingly, not extravagantly, but proudly and justly. Old dreams of ambition and romance came over her soul, dreams that had been dreamt and re-dreamt, and had awakened—old fancies of a desperate, whole-souled love, proud as her own, that was to meet her own and make surrender—that was to woo, plead, strive, and die for her, and be accepted. She thought of Mike, and in her daring mood as she was, the patient, gentle, watchful hunter was swept away with a rush of scorn. Too timid to dare for her, too careless to plead for her, too simple for an ideal, his love was the likings of a man, but no love for such as her. A man that she couldn't understand at times, a man that was too cautious to praise, too weak to dare anything for her, even a refusal —out on such a man! The consciousness of a secret liking that had made her leave Mike so hastily at Bonda Key when he had proffered the cat-skin, made her pride revolt and her scorning the bitterer. Then she was too proud to let him come nearer her because she was the daughter of a planter, and he a vagrant hunter. Now she was too proud even to think of him, for she was the child of misfortune, poor, and an orphan. It needs but a little excuse to let the proud heart work out its will. Lou Jackson had shown it rich and poor all the more because she could not rid herself of that unconfessed regard. There were other men that were bolder than Mike. The dark eyes that had flashed to her at St. Augustine, the ready tongue and fair words, were they not the signals of a higher life and warmer heart? Had this immense world no life and form in it that was perfect to her ideal?

"Fool—fool! I am a fool!" she said aloud, springing upon her feet. Taking a cloth from a locker, she began polishing the reflectors of the light, whistling some old air between the pauses of her duty.

"Donald, isn't it time to light up?" presently called her voice from the gallery of the lantern.

"Yes," answered her uncle from below, scanning the horizon with a long look to note the gathering shadows.

In a moment more it was dark, and the sailor pacing his watch on the ship in the offing called from the forecastle deck to the mate: "Cape Florida light, sir, on the port bow, ten miles away."

CHAPTER XXVI.

TRACKING THE ENEMY.

"For it is with feelings as with waters—
The shallow murmur, but the deep are dumb."

"Nine Injins and no squaws," quoth Mike, seating himself on one of the rolling sand hills that border Indian River, a little south of Cape Carnaveral, after a long examination of the surrounding shores.

On the same evening that we pitched our camp on the well-marked trail leading from the St. Johns River across to St. Augustine, Mike had disappeared. He had given no notice of his intention, unless the purchase of powder and ball from a trader camping at the same place might have been a notice. The place where he slept at the fire was vacant, and the dun hound and heavy rifle had disappeared with their owner.

We were safe from all doubt as to our course, and from all danger, for St. Augustine was but sixteen miles away, but we speculated much on the cause of the sudden flight. Had the trader or his men given him any bad news? No, they were only talking of the wars, of Tiger Tail's forays, and how the troops were drawing down in concert to destroy the Indians or drive them southward. We thought at first he had gone over to the town, but a missing canoe showed he had taken to the water. We mentally bade him farewell, and started over to the Spanish town of St. Augustine, and were soon pacing its narrow streets, under the moss-grown walls of the old fort, builded, as saith its inscription, by Field Marshal Don Alonzo Fernando Hereda, of noble fame.

In three days Mike stood under the moss-grown walls of the cypress trees that bastion the southern shores of Lake George, builded and mossed when Hereda's fort was in the quarry. He had retraced the course he had brought us in descending the river. Over the broad water of Lake George he passed like a gull before a northerly wind, holding up his blanket for a sail, and made the orange tree point where the St. Johns enters the lake from the southward.

Following the St. Johns beyond Lake Monroe, he passed in the night, and unobserved, the company of soldiers we met in descending the river. Their campfire was bright on the beach, and he could hear the sentries challenge as they marched to and fro under the stately trees, according to what Mike thought their unnecessarily ostentatious rules of camp government.

"Hulloain' like that in the woods when they ought to be hidin' away," said he to himself, as he noiselessly floated by; "that's all some folks knows."

Mike was like a good many quiet people—he liked his own company, and would talk to himself, little by little, in disconnected sentences, even when he refused to talk to any one else. The many days he passed alone encouraged the habit.

Thence still up the St. Johns, through all its winding course, he paddled, warily watching the shore and water, and often visiting either bank to look for signs. Wherever there was a bend in the river he kept close to the point around which the curve made, creeping around so slowly and cautiously that his eye took in all the reach of the river ahead before he could himself be discovered. He visited many old Indian camps, wandering around them, looking for little signs indicating the intention their occupants had at parting. Wherever there was a trail across the river he seemed to know or divine it, approached it warily, and only left it after a careful scrutiny.

When he built a fire to cook his food, it was made back from the river, and the fire was lit of the driest twigs, so that it raised no smoke, and at leaving he covered it over with ashes, and stamped out the mark his rifle had made in the sand. Sometimes he would not let his dog come ashore, or if he did, carefully rubbed out the tracks of his feet. He did not travel at night, unless in the early part of the evening, and never struck a light after dark, but carrying his canoe on shore, filled it with moss, and laid down in it with his dog at his side.

At the far upper end of the St. Johns, after the explorer has passed through innumerable expansion-like lakes, and crossed the beautiful waters of Lake Poinsett, he will find the St. Johns winding and twisting, overflowing the prairie here in shallow marshes, and running off into deep long tributary lagoons, fringed with canes, reeds, and flags of the most graceful shapes and dense growth. Some of the canes totter over, leaning their tall tips against the others for support, and so they reach entirely across the narrow creeks, shutting out the sun and air, and leaving the boatman to push his canoe as through a sewer. One such branch of the St. Johns turned eastward and reached nearly to the coast. This was the course taken by the Indians when making their journeys from the interior to the sea, and it carried them so near Indian River, a broad inlet of the sea that margins the Atlantic, that they had but a very short carry to get across. Mike was following this outlet. He had seen old fires a day or two back, and thought them, judging by the brands, about as old as the interval of time which he had taken to reach there after Tiger Tail had passed, providing the chief had come this way immediately after visiting Lake George.

Mike examined the narrow passage up which he was paddling with the instinct of a tracker without any positive signs, merely led on by his suspicion, mayhap by his heart. Every scratch on the canes he noticed, and floating bits of wood he picked up from the water to look at them, and then toss them back again. Where a flag had been broken, and half withered hung from its stem, he floated past with upraised paddle, calculating the number of days it would take a flag to wither that much.

At length a dint in the oozy bank he marked as made by the blade of a paddle, and marked it so exactly that when he saw another on the same bank he knew they were the blades of different paddles, and that there were more boats than one that had recently preceded him. By the inclination of the hole in the mud, he knew the direction of the stroke, and therefore the way the paddlers who left the marks were going. When there was an opening in the reeds he would raise himself to his feet and look out on the flatlands, watching the birds to see if they would indicate by their flight or their cries passers in the desert.

Where the creek ran out, the scout examined warily the landing. There were no marks or signs of any kind. He watched long and closely, but could see not a token that a footstep had been there for a month.

"Queer, that!" he said, and paddling back a little to an out-of-the-way elbow, pulled in his canoe in the reeds, and stepped ashore, leaving his hound tied in the boat. He then crossed over from the low land to the higher rolling sand of the coast, but found no signs of passers. Extending his walk a couple of miles down, he came upon footsteps plainly marked in the sand, going from west to east.

"Ha!" said he, coming to a halt, and bringing his hand to the cock of his rifle. His eyes followed the signs back and forth, and he smiled drily. He felt the compliment to himself, implied in the pains taken by the savages to conceal their trail.

"Tried to dodge—landed back and walked around. Somethin's up—wouldn't have been so pertickalar ef they'd been actin' honest."

The hunter followed the trail both back to the lagoon, or a branch of it, where they had left the ordinary course for secrecy, and then over the sands till where the footsteps faded out in the ripples of Indian River.

"Seven days out, jist!" said he, musingly. "Scratchin' along fast."

Seating himself on the sandy hillock, among the rough swaying grass, he mused on the thoughts suggested by the trail, and after a very long silence again repeated with a sigh, looking southward—"Nine Injins and no squaws—that means mischief."

The soft haze was over the landscape, and the cabbage trees on the distant beach loomed up like inverted mountains. The ripples on the sand whispered softly, and the air was burdened with the exhalations of the opening year.

Mike laid off his cap and drew back his matted curls, leaving his forehead open to the caressing air. "Seven days," he said. "Wall, seven days are a deal of time, and what's wrong done, is done bein' helped. I might as well go over and see. Somehow or nother, it don't seem nateral for that critter to come this way. Ef he's runnin' from the soldiers he'd gone west; he knows too much to be bothered by them. He's sent off the women folks for no good, but it mayn't be he's goin' so far. She'll think I'm s'pectin' danger when there ain't none.

"Wall, wall I might as well be down thar. She won't be any the worse for my bein' nigh her. Poor child, poor child! And ef thar's nobody about, why I can come away again without her knowin' it. It does a fellar good to know she is near, and maybe it will turn up as times go she may need me."

That night, Mike with his dog slept among some willows, kindling his fire from the half-burned brands that had served before to cook the food and dry the moccasins of the band he was pursuing. It seemed as if a sort of instinct guided him on the trail. One day he might not see it at all. Travelling, as they both were, by canoes, there were no signs left save where landings had been made to cook or sleep, or to carry over the little portages, the traversing of which so shortened the route between Indian River and Jupiter Inlet. But it was the knowledge of native character that guided the pursuer. He could tell on his day's journey just where such a band, impelled by Indian cunning, would land to conceal their fire. Had they been running carelessly, landing where accident led them, their course would have been more difficult of detection, but Mike was tracking them mentally, more by reason than by a trail perceptible to the eye, and as he ran his canoe to the beach, it would sometimes strike on the very footprints of the savages, and the hunter would give his satisfied ejaculation of "ha!" and quietly sit down to his meal without further examination.

Mike travelled faster than his predecessors. When he carried his canoe over the portage connecting Jupiter Inlet with the next creek to the southward, and examined the tracks where they had not been drifted over with the sand, he smiled, saying—"Gained a day." Presently his dog dug up from the sand a broken paddle. Mike patted the hound, and examining the paddle, knew why they had travelled so slowly that day; and a little search showed some shavings where a new one had been cut. His suspicions as to the leadership of the band and the direction they were taking had become confirmed, little by little, and he now baked his corn-bread, and rolled himself to sleep on his Spartan couch, satisfied to a certainty that his journey was not a needless one.

A boat is usually sent by the government, at regular intervals, to visit the different light-houses of the United States coast, and supply them with stores. Such a visit had just been made to the light-house at Cape Florida. Two barrels of oil, provisions for the light-keeper, a little powder and shot, some tools, cordage and oakum, a few fishing implements, and some books that had been sent for Lou Jackson, had been delivered and were lying in front of the little house, and the white sails of the schooner were again low on the horizon, leaving the light-house keeper and his niece to another month of solitude.

Lou's uncle was busily engaged storing the goods, some

in the house and some in the light-house, and the girl was in the lantern with a book on her knees and her eye wandering away along the reaches of the shore and of the past. The evening was lull, and even the gulls had settled down on the waters of the bay. Presently her eye caught a motion from over the palmetto bushes that ran down the island, and she watched for the cause. In a moment she saw a naked Indian creeping over the sands, running from a clump of bushes to one nearer the house. The fellow was painted vermilion and black, and from his gaudy color and crouching motion, looked like a leopard more than a man. Lou was not so ignorant of Indian ways but that she knew in an instant the meaning of the war paint and the subtile approach that never could have been seen from below. The blood rushed to her heart with a bound, and then her thoughts were as cool as before. This had not been a totally unforeseen contingency, and they had discussed the course to be followed, and had prepared for it in a measure. The door of the light-house had been made heavy and strong, and the arrangements in the upper story had been such that a person would find it a comparative shelter.

Lou leaned over the rail and called to her uncle in her ordinary voice, "Uncle!"

"Well, child?"

"Look up here, uncle."

The old man leaned over the coil of ropes he had in his hand, and looked up at the lantern.

"Don't move fast," said she, in a measured voice, "but come into the tower quietly; there are Indians in the palmetto bushes."

The uncle was not capable of self-control. He cast a hasty look around him, dropped the coil of rope, and ran to the light-house. It was well for him the door stood open wide, for as he ran a ringing shot came from the palmettoes, the bullet cutting his jacket, and another shot from another covert shattered a pane of glass beside Lou Jackson, and from every side broke out the war whoop, while half a dozen savages, whooping with their hands to their mouths, sprang from the palmetto bushes, and rushed across the opening to intercept the fugitive.

The old man slipped in, slamming and bolting the heavy door behind him, and was safe. The savages crowded up against the doorway, as an angry wave would sometimes do on a stormy night, and then fell back with tumult and sullen roar, baffled for the nonce.

CHAPTER XXVII.

SMOKING OUT THE ENEMY.

> "The creeping tide came up along the sand,
> And o'er and o'er the sand,
> And round and round the sand,
> As far as eye could see;
> The blinding mist came down and hid the land
> And never home came she."
> KINGSLEY.

IT was evening when Donald Laidlaw, Lou's uncle, effected his escape into the light-house, and the next morning found the two prisoners in the upper floor, vainly seeking to spy out their foes, who had disappeared like the uncouth shapes of a dream. The prisoners had listened and waited all night long, but there was no sound on the air but the low wash of the sea, and nothing could be discerned from the apertures of the tower save the sand and the trailing gleam of the lantern on the ocean.

Hour by hour glided by in perfect hush. The comorants flew past to their daily fishery, the gulls came in from sea, and the shore birds ran in and out with the ebbing tide as they were wont to do. Laidlaw emerged out on the upper floor of the light-house, and turned out the lamp, cautiously peering about him. He saw the goods strewn on the sand, just as they had left them, and the half-open door of the cottage still ajar. He descended again to the tower and told what he had seen; but his escape from the enemy had been so narrow on the previous evening, and Lou's knowledge of Indian character was so good that they concluded it was far from safe to venture out of their place of refuge. So they opened a bag of biscuit and made a frugal meal, from time to time peeping out of the crevices between the plastering and the floor above, and then turning again to each other to talk or dream away the day.

Noon had long passed when they became conscious of some one calling from below, and saw an Indian standing in front of the house, waving a white rag, and indicating by his motions a desire to speak. Laidlaw mounted the steps to the platform on which the light was placed, and which extended some distance over the tower, and moving cautiously to the edge in such a manner that only his head was exposed to observation from below, called out to the Indian to inquire his message.

"Indian wants to talk."

"Well, what is it? Go on," answered Laidlaw.

"Indian is going away—he wants peace. Indian will do no harm. Give him one blanket and he goes."

"Why did you fire at me last evening?"

"Indian was wrong—Indian much drink—Indian is sorry. Give Indian one blanket."

The savage held up one finger to denote the smallness

of his wants, and his other hand he pressed to his breast. His face was free of paint, and he carried no arms and spoke very pleasantly, and with a graceful gesture.

"What shall we do, Louisa?" asked the uncle, turning around to the trap-door, through which his niece's head appeared, as she listened attentively to the conversation.

"Tell him to take the blanket and go. We will see if he will do it."

Laidlaw told the Indian, who, after a pause, replied: "Indian can't take blanket—say Indian stole blanket."

"Uncle, it is all a cheat. Look out for them," whispered Lou.

"No, we will not come out to bid you good bye. Take the goods you want and be off."

The Indian seemed disappointed, judging from his manner as he turned on his heel and disappeared in the bushes, while the old man descended to the securer retreat of the tower.

The light-house in which Lou and her uncle were entrenched, was the ordinary columnar-shaped edifice that may be seen at intervals all along the coast at the present time. It was built of unhewn stone, to the height of about six feet from the sand, and then of concrete—a composition of broken shell and mortar—for forty feet more, slightly decreasing in size until within a few feet of the top, when it suddenly expanded to receive the bell-shaped lantern of glass that covered the lamps.

Under this lantern was constructed a stone platform,

overlaying the tower, and extending out till it formed a narrow ledge, and a single hand rail ran round its exterior edge, so that the light-keeper could walk the outside, polish the glasses, and keep undimmed the light. In the lantern stood the lamps on a pedestal, with their metal reflectors, a can of oil and a bundle of waste, for polishing.

At the base of the tower, and on the side from the sea, was a heavy oaken door, entrance to which was gained by a little flight of stairs, and the door was placed above the stone work, so as to be free from any extraordinary tides. On the level with the door in the tower was a pile of stores of divers kinds, some provisions and some necessary implements for the station. From this a winding stairs of wood ran up to the narrow opening that led to the lantern.

When Lou and her uncle took refuge from the savages, they remained at the bottom of the tower, reclining on the cordage or bales, save as they were occupied in trying to make discoveries of the savages through the narrow windows that here and there were cut, like arrow slits, into the walls for the purpose of light. It was hither they descended when the unsuccessful Indian diplomatist departed, and they were left once more to their own anxious expectations, and to the renewed machinations of their foes.

It was not a great while they had to wait before they heard on the exterior the guttural voices of the savages, and felt the door vibrating under their tests of its

17

strength. Presently they heard heavy blows as though from a stick of timber, and then the sharp rap of a hatchet. Laidlaw started up, and arming himself with the only weapon he possessed, an old fowling-piece, prepared to do battle when the door should no longer be a security. Lou retreated up the steps toward the lantern. But the door was of live oak, studded with nails, and the Indians did not care to risk their hatchets on so stern a material, and even the blows of the timber presently ceased, the assailants finding it difficult to make their battering ram work effectively from the narrow platform afforded by the steps on the exterior.

The prisoners congratulated themselves on their security, and again seating themselves on the cordage, renewed their council, and even jested upon the futile attempts of their enemies. An hour or more had passed away in most perfect quietness, and saving the occasional visits to the loop-holes of the tower, Lou had relapsed into a dreamy state of half wakefulness, while her uncle, with the caution of years, sat close to the door-way with his duck gun across his knee, and his ear to the crack.

"Don't you smell something strange, uncle?" said the girl, after a pause.

"No," whispered the old man. "What like?"

"I thought I smelt wood burning. What is that I see on the floor?"

Her uncle looked down on what seemed a carpet of lamb's wool, white and flaky, gradually spreading itself over the floor. Laidlaw leaned down his face until he could look out through the crack beneath the door. Then raising up his head suddenly, he stared at his niece, exclaiming in a whisper—"They have set fire to the door."

There was a long pause, and the two doomed people gazed at each other in silence. As they sat they could hear from without the dull rumbling of the flames as they gathered volume, and then at intervals the whoop of the savages in mocking tones.

The thoughts that chased each other through the minds of the prisoners were stern and hurried. There was no water or other means of putting out the fire, and even had there been it was on the outside of the door and constantly supplied with fuel by the savages. In a little while the flames became perceptible through the crevices of the door as the panelling shrunk from the heat. The knots fell out, and through the openings left they could see the savages passing and repassing. Lou's mind likened them to devils in the flame of the pit, and her soul went up in an unsyllabled prayer for deliverance from a death to which only the torments of the lost bore any likeness.

Had Laidlaw been a man like the men that the wild scenes of those days often engendered, he would have been plotting against the savages, or at least been prepared for this emergency and capable of inflicting a salutary revenge; but he was mild and gentle, having outlived many of his friends and ambitions; he returned to gentle pursuits and dreamy musings to fill his vacant mind.

His only attempt now was a trial of endurance without any retaliation upon the savages, and laying aside his fowling-piece he assisted his niece in carrying up to the lantern a few things that a protracted stay might render necessary. A few bags of biscuit and boxes of figs, a canvas sail and a rope were brought up, and two or three glass reflectors of heavy weight and much value, were lifted up, with great labor, to the topmost platform.

"I have forgotten my gun," said Laidlaw, descending for the last time the winding steps, blurred with smoke and dusky with the twilight, while Lou crouched down in the lantern to avoid being seen from the sands.

"And bring up some tobacco for your pipe, uncle," she called after him, down the stairs.

"I can't find the gun. Lou, did you see where I put it?" he called from below.

"Is it not leaning against the centre post?" she called.

The answer to her question was sent back up the confined tube of the tower, multiplied into infinite echoes by the hollow walls, in an Indian war-whoop.

The savages had effected an entrance from below. Where was her uncle? She listened, but there was no sound of struggle or pleading, no prayer or groan, only the war-whoop came up in the darkness, echoing and re-echoing from vermilion colored lips and stony walls. She leaned her head down the trap door that communicated from the lantern to the stairs, calling, "Uncle, dear uncle, shall I come to you?" But no voice or sound replied; even the Indian yell died away. The fire at the door had been trampled out, and there was a most perfect hush, contrasting fearfully with the yells and tumult a moment before. Lou listened and watched, but the tower was thick with smoke, and darkness had settled over all the world. She did not dare to descend, knowing it would be a useless sacrifice and no help to her kinsman. She did not dare to go to the edge of the lantern, for doubtless the savages were watching her from below. She only fulfilled her woman's mission and waited and hoped.

She had been thus lying on her breast by the trap door an hour or more, during the most profound silence. The moon had arisen, and by its rays the winding stairs came partially out of the obscurity. Here and there down the black vault, a narrow slit of pale light came across the darkness, from the windows, and made a freckle on the stairs. Something moved past one of these bars of light, far down the tower. A moment after it passed another opening on the moonward side of the tower. Again, though without noise, it had mounted nearer, and where the bar of moonshine crossed it, Lou recognized the vermilion daubed face and braided scalplock of an Indian. In an instant after, it disappeared in the dark. She drew back as from an apparition, or from the arch fiend himself. She shut her eyes, and yet by her mental vision saw the brindled shape mounting nearer.

She would have prayed, but she scorned to address in

her extremity One she did not openly petition in her pride of life. Her mind swept around the whole circuit of her years, summing up in a second an age of being, and millions of defences that might have aided her had they been there. Trees, woods, air and the ocean, love, hope, and books, flashed through her mind as quickly and brightly as the light in a summer cloud, and yet she was conscious without seeing him, of the approach of the dread shape that was climbing from below. It was the fascination of a fate that could not be averted.

In a moment her eye fell upon a weight that had been used as a balance to the mechanism of the lamp. It was a heavy cannon ball, with a ring in it. She rolled it to the edge of the trap door, and when next the figure below passed the light of a window she let it fall. Downward it flew with swift gathering velocity, until it struck the savage on the bare forehead, when he was hurled with it to the bottom, striking from side to side a lifeless mass.

As one throwing a stone in a marsh will wake to shrill clattering, the rails hiding in its lonely coverts, and as their mocking cries, answered from tussock and reed, immediately hush into silence again, so the two bodies, hurled with a dull blow to the base of the tower, awoke the silence of the night with the baffled whoop of the savages who were waiting below; their cries were answered from other hiding-places, and immediately after the war whoop ceased, and a hush as of death reigned as before.

Lou listened to the wailing cry and sank back appalled

at her own act of desperation. The darkness wrapped her as a mantle, not protecting her but pinioning her arms in helplessness. It seemed the greater from the contrast with the beacon light that usually shone from the lantern brightening even the distant sea. She struck a match and lit the great lamp of the lantern, and as its flash broke out on the night her heart grew lighter at its accustomed cheerfulness. She could once more see the white walls of her house, and the ranks of marching breakers that knelt along the beach, discharging their regular volleys of noise and foam. She laid down on the floor so as to be secure from any shot from without, and watched the narrow winding steps of the tower.

Where was her uncle! There had been no voice or sound of him since they had parted. There was but one opinion as to his fate; she could not think of it, and sternly shut it back lest she might be totally unnerved.

A few hours sped by, and a motion at the base of the tower indicated some new attempt on the part of the besiegers. The experiment developed itself in a cloud of smoke that gradually mounted the tower and found vent through the trap door. Then a flame was seen below, and in a moment more the winding stairs were in a blaze. The fortress they dared not storm, was to be burned out. The girl looked around her as the smoke accumulated, and opened the windows and the door that led to the gallery to give it vent. The flames roared up through the aperture as through a hollow tree, above which the lantern, like the topmost boughs, came out against the night sky in bright relief or was wrapped in darkness as the flame or the smoke successively lighted or enveloped it. The girl cowered away from the flames as they came up the trap door, to the fullest extent of the tower. The smoke became denser and the stone beneath her warm. She wrapped a blanket around her and kept her face down to the floor. The fresh air that stole through the broken sash struggled with the smoke that curled around her. Her ear caught the whoop of the Indians exulting in their carnival, and an occasional shot that was fired at the lantern, more in triumph than with the intent to slay. She heard the surf, and the peevish cries of the sea birds that circled around the unusual light. Her brain reeled with the smoke, and she became insensible.

When she recovered her senses the morning had broken and the world with its thousand happy tenants had awakened to the joys of another day. The slight wooden staircase in the tower had burned out, leaving the column of stone and mortar with its iron ribbed lantern as strong as before. The girl looked down the column and found herself cut off from the earth. She looked out on the strand and there was no living being in sight. The lamp had gone out in the smoke. She looked out for her late enemies, but could see none. The world below her was beautiful to see, replete with rolling breakers, shells and sands, flowering palmettoes, and the long lagoon, with its little island, dreaming a hundred yards from shore.

CHAPTER XXVIII.

BESIEGING THE LIGHT-HOUSE.

"And that unknowing what he did,
He leaped amid a murderous band,
And saved from outrage worse than death
The lady of the land."
COLERIDGE.

THERE are some positions in which one is thrown so hopeless, and so complicated in the abundance of their misfortunes, that the heart gives up resistance and lamentation. Then, after a little, there arises a pride of superiority, and the heart grows greater from its conscious scaling of these disasters. They cease to afflict, and are the sources of a pleasurable pride.

So from her house of refuge by the sea Lou Jackson's mind ran over her lonely life, her position of disaster so singularly great, and her desolate feebleness against a nation of foes. Her mind recovered its tone, she became proud of herself, matching her feeble endurance against war, fire, and the girdling waves. She did not flaunt her new-found hardihood, but used the arm of the feeble, and kept concealed in the bottom of the lantern, yet proud of her own endurance and fortitude. She knew that Indian eyes were on the tower, and that the bushes, seemingly inhabited only by the cardinal birds, were sheltering her enemies as well. She peered out from the crevices of the tower, watching her foes or the passing sails that, unconscious of her fate, crept along the horizon, and the sea, in glassy undulations murmured to the shore.

As noon rode in the dazzling air and the hollow tower still stood, blackened by the fire, yet seemingly deserted, the Indians, satisfied by the death-like stillness, stole from their hiding-places to examine their work of destruction. First one crept out, with his rifle in his hand, winding around different covers until he reached the base of the tower, and looked up its lofty cone. The embers still smoldered in its base, and up the darkened trunk he could see the square hole that led to the platform, and through it the blue of the sky. Then another savage came out, and another, and they gathered together and talked long at the base of the tower. Lou saw them from where she lay, and could have thrown her lamp-scissors on their heads, but she kept quiet and concealed. The savages, tired of their siege, and satisfied that they had destroyed the only occupants of the light-house, collected together the spoils from the dwelling-house, and putting them in their canoes, prepared to start. Lou watched them eagerly, thinking she might see her uncle a prisoner among them. She saw the patchwork coverlet from her bed go down wrapped around a painted chief. She saw some of the little mantel ornaments, her uncle's large brass compass, the family kettles and pewter plates. She saw many a little article of grace and comfort, endeared to her by gift or use, passed through brutal hands and stored in the canoes lying in the lagoon, but her uncle was not there. The faint hope that had arisen in her soul faded away, and the mercury of her heart fell back with a cold chill.

The Indians paddled off fast, to get to the main land, for the weather was changing; a cold wind was blowing, and they preferred the shelter of the main to their exposed camp on the Key. In a little while their canoes looked like a train of ducks gliding over the black waters of the bay, and the curling waves came in from seaward with a hollow sound, booming out at sea, and hissing on the sands. Far beyond the regular shore-breakers, white spots on the ocean and curling ridges showed where the coral reefs reared their backs and made maëlstroms of boiling waves tangled with sea-weed and brightened with foam.

The sun set before its time in clouds. The air was all a haze. The gulls flew about hither and thither, like bits of white paper tossed on the winds.

"A hard night at sea," said Lou, gathering herself up and looking round her citadel. The wind blew up the trap-door with spatters of the salt water, and found egress through the shattered lantern. She drew some planks over the hole, and after a fashion stopped the broken windows with pieces of boards or glass. The activity calmed her mind. She saw she was safe if she could hold out until some one came to her relief, or until the store-ship returned again. There were a bag of crackers and several cans of lamp oil safe from the flames stored in the lantern, but they formed a meagre diet. She trimmed her lamp as was her wont, from time to time stopping to watch the rising sea or scan the distant shore, where the Indians had disappeared. The night was a severe one for coasting vessels. Many a wreck would strew the Keys by the morrow, now that the good light was destroyed. Many a brave ship with its light hearts and cabins full of mirth would "crash together the keel and the mast to be tossed up aloft in the glee of the wave;" a sense of duty and self-sacrifice came over her mind, strengthening her to action. "The ships, at least, should have the benefit of the light as long as she was there," spoke the girl; and so, when everything was made as secure in the lantern as her means admitted, she touched the wicks with turpentine, and then with a match. In an instant, like the electric contagion of a heroic deed, the bright light flashed over the seething main, in a long train of splendor; and the watching mariner who had been longing, yearning, for that light from his reeling deck, saw it and blessed it aloud, though he wist not the enduring heart that bade it burn.

Down among the tangled foliage of one of the islands close bordering the far shore was crouched a band of Indians. Over the fire cooked their supper. Their canoes, inverted, lay along the shore. Their blankets

and the plunder of their foray were scattered around
them. The dense hedge of palmetto with its fan leaves,
and the matted cane, bent over them, screening them
from the wind, and though on the pulses of the gale they
could hear the sobbing of the distant sea, they were
secure from the tempest and from want, laughing low
with humor, smoking their pipes, drying their leggins and
stretching and basking like cats in the genial warmth and
light of the fire. They too saw the bright flash of the
light-house, as it stepped to its place in the heavens as did
Herod the star over the cradle of Bethlehem. With their
harshly uttered accents of surprise, they started to their
feet and peered out from the foliage on the light they
thought had darkened forever. The whole temper of
their meal was changed, and with diverted glances and
low conference they ate their food and glowered at the
star that shone so placidly in the horizon.

Still another party, besides the sailor on the sea and
Indians at their camp, saw that star take its accustomed
place in the dark.

Mike was coming down the same lagoon when the
far-floating specks of the Indian canoes caught his eye,
and drove him to cover. He hid his little craft in the
palmetto bushes on the land, and squatting beside it with
his hound, the two watched the savages pass and land
on the beach opposite to him. There were three canoes
—that was the same number he had been tracking,
there were no women with the party—that again tal-
lied, but here were eight men, and there had been

nine in Tiger Tail's party. Had they sacked the light and left with the spoils, after losing one man? This seemed to be probable. This would be a likely result, in case the two inhabitants of the Key were attacked in such a manner that they could return but a single blow before they were overpowered.

"Or it might turn up," quoth Mike, to himself, "that they treed more'n they could ketch, and were goin' off for a time on a make-believe, leaving one to ketch the old man when he cum down. That's like 'em. Cum back, Yowler; don't show your ugly mug to them critters; they know you better'n their own squaws."

And the old dog obediently resumed his place at his master's side, and the couple quietly watched the open sound that had now become too rough to cross in a canoe.

"No, taint it," continued Mike, to himself. "They've been here four or five days. They wouldn't have sot there all that time and done nothing. Wall, wall, time'll show."

The hunter nibbled his jerked venison, giving a bit now and then to his dog, who sat with his head in his master's lap. He saw the screaming gulls come landward, and the darkness gather like a pavilion. He saw the light of the Indian fire, and the long reach of Key Biscayne like a log on the wrathful sea, and the breakers combing over either end.

When the lantern suddenly looked down at him with its tranquil eye, he sprang to his feet, exclaiming—"God is good! God is good to sinful critters. No daylight was ever so pretty to a lonesome bein'. Ha! they've got a long pull to make yet, before they can blow out that ere light."

He conned over again the devices of the Indians, and came back to his first conclusion that there was one watching the light-house, while the rest had left on a *ruse*.

"Don't think that ere Injin is in a very safe spot," said he to himself, rubbing down the barrel of his rifle with his rough hand, and looking at the waves that kept him still on shore.

When the morning came, Tiger Tail with his band came back to the island to complete his revenge, but Mike had already gone down along the lee shore during the night, and was waiting for him.

The Indians, well knowing who was in the tower, made no secret of their approach. They landed just back of the house, and walked around the tower, and in and out the little building where Lou had so pleasantly lived. They entered the base of the tower whooping and yelling, and looking with eager eyes toward the aperture that led to the lantern. The sea was still rolling in its heavy billows; as they toppled over and danced in foam, the impetus of the waters behind them carried them up to the base of the tower, when they climbed up like a sheaf of white feathers, and then raced back down the sands to gain force for another attempt. The outer side of the tower was in a measure protected by the surf from the savages, and they confined their attack to that side that looked out toward the little island in the bay.

In the dwelling-house they found implements to aid them in their schemes. A beam was brought out and laid endwise against the tower. On this an Indian walked up and drove a spike into the plaster wall. He then mounted on the spike, the inclination of the tower permitting him to lean inward and drive another at such a height he could just reach it with his hand. With his hatchet he then cut out a stepping-place for his foot, and mounted on to the second spike, and then another, until he climbed up to the overhanging ledge of the tower under the lantern.

Thence throwing down his hatchet to his comrades he gradually extended one hand out until he could feel the edge of the overhanging eaves. This gave him a support. Then reaching out the other hand, and dropping his feet from their support, he swung out pendent from his hands, and gradually raised himself up until he could see into the lantern.

Lou had been all this time not unconscious of the plots of her foes, but she did not dare to overlook the eaves to see what they were intending, and therefore could not tell precisely how the blow was to fall. She lay down on the floor and waited, trusting to the Providence that had kept her thus far to preserve her to the end.

While thus waiting and listening, her eyes fell upon the savage at the ledge of the platform. The crest of eagle feathers, the circles of black and vermilion, and the glaring eye, had something in it of so paralyzing a horror that she only gazed as she would have gazed in the dilating pupils of a lion, without making a motion of defence.

At this instant there came to the ear of the girl the crack of a rifle. The surf roared so heavily on the beach, and the wind rushing so fiercely through the palmettoes, and wrestled with the cocoa-nut tree, that the report of the rifle could just be heard by the crouching girl in the lantern, and not at all by the crowd assembled on the noisy strand.

But the Indian clinging to the tower heard it, and sprang half his length above the ledge by the contraction of his arms alone. He writhed around so that his back turned toward the wall. His eyes searched the thickets and the little island that lay near by in the bay. He attempted to sound the war-cry, but the blood bubbled out of his mouth and fell pattering on the astonished staring group below. One hand fell off from its grasp on the stone coping. He tried to reach it back again, but it wavered in the air half lifted. His eye, filming with death, caught sight of the white sea-gulls that, drawn by the strange sight, balanced in the air above him, uttering their plaintive cries. He saw in them the pure spirits of the happy Hunting Grounds promised by his religion. His body swung around in the wind. The head fell back, and the fingers slipped their hold, while the dead corpse fell with a heavy thud on the sands.

During the occurrence the savages stood in horror

looking on the unaccountable spectacle. When the body was hurled to the ground they paused a little, and then crept up to it, leaning over it and examining it. One pointed out with his finger the little blue spot under the arm that a rifle bullet makes. A guttural " ugh!" proclaimed their assent and surprise. They lifted up their dead comrade and retired to the dwelling-house, setting him up against its walls, and held a long consultation.

Lou crept up to the edge of the lantern and peered down through the crevices. She saw the dead warrior, and the council of the survivors, and their revengeful glances at the tower. She looked all around for the source of the rifle shot, but could see no living or moving thing. The same crash of waves on the one side, and the same monotonous line of coast and bay on the other. The little island stood off the shore, its palmetto bushes rustling and waving in the wind. The cocoa-nut tree bent and twisted, and far out at sea, past the Babel of noise and the tumbling waves, a happy white-sailed ship stood immovably on the horizon, passing from the north to some of the summer ports of the Indian islands.

A movement among the Indians announced the termination of the conference, and another attempt on the tower. A young man came out with his rifle hung over his back with a sling. Like his predecessor, he was naked to the waist, only dressed in his leathern breeches, and as he walked he drew off his moccasins. Another Indian climbed up on the roof of the house, and with his rifle resting on the chimney seemed to keep guard over the lantern. The others scattered about, each one in a different direction, thus commanding the tower from all sides. The young man who had first advanced walked up to the cocoa-tree, and keeping on the side furthest from the tower, commenced to ascend it.

The beleaguered girl saw at a glance the intent of the savage, for the tufted head of the tree where hung the huge cocoa-nuts was nearly on a level with the base of the lantern, and lying as close as possible, she would not be able entirely to hide herself from his shot.

She saw him mount slowly up, only his arms and legs exposed to her view, looking like bronze serpents enlacing the tree. He had reached the top of the trunk, the long spinous leaves waved and tossed their bending fans above him, and hid him from her view. He unslung his rifle from his back. There came a lull in the wind. The cocoa-tree resumed its upright position, and the marksman steadied himself for a shot. Again sounded the crack of a rifle—it came from the islet in the bay— and the young Indian dropped motionless to the sands beneath, like the fruit of the tree when it is fully ripe.

There was no doubt in the minds of the savages now as to whence came the blow. They had heard the report of the rifle, and each one, with a whoop, sprang off to a cover, and the one behind the chimney on the house-top jumped from his exposed position with a celerity that showed more fear than courage. In a moment more there was not a savage to be seen; only the two dead bodies lay on the beach.

CHAPTER XXIX.

MIKE AND TIGER TAIL PLAY CHESS.

"*Falstaff.* These nine in buckram that I told thee of, began to give me ground.
Prince Henry. O monstrous!"
KING HENRY THE FOURTH.

There are some peculiarities in the Indian character that resemble those of a cat. The Indian is patient, and untiring in pursuit of prey, not seizing it by force but by surprise. He never openly attacks an equal, but waylays him, nor risks a life to take another, though the taking of that other may have been his sole occupation for days. The knowledge of these feline qualities of the savage mind gives to some backwoodsmen their great success in Indian warfare, and a reputation that, like Cœur de Lion's, is handed down from generation to generation among obscurer nations than those that knew the great Crusader.

Mike was a philosopher in this lore. A saying of his was, "I know what an Injin's up to by his paint," meaning that his war paint, his trappings, the arms he carried, the decoration of his dress, or its freshness, would show the errand on which its bearer was bent.

So when the savages fell back from the tower, leaving the bodies of their two comrades on the sand, Mike slowly and methodically loaded his rifle, under the cover of the palmetto-bushes that covered the little islet, measuring the charge of powder in an alligator's tooth that hung at his girdle, and trimming off the spare corners of his greased patch after the ball was fitted as carefully as though he was shooting for a Christmas turkey, and then taking out his store of venison from his hunting shirt, made his morning meal, as assured of a truce as though in his cabin. The islet he was concealed upon was scarcely twenty yards across, and yet so luxuriantly had the palmetto overgrown it that no single bit of sand could be seen. It looked like a floating garden. Under the broad fan-like leaves of the plants the hunter had made a pathway like an otter from the outer side to the landward edge, and thence he looked out on the light, a hundred yards across the open water and the long extended beach.

No boat could appear on the open water, or any approach be made to the lighthouse without its being seen from the island. Mike knew that the Indians would not expose themselves either in the one way or the other, although they outnumbered him six to one. That they were watching him he was perfectly assured, and he did not give them the opportunity of seeing his hiding-place, by any unwary motion, as it would only draw their bullets. He merely stretched out an arm over the deep muzzled head of his hound, and slept.

From the other side of the narrow straits the Indians frowned on the island, consulted together, or passed from clump to clump to examine it the more closely, carefully screening their bodies from the hunter, though careless as to all observation from the light-house. Among them, preëminent in gracefulness of figure, was one who wore on his breast a silver medal, like those given to Indians of distinction by the government of the United States, as a reward, or inducement to fidelity. He had crawled down almost to the beach, and from behind some broken timber kept a steadfast watch of the island. Although they had seen neither the marksman, his trail, nor any of his signs, there was no doubt in the Indians' mind as to whom the island concealed. Mike's character was too well known to doubt whose daring act had cost the band two of their best warriors. Even had they not known his intimacy at Far Away, or been warned by the diamond cut, his well known monogram, that he had marked on their canoe. Tiger Tail would have given his rifle and squaw for the scalp Mike wore, and yet there slept the scout, almost in sight of him and his band, and they dared not go and take him.

Had a stranger looked on the scene he would have considered the beach a desolate ruin, never more to be inhabited. The lonely tower was blackened and marred, the place was deserted, and the two dead bodies lay on the sand, watched by the vultures that, with braced wings, crept in slow circles like motes in the upper air. The storm of the previous night had passed away.

The descending sun sullenly set in the everglades, the **wind lulled, and a gentle rain fell** like a mist. The trees and light-house loomed **large in** the obscurity, and the white reefed **breakers on the** reefs, spitting their frothy **spume into** air, could not be distinguished from the drifting scuds that settled down on the sea. A tangled path would the ocean be for the ships that walked its waters **that** night.

Lou Jackson shivered on the stone flooring of the tower. The meagre diet of biscuit, the drink of rain water lapped up from the hollows of the stone, the excitement and terror, had begun to work on her system. Her hand trembled, her eye was sunken and brilliant, and her mind, excited unduly, ran riot with fancy and vision, and became morbidly sensitive to the slight**est** indication of passing events. She knew that some one was near and had fired on the Indians. Who or from where she had not descried. **She** could see the bodies of the two Indians lying on the sands, and others walking about, and she knew she was still a hunted animal, and, with the instinct of a quarry, hid as best her reason taught her.

But another thought came to her with the closing day and the darkening sea. She thought of the happy homes on the open main, and her mind took in the children's laugh, and the lighted cabin with its music and books, and the foretop with its hanging sailors prying about for Cape Florida light. Her own mother went to sea when Lou was yet a child; whether she went down crushed under toppling seas, whether she was captured by pirates, or still floated over the waves, watching for her native harbor, Lou did not know, only her feverish mind pictured her leaning over the taffrail, and saw her pale face looking for shore. When night came down, trailing her black robes heavy with the sea fog, and shutting out the earth, the vision came stronger still. Her mother's voice calling to her in the wind to save her—the sea bird "lone watcher of despair" piped to her in plaintive cries for help. It was the call of the remembered voice. The feeling was so strong she knew her mother was careering past the reefs; she saw the sheeted ship among the spume, and started to save her. She arose from her hard bed, and taking her scissors and oil can, trimmed the great lamps and wiped dry the reflectors. She touched them with spirits and then striking a match, the fair light flashed out to sea, and the light-keeper again sank to her hiding-place. The darkness had protected her while trimming the lamps, and when the light came she sank so quickly to the floor, the Indians could as easily have shot one of the bale-fires that sometimes hung about the tower, as she. As if in answer to her act of devotion a moment after, from so far at sea, it looked like a thread of gold, a rocket went up into the air, parted its trident rays, and dropped again into darkness.

"Mother mother!" called the girl stretching her thin hands seaward toward the signal light of the ship, "I come, I come"—but only the billows thundered back their responses, and her wavering mind flickered between **reason and madness.**

When the lamp shone out from the tower, the scout, **satisfied of the safety, as** he supposed, of Laidlaw and his niece, **carefully backed out from his** concealment, and **drawing his canoe** from under the rank foliage, noiselessly embarked and disappeared in the **darkness** like a **wraith.** The fog and darkness concealed his movements from all observation. He knew that with the darkness **he** would be attacked by the savages, and that they would leave unmolested the tower until he was taken or driven from the neighborhood. Having the first move, he moved away like a knight on the chess board, with a great zig zag that carried him far out into the sound, and then back to where he had seen the Indian canoes lying during the day-time.

This detour cost him much time, moving with **the caution that** he thought necessary. When he had floated into one of the narrow creeks, or ditches, **that ran up into** the beach, he left his canoe and the **hound,** and crept down the shore to where **he** had seen the Indians landing. Their canoes were gone. "Ha, I knowd it," said Mike to himself, "they've **given over the fawn and** are trailin' the painter now."

He crept on slowly from bush to bush toward the tower, and soon came out from the grove to **the cleared** land, and warily examinined on every side for the rear guard left by the enemy. There appeared to be none.

"Six agin one," said Mike, smiling to himself, "that's hardly fair play."

Then straightening himself up under some heavy foliage he looked long up into the lantern. There was no sound or motion from there, only the light burned on tranquilly, falling aslant on the heavy waves that crumbled over and hurried up the beach, simmering with the phosphoric fire that made them blue and white.

"Wall, wall, them folks are roostin' higher 'en turkey cocks; I wonder ef I could crawl up thar."

He crept along the house and found it sacked, and finally reached the foot of the tower. Drawing his hunting knife he stepped inside, and felt around with his hands. Nothing but ashes and cinders met his hand. "Burned out the hollow tree," said he, and then looking up at the little glimmer of light that came down through the trap door, he continued, "but didn't smoke out the coons."

Turning to go, his foot encountered something soft. He leaned down and felt it with his hands. It felt like a human body, and a taint of corruption emanated from it that burdened the heavy air. A fearful idea seized the hunter; he grasped the body with both hands and carried it into the light. There was just light enough to see that it was the body of a man. The hunter felt the head and it was scalped. He stood up for a moment and drew a long breath, repeating his favorite prayer of thanksgiving and praise, "God is good, God is good to sinful creeturs."

A stranger would have wondered what the simple man could have found in the mangled corpse to call forth so fervent an ejaculation of praise and of joy.

Then carrying back the body and placing it just where he found it, he glided back to the bushes and was soon hid in his canoe under the mangrove roots that laced and interlaced the crumbling banks.

It was growing toward morning when the hunter heard the Indians returning. He saw the boats glide past without noise, seeking their former landing. From where he lay hid he could have reached out and touched them with his paddle. He counted the Indians as they passed—there were but five.

"Where's that t'other one?" questioned he in a whisper. No one answered his question, and when the boats were out of sight Mike shot out into the open water, and the strong long pushes of his paddle soon swept his canoe around opposite the island he had lain on during the day. The light from the lantern guided him so that he lost no time, and when the little islet could be discerned he halted, backed out a little, and softly let down a stone anchor attached to a string to keep his canoe from drifting from its place. Then throwing off his hunting shirt and moccasins, and armed only with his knife, he cautiously let himself down into the water and floated toward the island. As he reached it he quietly drew himself up out of the water and wormed his way under the palmetto leaves toward the shoreward end of the island. In a moment more there was a guttural sound from the darkness, and the dense foliage was violently agitated as if two bodies were struggling beneath. The noise could not be heard on the shore for the sound of the surf. But backward and forward on the islet swayed the heavy leaves of the sea-rocket, that reared its red head from the palmettoes, and Yowler, the hound, stretched his head shoreward from the boat and snuffed the air with quivering nostrils, and his eyes glowed like a lion's. Presently Mike crawled out again from the foliage, dragging down to the water's edge the pliant lithe body of an Indian that he left under the leaves, and then he swam out and drew up his boat to the island and hid it where it had been before, under the tangled leaves.

Then the red flush came out of the sea, and the morning wind, and like an army with banners, the great sea fog rolled up its masses and trailed away over the everglades, leaving the tower, and the beach, and the tumbling seas, rejoicing in the beauty and the joy of a Sabbath morning.

In a little while after the light appeared, the warriors of Tiger Tail's band showed themselves among the coppices on the beach, carefully beating up every spot that might afford a cover for the scent they had spent the night in searching for. They went into the ruined dwelling, and then into the light, and away down to where the point of land dwindled into the surf, and finally, as if satisfied with their search and ashamed of the flight of their foe, they resumed their positions around the tower, and one of them, laying his rifle down, prepared to make the ascent of the outer wall to the light, that still burned dimly and fitfully in the lantern, like the morning star in the sky. The forest matador carefully prepared himself for his task by laying aside his hunting-shirt that the Seminoles wore, contrary to the usual habit of dress among native tribes. He took off the necklace of coins with a pendent crescent of silver that ornamented his breast. He threw aside his wrought belt with its bullet-pouch and sheath, and putting his knife between his teeth, like a butcher, with a cat-like bound ran up the timber that still leaned against the tower, and carefully mounted the first of the iron spikes driven into the wall. His tight buckskin leggins were fringed with blue, his naked chest and arms glistened with sweat, and the sunshine and the vermilion-colored painting on his face and breast made him resemble an ocelot climbing a tree. He found the ascent very easy, until he reached the top of the tower, where it curved out to form the little gallery that ran round the lantern. Here he paused for a moment, adjusting his feet and inserting a hand in a crevice of the wall to support him, while he reached out with the other to fix his hold in the ledge, and here he met the bolt of fate from Mike's rifle, that with its clear ringing knell proclaimed to the astonished band that not only was their comrade on the tower death-stricken, but that necessarily the outpost they had left on the island in the night had first fallen before the same avenger.

Sometimes, when one is hunting squirrels, and has made his shot at some determined nut-cracker in a stately hickory, he will see the wounded animal shiver and drop the unopened nut it held in its teeth, then move on a little and lay flat on the limb, then one by one its feet relaxing their hold, until it slips from the cradling bough, still clinging by one paw, and when that loses its grasp, catching at a lower branch with the other, while on the forest leaves, with a slow patter, the red drops fall until the still wrestling animal hurtles from its retreat, crashing through the leaves to the earth beneath, never more to wake the morning with its shrill bark, or shower down the hanging dew beneath its dizzy leap.

So the Indian on the tower at the crack of the rifle shivered and dropped his hunting-knife from between his teeth, and reluctantly quitted his hold and fell to the earth below. His comrades had already fled to cover, and lying there in the sun he clenched the sand, gave a few convulsive sobs, and lay still forever.

An hour passed by when Mike saw from his concealment the four Indians that remained crossing the sound in their boats, they had considered it safest to beat their retreat while they knew precisely where their foe was intrenched. They carried their dead with them, save the body of the one lying by Mike on the islet, and fled in the direction they were taking when the light in the lantern recalled them to complete their revenge.

The hunter watched their course until they faded into the distant shore, and then coming out of his retreat, crossed over to the beach. For the first time since his arrival he seemed in a hurry. When he hailed the tower and called Lou Jackson by name his voice trembled, and when no answer came down to his repeated questions, he threw off his coat and climbed up in the same way so ineffectually tried by the savages.

Lou heard him call, and recognized his voice. She was lying on the stone floor, and her mind had returned with the soothing daylight, yet she retained the consciousness of its wanderings, and thought she was dreaming. The vision was so pleasant to her she held her breath that it might not go away. Others had come to her and gone during the night, and left her alone to the terrors of death. She dreaded lest this one might also go. Presently she heard the brushing of garments against the outer wall, and the breathing of some one near her, and then she knew the vision was gone, and dreaded the spectre head she had before seen rising in the self-same place. She drew back in fear, and closed her eyes to shut out the Medusa head that was to transfix her with horror. She heard a sudden bound, as though something had swung itself onto the gallery, and then in her vision came the brown face of Mike the hunter, and she heard his low voice as he stooped over her, saying, as he lifted her in his arms:

"Lou, child, they haint put out the light yet."

Sometimes, when one is hunting squirrels, and has made his shot at some determined nut-cracker in a stately hickory, he will see the wounded animal shiver and drop the unopened nut it held in its teeth, then move on a little and lay flat on the limb, then one by one its feet relaxing their hold, until it slips from the cradling bough, still clinging by one paw, and when that loses its grasp, catching at a lower branch with the other, while on the forest leaves, with a slow patter, the red drops fall until the still wrestling animal hurtles from its retreat, crashing through the leaves to the earth beneath, never more to wake the morning with its shrill bark, or shower down the hanging dew beneath its dizzy leap.

So the Indian on the tower at the crack of the rifle shivered and dropped his hunting-knife from between his teeth, and reluctantly quitted his hold and fell to the earth below. His comrades had already fled to cover, and lying there in the sun he clenched the sand, gave a few convulsive sobs, and lay still forever.

An hour passed by when Mike saw from his concealment the four Indians that remained crossing the sound in their boats, they had considered it safest to beat their retreat while they knew precisely where their foe was intrenched. They carried their dead with them, save the body of the one lying by Mike on the islet, and fled in the direction they were taking when the light in the lantern recalled them to complete their revenge.

MIKE AND TIGER TAIL PLAY CHESS.

The hunter watched their course until they faded into the distant shore, and then coming out of his **retreat**, crossed over to the beach. For the first time since his arrival he **seemed in a hurry.** When he hailed the **tower and** called Lou Jackson by name **his** voice trembled, **and when** no answer came down to his repeated **questions,** he threw off his **coat and climbed** up in **the same** way so ineffectually tried by the **savages.**

Lou heard him call, and recognized his voice. **She** was lying on the stone **floor, and her** mind had returned with the **soothing daylight, yet she retained the** consciousness **of its wanderings, and thought** she was dreaming. **The** vision was so pleasant to her she held her breath **that it might not go away. Others** had come to her and gone **during the night,** and left her alone to the terrors of death. She dreaded lest this one might also go. Presently she heard the brushing of garments against the outer wall, and the breathing of some one near her, and then she knew the vision was gone, and dreaded the spectre head she had before seen rising in the self-same place. She drew back in fear, and closed her eyes to shut out the Medusa head that was to transfix her with horror. She heard a sudden bound, as though something had swung itself onto the gallery, and then in her vision came the brown face of Mike the hunter, and she heard his low voice as he stooped **over** her, saying, as he lifted her in his arms:

"Lou, child, they haint put out the light yet."

CHAPTER XXX.

THE SURRENDER AT DISCRETION.

"Of bowe and shafte he bin bereft,
And eke of bugil horne;
A goodlye wighte, by craftie slyghte
Alake! is overborne."   OLD BALLAD.

THE reader must carry his mind over three years that had flown between the events narrated in our last chapter and those about to be in the present. A few more grey hairs had interspersed the Doctor's curls, another wrinkle marked Mike's eyelid, and a little of the freshness of my life had wasted, when the Christmas festivities of a happy house brought us all once again together.

We met at the Moorlands, a sea-island plantation, one of many that from underneath the live oaks are visible from the arms of the sea that indent the Georgia coast. Happy, dignified homes, at once the centre of an extensive agriculture and an abundant and unostentatious hospitality. Boys were home from college; packages of northern goods and books had arrived; the negroes were gay with their Christmas gifts and privileges; the ladies bright with the excitement, and the world with sunshine; the gentlemen were boisterously preparing for the snipe and partridge shooting, and even Mike—the quiet, satirical Mike—had awakened to the uses of the holidays.

Mike, agreeably to a promise to spend the Christmas days at the Moorlands, had come as punctual as the year itself, and his wild, droll stories woke the fireside to peals of laughter when we nightly fought our battles o'er again. The house we were visiting was a portion of an estate that had reverted to Lou Jackson, and that from poverty had raised her again to wealth, and the feast that had lasted for a week was made doubly joyful by seeing our hostess of Far Away the head of the old homestead.

The allotted time of our visit, spent in a round of pleasure, had flown away, and it was now the middle of the night preceding New Year's day. The moon, "sweet regent of the sky," overlooked the Moorlands, and her reflections flecked the lawn, whitened the house, brightened the whitewashed negro cabins, and made the Altamaha a belt of silver among the rice-fields. The air was still, and all the household realized in dreams the hopes of the incoming year. The great house itself seemed to slumber, with its half-open doors, its smokeless chimneys, its scattered implements of labor, shadowed by trees, and lost in the forgetfulness of the early morning. Its young mistress lay in her bed, with her head pillowed on her hand. The door of her room opening on the piazza was ajar, and the moonshine in a flood came in, revealing the turned down book on the stand, and the white garments upon the chair, yet warm and conscious of the sleeper. Around the room were scattered many a memento of the maiden's former life—skins, and sketches, and Indian ornaments, the little indications of tasteful womanhood that make a house retain the image of the owner even after the owner may have gone to the house not made with hands.

Something disturbed the sleeper, her lips moved, and her regular breathing was stopped. She drew her white shoulders under the cover. The dream within her was strong, for her color changed, and a short, quick-drawn breath heaved her bosom, her eye half unclosed, and she seemed to see Mike standing in her room by the window, with his cap in his hand and his rifle on his arm. She lay still with her body, though her thoughts recovered their intensity in a second, and gathered up the past like a garment. The old days came back to her as they troop past a person in a fever, and woods and water, the moving sea, danger and childish fancies. Her life had nurtured her originally bold imagination until it ran wild, and her reason then made her control herself until she appeared to strangers to maintain a stoical reserve. Years agone she had sat by Mike, with her hand on his knee, listening to his wild tales, like Desdemona, "still questioning him the story of his life." As she grew older she drew the hand away, yet listened still, or counted the times and seasons of his coming and going. Older still she grew, and the distance between her and a mere scout became perceptible to her mind, and then pride came, doubt of herself, and experience, and she drew back; drew back in form, though **her heart did not.** She knew her heart **did not,** and so for that knowledge the more severely she kept herself from his contact.

Then came a change in her position in life. **The Indian** bullet made her an orphan child, and, like him, a **vagabond, not** knowing where to shelter herself. Guided **by** his woodcraft to **Tampa Bay, she** needed all the remembrance of her former hauteur and superiority to guard the safety of her heart. She reasoned to herself, and shamed herself to thinking that where she once felt so superior she could never feel just equal. Her sorrow **at her father's** death was with her, and she was glad to **flee from** us away to civilized life, where no such wild imaginings could come across her mind.

Once again the thoughts of her heart underwent a **change.** When the hunter came to her in her darkest **hour of distress** in the light-house, when he nursed her with the tenderness of a woman, when he guarded her with the loyalty of a knight, and after weeks of a simple, **humble devotion that was past all** show, and silent in words, though ceaseless in acts, finally restored her to life, to wealth, and to her kindred, then Lucy Jackson became conscious **to** herself, and blushed at the knowledge. She was all unveiled to her own eyes; she floated in his approbation, and was crushed by his unimpassioned **look.**

But while *she* had been changing, he, too, had changed, and, like her, acquired a pride all of his own. He was conscious that he had been kept at **a** distance at Bonda

Key, he was not analyst enough to tell how; this, to his sensitive heart, was a refusal, abject, persistent, unreasonable. He felt that in her was a certain pride, and, loving her, acquired it himself. When he became the means of her salvation at Key Biscayne, that pride grew side by side with a species of knightly honor that would not allow him to avail himself of the gratitude of the person he had benefited. Such a coercion would be like selling his bold deeds for his own advantage. She was helpless, weak, and distressed; he refused to ask what might be conceded as a right, and what he had not, when pleading as an outcast before a superior being, received before. So modest he was, he saw not the longings that he had awakened—so mutely, devotedly humble, he never dreamed of success after his first hope was thwarted. He walked by her side a servant, and turned back to the woods again when the service was done, leaving her rich in substance, yet poor in spirit, bowed down with a feeling of being scorned, and yet of having caused that neglect by her own act.

Three years had passed since then, and had brought no change to her feelings, though much to her wisdom. Three years had given her wealth and acquaintance, and a world of social life that had a bustle and a wakefulness about it disconsonant with a mind that had passed so many years in the quiet enjoyment of nature. She attended races and regattas, travelled and visited, but to her mind would come the moaning of the sea, and to her eye almost nightly would appear a camp-fire with its appurtenances of dogs, and trees, and slumbering figures, or the lonely lamp in the lantern would loom out of the **brine of her tears.** It was the ghost that would not down, and all the while came back to her again and again in every form or tone the scene at Bonda Key, where she had repulsed the single hope she now would give her life to recall.

Mike's measured, quiet demeanor that is natural to the woods, protected his feelings from scrutiny during his visit to the Moorlands, if he had any that he wanted to conceal. His frankness was like an armor that made fall to the ground all questions and suspicions. Lou watched him with a carefulness that left no act or word unnoticed, and yet with all, learned nothing of his hopes or his inner thoughts. He seemed to tell all, yet she sus**pected and** watched for more that might be unsaid. When she had his familiar company she feigned to herself that it was of little value, but when she had it not, its absence left her life vacant, and his deference was a burning reproach. She **knew** he was going soon back to whence he came. He seemed "weary of the rolling hours." As a migratory bird that sees the passing flocks against the sky, or a traveller that hears the airs of his native land, he seemed to be looking southward and counting the time. The knowledge of his going kept Lou's eye anxious, and made her toss and mutter in her sleep. Was it a consciousness he was by, that bade her wake? Did a paining of the heart make her feel he was nearing her in her sleep? **Was it a** conscious presence

—was it a communication like that which tells one that some one behind his back is watching him—or that calls at night in the misty woods of June to the trysting hunter, Come—come? Or was it that electric flash of pleasure from eye to eye that makes you feel and know that some one you are talking to is pleased and pleases, and is very like you, though he is a stranger? Her heart almost ceased its beating, when she saw him stand there in her room, every nerve was conscious of his presence, and throbbed, her ear heard his heart beating, her nostril detected the scent of his person, her fingers seemed to feel of his arm, the texture of his coat, and the fur of his cap. Was it a dream? Then, dear dream, stay forever. I will not move, lest I affright you. No! it was no dream, for in a moment the figure moved—it came nearer, laid something down on the stand by the bed, and taking up a lace sleeve of hers that was lying there, put it in its bosom, glided back to the window; the moonshine glinted on rifle and belt, and it was gone.

Lou Jackson sprang to the table ; on it she saw a fan, such as are only made in Florida, of the tail of the roseate spoonbill, the head, with its broad bill, being so fastened that it served as a handle.

Years before she had told Mike to get her such a fan, making some laughing promise if he succeeded. Had he mutely claimed the promise? She ran to the window, and saw him following the path that led to the boat landing. His pack was on his arm, his hound was following him,—he had gone. Where was the proffered promise?

was it thrown back to her in scorn? His humble devotion rebuked the thought. A moment of sinking horror, an upstart of wild hope, and Lou, wrapping a dressing-gown about her, was fleeing down the path he went. The cockspurs stung her feet, but she did not feel them, the dank smell of the salt grass recalled the Drowned Lands of Ouithlacouchee, and its memory of pleasure, but like a wraith she fled onward between the low drooping moss that overhung the path down to the Altamaha and came out on the open glade that margined the river. The moonlight stared her out of countenance with the boldness of her act, and she halted and turned back to the shadow. Suppose he should look coldly on her—what scorn would there be like that? She looked at her naked feet, and retreated into the obscurity. The glow-worm turned his eye on her, the palmetto pointed its long finger at her. Custom, instinct, and doubt, blew in her face with the salt air, and made her shiver. They tied her there as to a stake, while she knew he was being banished forever. A chain clanked on the shore. She knew it was the boat's chain he had unfastened.

"One word, oh! one word—I would die for one word. I love him so I will take shame for him, scorn from him, anything but this doubt," she said, half aloud, and again hurried toward the beach. Mike stood with his foot on his boat, wherein were lying his gun and his dog.

He started as the hound challenged the comer with a growl, and the girl placed her hand on his shoulder, calling to him: "Mike! Mike! where are you going?"

"Back home," answered the hunter, dropping the boat's painter in his surprise, and speaking in a half whisper.

"Take me with you, Mike—take me with you?"

"Child, would you go in the night and alone?" said Mike, drawing her robe together where it was falling from her shoulder?

"Oh! Mike, are you blind, or am I mad? Take me—take me—don't leave me!" and as the hunter put his great arm about her, she whispered, "Take me and love me," and her head fell on his breast.

He gathered her up in his arms, and carried her back from the wet shore, like an infant whispering in a broken voice, while his tears fell down on her hair: "God is good, God is good to sinful creeturs!"

The roseate fingers of the morning unclasped from beneath the ocean horizon, and a hundred tongues from copse and grass anthemed the dawn of a new day and a new life.

THE END.

www.ingramcontent.com/pod-product-compliance
Lightning Source LLC
Chambersburg PA
CBHW022103290426
44112CB00008B/534